HEALTHIER COOKING
ANNUAL RECIPES

Taste of Home

RDA ENTHUSIAST BRANDS, LLC • MILWAUKEE, WI

HEALTHIER COOKING
ANNUAL RECIPES

50

131

© 2020 RDA Enthusiast Brands, LLC.
1610 N. 2nd St., Suite 102, Milwaukee WI 53212-3906

Visit us at **tasteofhome.com** for other Taste of Home books and products.

ISBN:
D 978-1-61765-941-6
U 978-1-61765-942-3
Component Numbers:
D 117900055H
U 117900057H
ISSN: 1944-7736

Executive Editor: Mark Hagen
Senior Art Director: Raeann Thompson
Editor: Christine Rukavena
Art Director: Maggie Conners
Designer: Arielle Jardine
Senior Copy Editor: Dulcie Shoener
Senior Food Editor: Peggy Woodward, RDN

Cover Photographer: Mark Derse
Senior Set Stylist: Melissa Franco
Food Stylist: Josh Rink

Pictured on front cover:
Contest-Winning Greek Pasta Bake, p. 161.

Pictured on title page:
Spicy Sausage & Rice Skillet, p. 124.

Pictured on back cover:
Garlicky Chicken Dinner, p. 175; Chicken Chili with Black Beans, p. 62; Soft Fish Tacos, p. 126; Chocolate & Raspberry Cheesecake, p. 233; Rise & Shine Parfait, p. 12.

Printed in USA
1 3 5 7 9 10 8 6 4 2

LIKE US
facebook.com/tasteofhome

FOLLOW US
pinterest.com/taste_of_home

SHOP WITH US
shoptasteofhome.com

VISIT US FOR MORE!
tasteofhome.com

TWEET US
@tasteofhome

SHARE A RECIPE
tasteofhome.com/submit

E-MAIL US
bookeditors@tasteofhome.com

Contents

Get inspired to try something fresh and healthy with this all-new collection of 360 heart-smart recipes! You will love discovering favorite dishes for weeknight dinners, holiday entertaining, vegetarian cooking and more.

58

A 'Healthier' Take on Cooking

Find out why we made the shift and what it means for our recipes.

Health and nutrition professionals can't always agree on the hallmarks of a healthy diet. But most of them can agree that a healthy diet is on a spectrum of sorts. At one end are foods loaded with vitamins, minerals, lean protein, fiber and healthy fat, like our  "power-packed" recipes. At the other end of the spectrum? Foods that provide energy from calories, but not much else.

PRACTICE DOESN'T MEAN PERFECT

All foods on the spectrum can fit into a healthy diet. It's up to us as individuals to make choices at our meals that, when added up over the days, weeks and months, land us toward the nutritious end of the scale. This is the healthier end, where we want to be. Much like the "practicing" of meditation or yoga, healthy eating is an ongoing process. It changes, it's imperfect, and it's the sum of hundreds of small choices we make. It is not a single meal, snack, food group or dessert.

MAKE IT PERSONAL

So what's your idea of healthy eating? It could include specific dietary needs, health goals, sustainability objectives, and more. No matter how you define a healthy diet, this collection of recipes can help you keep on track. Your own healthy eating path won't be the same as anyone else's.

Our switch to *Healthier Cooking Annual Recipes* puts the idea of a healthy, well-balanced spectrum front and center. It's about making better choices most often, like the power-packed **GRILLED GARDEN VEGGIE PIZZA (P. 196),** but still feeling good about having **CONTEST-WINNING FRESH BLUEBERRY PIE (P. 250)** for dessert sometimes.

Happy Cooking,

Peggy

Peggy
Woodward, RDN
Senior Editor/
Food

196

250

About Our Nutrition Facts

Healthier Cooking Annual Recipes provides a variety of recipes to fit in a healthy lifestyle. Here's how we arrive at the serving-size nutritional information at the end of each recipe.

- Whenever a choice of ingredients is given (such as ½ cup sour cream or plain yogurt), we use the first ingredient in our calculations.

- When a range is given for an ingredient, we calculate using the first amount.

- Only the amount of a marinade absorbed is calculated.

- Optional ingredients are not included in our calculations.

- Sugars provided in the Nutrition Facts represent both added and naturally occurring sugars.

* HEALTH TIP * Peggy shares her best secrets to help you make healthy eating choices throughout the week.

SPECIAL INDICATORS

Power-Packed Each dish contains a whole grain or legume, a lean protein, and a healthy dose of fruits or vegetables.

Meatless Indicates breakfast, lunch, dinner and snack-time options that don't use meat or meat products.

Fast Fix Dishes are table-ready in 30 minutes or less.

Slow Cooker Dozens of slow-simmered recipes use the favorite appliance.

Dig in and discover healthier choices like these.

See for yourself why our online users love them!

"This is now my go-to recipe for 'fried chicken.' My family loves it!"
—sandy65

150

"Awesome! I've been looking for vegetarian baked beans, and this recipe did not disappoint! I will be trying it with prepared dried beans and doubling the recipe soon."
—Sherry

88

"I have made this recipe several times. My family loves it and my co-workers are loving it as well. It is a great alternative to fatty dips."
—brendadsnyder

37

"My sweetheart, who has prediabetes, loved this!"
—MrsJohnG8958

158

"It will become part of our regular menu. Yum! Plus the calories are not crazy. Thank you for sharing this gem."
—nancy headlee

231

"Took these bars to a potluck and came home with compliments and an empty pan. Gluten-free eaters really appreciated the new recipe."
—aksunflower

19

GOOD
MORNINGS

"*I love pumpkin, and it is so good for you. I wanted a way to have my pie and eat it too—for breakfast! Add a sprinkle of granola for an extra treat.*"
—Alisa Christensen, Rancho Santa Margarita, CA

**POWER BERRY
SMOOTHIE BOWL**

POWER BERRY
SMOOTHIE BOWL

*While you can't taste the spinach in these
smoothies, you get all its nutrients with
big berry flavor.*
—Christine Hair, Odessa, FL

....

Takes: 10 min. • **Makes:** 3 servings

½ cup orange juice
½ cup pomegranate juice
1 container (6 oz.) mixed berry yogurt
1 cup frozen unsweetened
   strawberries
1 cup fresh baby spinach
½ medium ripe frozen banana, sliced
½ cup frozen unsweetened blueberries
2 Tbsp. ground flaxseed
   Sliced fresh strawberries, fresh
      blueberries, flax seeds and granola,
      optional

In a blender, combine first 8 ingredients;
cover and process for 30 seconds or until
smooth. Pour into bowls; top as desired.
Serve immediately.
1 cup: 172 cal., 3g fat (0 sat. fat), 3mg chol.,
47mg sod., 35g carb. (28g sugars, 4g fiber),
5g pro.

OMELET LORRAINE

*I lightened up quiche Lorraine by making
it without the pie crust. This bacony
breakfast has the classic taste that folks
love. It's a winner for a late-night snack
as well as for a brunch dish.*
—Diane Hixon, Niceville, FL

....

Takes: 20 min. • **Makes:** 2 servings

3 large eggs, lightly beaten
2 Tbsp. fat-free milk
1 Tbsp. dried minced onion
⅛ tsp. salt
⅛ tsp. pepper
2 bacon strips, cooked and crumbled
¼ cup shredded reduced-fat Swiss
   cheese
1 tsp. dried parsley flakes

1. In a small bowl, beat the eggs, milk,
onion, salt and pepper. Lightly grease
a 10-in. nonstick skillet and place over
medium heat. Add egg mixture. As eggs
set, lift edges, letting uncooked portion
flow underneath.
2. When eggs are set, sprinkle bacon,
cheese and parsley over 1 side; fold
omelet over filling. Cover and let stand
for 1 minute or until cheese is melted.
½ omelet: 193 cal., 11g fat (4g sat. fat),
293mg chol., 440mg sod., 4g carb. (2g sugars,
0 fiber), 18g pro. **Diabetic exchanges:**
3 medium-fat meat.

APPLE SPICE MUFFINS

When I ran out of muffin mix, I came up with this recipe by improvising with ingredients I had on hand. I was so happy with the results! I love that they keep in the freezer so we can enjoy them anytime.
—Beckie Lapointe, Abbotsford, BC

Prep: 15 min. • **Bake:** 20 min.
Makes: 1 dozen

- 2 cups all-purpose flour
- 1 cup granola without raisins
- ⅔ cup sugar
- 3 tsp. baking powder
- 1 tsp. salt
- ½ tsp. ground cinnamon
- ¼ tsp. ground nutmeg
- 2 large eggs, room temperature
- ⅔ cup unsweetened apple juice
- ¼ cup canola oil
- 1½ cups grated peeled apples

1. In a large bowl, combine the first 7 ingredients. In another bowl, whisk eggs, apple juice and oil. Stir into dry ingredients just until moistened. Fold in the apples.
2. Fill 12 greased or paper-lined muffin cups three-fourths full. Bake at 400° for 18-20 minutes or until a toothpick inserted in the center comes out clean. Cool for 5 minutes before removing from pan to a wire rack. Serve warm.

Freeze option: Freeze cooled muffins in tightly sealed freezer containers. To use, thaw at room temperature or, if desired, microwave each muffin on high for 20-30 seconds or until heated through.

1 muffin: 228 cal., 7g fat (1g sat. fat), 31mg chol., 333mg sod., 38g carb. (16g sugars, 3g fiber), 5g pro.

APPLE-CINNAMON QUINOA PANCAKES

My daughter and daughter-in-law got me hooked on quinoa. I dressed up a regular pancake recipe to create these delicious apple-cinnamon breakfast treats. The shredded apple remains slightly crunchy with the short cooking time, but it really compliments the chewiness of the quinoa.
—Sue Gronholz, Beaver Dam, WI

Prep: 15 min. • **Cook:** 5 min./batch
Makes: 10 pancakes

- ¾ cup all-purpose flour
- 2 tsp. baking powder
- 1 tsp. ground cinnamon
- ½ tsp. salt
- 1 large egg, room temperature
- 1 large egg white, room temperature
- ⅓ cup vanilla almond milk
- 2 Tbsp. maple syrup
- 1 Tbsp. canola oil
- 1 tsp. vanilla extract
- 1 medium Gala apple, shredded
- 1 cup ready-to-serve quinoa
- 1 Tbsp. butter or canola oil

1. Whisk together the flour, baking powder, cinnamon and salt. In another bowl, whisk together egg, egg white, almond milk, syrup, canola oil and vanilla. Add to flour mixture; stir just until moistened. Stir in apple and quinoa.
2. In a large nonstick skillet, heat the butter over medium heat. Pour batter by ¼ cupfuls onto griddle; cook until bubbles on top begin to pop and bottoms are golden brown. Turn; cook until second side is golden brown.

2 pancakes: 222 cal., 8g fat (2g sat. fat), 43mg chol., 538mg sod., 32g carb. (10g sugars, 3g fiber), 6g pro. **Diabetic exchanges:** 2 starch, 1 fat.

TEST KITCHEN TIP

This recipe was tested with Suzie's Ready-to-Eat Quinoa. Substitute leftover cooked quinoa if desired.

APPLE SPICE MUFFINS

MIXED FRUIT WITH LEMON-BASIL DRESSING

A slightly savory dressing really complements the sweet fruit in this recipe. I also use the dressing on salad greens.
—Dixie Terry, Goreville, IL

Takes: 15 min. • **Makes:** 8 servings

- 2 Tbsp. lemon juice
- ½ tsp. sugar
- ¼ tsp. salt
- ¼ tsp. ground mustard
- ⅛ tsp. onion powder
  Dash pepper
- 6 Tbsp. olive oil
- 4½ tsp. minced fresh basil
- 1 cup cubed fresh pineapple
- 1 cup sliced fresh strawberries
- 1 cup sliced peeled kiwifruit
- 1 cup seedless watermelon balls
- 1 cup fresh blueberries
- 1 cup fresh raspberries

1. Place the lemon juice, sugar, salt, mustard, onion powder and pepper in a blender; cover and process for 5 seconds. While processing, gradually add oil in a steady stream. Stir in basil.
2. In a large bowl, combine the fruit. Drizzle with dressing and toss to coat. Refrigerate until serving.

¾ cup: 145 cal., 11g fat (1g sat. fat), 0 chol., 76mg sod., 14g carb. (9g sugars, 3g fiber), 1g pro. **Diabetic exchanges:** 2 fat, 1 fruit.

SLOW-COOKER HONEY NUT GRANOLA

I lightened up a friend's recipe and changed the add-ins to our tastes. It's now a family favorite! You can vary the recipe as you want, changing the nuts, seeds or dried fruits.
—Tari Ambler, Shorewood, IL

Prep: 20 min. • **Cook:** 1½ hours + cooling
Makes: 8 cups

- 4½ cups old-fashioned oats
- ½ cup sunflower kernels
- ⅓ cup toasted wheat germ
- ¼ cup unsweetened shredded coconut
- ¼ cup sliced almonds
- ¼ cup chopped pecans

SLOW-COOKER
HONEY NUT GRANOLA

- ¼ cup chopped walnuts
- ¼ cup ground flaxseed
- ½ cup honey
- ⅓ cup water
- 3 Tbsp. canola oil
- 1 tsp. ground cinnamon
- 1 tsp. vanilla extract
- ½ tsp. ground nutmeg
  Dash salt
- ¾ cup dried cranberries
- ¾ cup raisins
  Yogurt, optional

1. In a 3- or 4-qt. slow cooker, combine the first 8 ingredients. In a small bowl, whisk honey, water, oil, cinnamon, vanilla, nutmeg and salt until blended; stir into the oat mixture. Cook, covered, on high until crisp, 1½-2 hours, stirring well every 20 minutes.

2. Stir in cranberries and raisins. Spread granola evenly onto waxed paper or baking sheets; cool completely. Store in airtight containers. If desired, serve with yogurt.
Note: Look for unsweetened coconut in the baking or health food section.
½ cup: 267 cal., 12g fat (2g sat. fat), 0 chol., 43mg sod., 39g carb. (19g sugars, 5g fiber), 6g pro.

TEST KITCHEN TIP

For even cooking, be sure to thoroughly stir the granola mixture every 20 minutes.

RISE & SHINE PARFAIT

Start your day with a smile. This fruit, yogurt and granola parfait is so easy to make. If you like, use whatever favorite fresh fruits are in season and are looking best at the supermarket.
—Diana Laskaris, Chicago, IL

Takes: 15 min. • **Makes:** 4 servings

- 4 **cups fat-free vanilla yogurt**
- 2 **medium peaches, chopped**
- 2 **cups fresh blackberries**
- ½ **cup granola without raisins or Kashi Go Lean Crunch cereal**

Layer half of the yogurt, peaches, blackberries and granola into 4 parfait glasses. Repeat layers.
1 serving: 259 cal., 3g fat (0 sat. fat), 7mg chol., 6mg sod., 48g carb. (27g sugars, 7g fiber), 13g pro.

PEACH-STUFFED FRENCH TOAST

PEACH-STUFFED FRENCH TOAST

With its make-ahead convenience and scrumptious flavor, this recipe is ideal for holiday brunches—and for busy brunch hosts with a hungry crowd to feed!
—Julie Robinson, Little Chute, WI

Prep: 25 min. + chilling • **Bake:** 25 min.
Makes: 10 servings

- 1 **loaf (1 lb.) French bread, cut into 20 slices**
- 1 **can (15 oz.) sliced peaches in juice, drained and chopped**
- ¼ **cup chopped pecans**
- 4 **large eggs**
- 4 **large egg whites**
- 1½ **cups fat-free milk**
- 3 **Tbsp. sugar**
- 1¼ **tsp. ground cinnamon, divided**
- 1 **tsp. vanilla extract**
- ¼ **cup all-purpose flour**
- 2 **Tbsp. brown sugar**
- 2 **Tbsp. cold butter**
  Maple syrup, optional

1. Arrange half of the bread slices in a 13x9-in. baking dish coated with cooking spray. Top with peaches, pecans and the remaining bread.
2. In a small bowl, whisk eggs, egg whites, milk, sugar, 1 tsp. cinnamon and vanilla; pour over bread. Cover and refrigerate for 8 hours or overnight.
3. Remove from refrigerator 30 minutes before baking. Bake, uncovered, at 400° for 20 minutes.
4. In a small bowl, combine the flour, brown sugar and remaining cinnamon; cut in butter until crumbly. Sprinkle over French toast. Bake 5-10 minutes longer or until a knife inserted in the center comes out clean. Serve with syrup if desired.
1 piece: 267 cal., 8g fat (3g sat. fat), 92mg chol., 368mg sod., 39g carb. (13g sugars, 2g fiber), 10g pro. **Diabetic exchanges:** 2½ starch, 1½ fat.

LOADED QUINOA BREAKFAST BOWL

After I was diagnosed with multiple sclerosis in 2001, I embarked on a journey to live a healthy lifestyle. I started developing recipes that were not only deliciously satisfying but also anti-inflammatory and highly nutritious.
—Chantale Michaud, Guelph, ON

....

Prep: 15 min. + soaking • **Cook:** 15 min.
Makes: 1 serving

- ¾ cup water, divided
- ¼ cup tri-colored quinoa, rinsed
- 2 Tbsp. dried goji berries or dried cranberries
- 1 small banana
- ¼ cup unsweetened almond milk
- 1 Tbsp. maple syrup
- ⅛ tsp. ground cinnamon
- ⅛ tsp. vanilla extract
- ¼ cup fresh or frozen unsweetened blueberries
- 1 Tbsp. chopped walnuts
- 1 Tbsp. slivered almonds
- 1 Tbsp. fresh pumpkin seeds
  Additional unsweetened almond milk and maple syrup, optional

1. In a small saucepan, bring ½ cup water to a boil. Add quinoa. Reduce the heat; simmer, covered, until liquid is absorbed, 12-15 minutes. Meanwhile, soak berries in remaining water for 10 minutes; drain. Halve banana crosswise. Slice 1 banana half; mash the other.
2. Remove quinoa from heat; fluff with a fork. Mix in mashed banana, almond milk, maple syrup, cinnamon and vanilla. Transfer to an individual bowl; add the blueberries, walnuts, almonds, pumpkin seeds, banana slices and goji berries. If desired, serve with additional almond milk and maple syrup.

1 serving: 475 cal., 13g fat (1g sat. fat), 0 chol., 85mg sod., 83g carb. (35g sugars, 10g fiber), 13g pro.

EARLY-RISER OVEN OMELET

Everyone will rush to the table when you serve this big fluffy omelet. Packed with tomato, broccoli, ham and cheese, it makes a hearty brunch dish that easily serves a bunch.
—Wendy Fawcett, Gillam, MB

....

Prep: 15 min. • **Bake:** 35 min.
Makes: 6 servings

- 10 large egg whites
- 5 large eggs
- 1 cup fat-free milk
- ¼ tsp. seasoned salt
- ¼ tsp. pepper
- 1½ cups cubed fully cooked ham
- 1 cup chopped fresh broccoli
- 1 cup shredded reduced-fat cheddar cheese
- 1 medium tomato, seeded and chopped
- 3 Tbsp. finely chopped onion

In a bowl, beat egg whites, eggs, milk, seasoned salt and pepper. Pour into a 10-in. ovenproof skillet coated with cooking spray. Sprinkle with the ham, broccoli, cheese, tomato and onion. Bake, uncovered, at 350° for 30-35 minutes or until eggs are almost set. Broil 4-6 in. from the heat for 1-2 minutes or until the eggs are set and top is lightly browned.

1 slice: 230 cal., 10g fat (5g sat. fat), 210mg chol., 893mg sod., 6g carb. (0 sugars, 1g fiber), 27g pro. **Diabetic exchanges:** 4 lean meat, 1 vegetable.

LOADED QUINOA BREAKFAST BOWL

CRANBERRY EGGNOG MUFFINS

CRANBERRY EGGNOG MUFFINS

No one in my house wants to finish the leftover eggnog or cranberry sauce, so I use those ingredients to make warm muffins that vanish.
—Nancy Mock, Colchester, VT

Takes: 30 min. • **Makes:** 1 dozen

- 2 cups all-purpose flour
- ¾ cup sugar
- 3 tsp. baking powder
- ½ tsp. salt
- ¼ tsp. ground cinnamon
- 1 large egg, room temperature
- 1 cup eggnog
- ¼ cup butter, melted
- ¾ cup whole-berry cranberry sauce

1. Preheat oven to 400°. In a large bowl, whisk the first 5 ingredients. In another bowl, whisk egg, eggnog and melted butter until blended. Add to flour mixture; stir just until moistened.
2. Spoon 1 Tbsp. batter in bottom of each of 12 greased or paper-lined muffin cups. Drop 1 tsp. cranberry sauce into center of each; top with remaining batter and cranberry sauce. Cut through batter with a knife to swirl.
3. Bake 15-18 minutes or until a toothpick inserted in center comes out clean. Cool 5 minutes before removing from pan to a wire rack. Serve warm.

Note: This recipe was tested with commercially prepared eggnog.

1 muffin: 208 cal., 5g fat (3g sat. fat), 38mg chol., 275mg sod., 37g carb. (19g sugars, 1g fiber), 4g pro.

BREAKFAST BANANA SPLITS

I can't brag enough about this recipe. It's elegant enough for a formal brunch, yet simple and nutritious. With different fruits and cereals, the variations are endless.
—Renee Lloyd, Pearl, MS

Takes: 10 min. • **Makes:** 2 servings

- 1 medium banana
- ⅓ cup each fresh blueberries, halved seedless grapes, sliced peeled kiwifruit and halved fresh strawberries
- 1 cup vanilla yogurt
- ½ cup granola with fruit and nuts
- 2 maraschino cherries with stems

Cut banana crosswise in half. For each serving, split each half lengthwise and place in a serving dish. Top with the remaining ingredients.

1 serving: 337 cal., 6g fat (1g sat. fat), 6mg chol., 96mg sod., 66g carb. (42g sugars, 8g fiber), 12g pro.

COUNTRY CRUNCH PANCAKES

I adapted a basic pancake recipe and came up with this tasty favorite. Kids love them!
—Anita Harmala, Howell, MI

....

Takes: 30 min. • **Makes:** 16 pancakes

- 2 cups all-purpose flour
- ⅓ cup whole wheat flour
- ⅓ cup quick-cooking oats
- 2 Tbsp. sugar
- 2 tsp. baking powder
- 1 tsp. baking soda
- 1 tsp. salt
- 1 tsp. ground cinnamon
- 2¼ cups buttermilk
- 2 large eggs, room temperature, lightly beaten
- 2 Tbsp. canola oil
- 1 cup fresh or frozen blueberries, optional

CRUNCHY TOPPING
- ½ cup quick-cooking oats
- ¼ cup chopped slivered almonds
- ¼ cup packed brown sugar
- 1 tsp. ground cinnamon

1. In a bowl, combine flours, oats, sugar, baking powder, baking soda, salt and cinnamon. Combine buttermilk, eggs and oil; stir into dry ingredients just until blended. Fold in blueberries if desired.
2. Combine topping ingredients; sprinkle about 1 tsp. for each pancake onto a lightly greased hot griddle. Pour ¼ cup batter over topping; immediately sprinkle with another teaspoonful of topping. Turn when bubbles form on top of pancake. Cook until second side is golden brown.

2 pancakes: 298 cal., 8g fat (1g sat. fat), 56mg chol., 644mg sod., 47g carb. (14g sugars, 3g fiber), 10g pro.

FRESH VEGETABLE FRITTATA

This breakfast dish is perfect if you want to incorporate more fresh veggies into your meals.
—Pauline Howard, Lago Vista, TX

....

Prep: 15 min. • **Bake:** 20 min.
Makes: 2 servings

- 4 large eggs, lightly beaten
- 1 cup sliced fresh mushrooms
- ½ cup chopped fresh broccoli
- ¼ cup shredded reduced-fat cheddar cheese
- 2 Tbsp. finely chopped onion
- 2 Tbsp. finely chopped green pepper
- 2 Tbsp. grated Parmesan cheese
- ⅛ tsp. salt
   Dash pepper

1. In a large bowl, combine all ingredients. Pour into a shallow 2-cup baking dish coated with cooking spray.
2. Bake, uncovered, at 350° for 20-25 minutes or until a knife inserted in the center comes out clean. Serve immediately.

½ frittata: 216cal., 10 fat (4g sat. fat), 183mg chol., 805mg sod., 6g carb. (4g sugars, 1g fiber), 25g pro. **Diabetic exchanges:** 3 medium-fat meat, 1 vegetable.

COUNTRY CRUNCH PANCAKES

POTATO OMELET

APPLE PIE STEEL-CUT OATMEAL

I absolutely love this slow-cooked oatmeal. The steel-cut oats have so much flavor and texture. My family sprinkles toasted pecans on top whenever possible.

—Angela Lively, Conroe, TX

Prep: 10 min. • **Cook:** 6 hours
Makes: 8 servings

- 6 cups water
- 1½ cups steel-cut oats
- 1½ cups unsweetened applesauce
- ¼ cup maple syrup
- 1½ tsp. ground cinnamon
- ½ tsp. ground nutmeg
- ⅛ tsp. salt
- 1 large apple, chopped
  Sliced apples, toasted pecans and additional maple syrup, optional

In a 4-qt. slow cooker, combine the first 7 ingredients. Cover and cook on low for 6-8 hours or until liquid is absorbed. Stir in chopped apple. If desired, top servings with apple slices, pecans and syrup.

1¼ cups: 171 cal., 2g fat (0 sat. fat), 0 chol., 39mg sod., 36g carb. (13g sugars, 4g fiber), 4g pro.

* HEALTH TIP * Boost protein with a dollop of vanilla Greek yogurt (it will help you stay full longer).

> **TEST KITCHEN TIP**
>
> Keep an eye on this as it nears the end of cooking to prevent overcooking at the edges, especially if your slow cooker runs hot.

POTATO OMELET

Even folks who don't care for eggs will like this dish. The comforting tastes of onions, garlic and potatoes come through.

—Edie DeSpain, Logan, UT

Takes: 30 min. • **Makes:** 4 servings

- 2 medium potatoes, peeled and diced
- 2 Tbsp. olive oil
- ½ cup sliced green onions
- ¼ cup minced fresh parsley
- 1 garlic clove, minced
- 6 large eggs
- ¼ cup water
- ½ tsp. salt
- ⅛ tsp. pepper
  Sour cream and crumbled cooked bacon, optional

1. In a 10-in. skillet, cook potatoes in oil over medium-high heat for 10 minutes or until golden brown, stirring occasionally. Add the onions, parsley and garlic; cook until tender. Reduce heat to medium.

2. In a bowl, beat eggs, water, salt and pepper. Pour over the potato mixture; cover and cook for 8-10 minutes or until completely set. Cut into wedges. Serve with sour cream and bacon if desired.

1 piece: 236 cal., 14g fat (3g sat. fat), 279mg chol., 408mg sod., 16g carb. (2g sugars, 1g fiber), 11g pro. **Diabetic exchanges:** 1½ fat, 1 starch, 1 medium-fat meat.

APPLE PIE
STEEL-CUT OATMEAL`

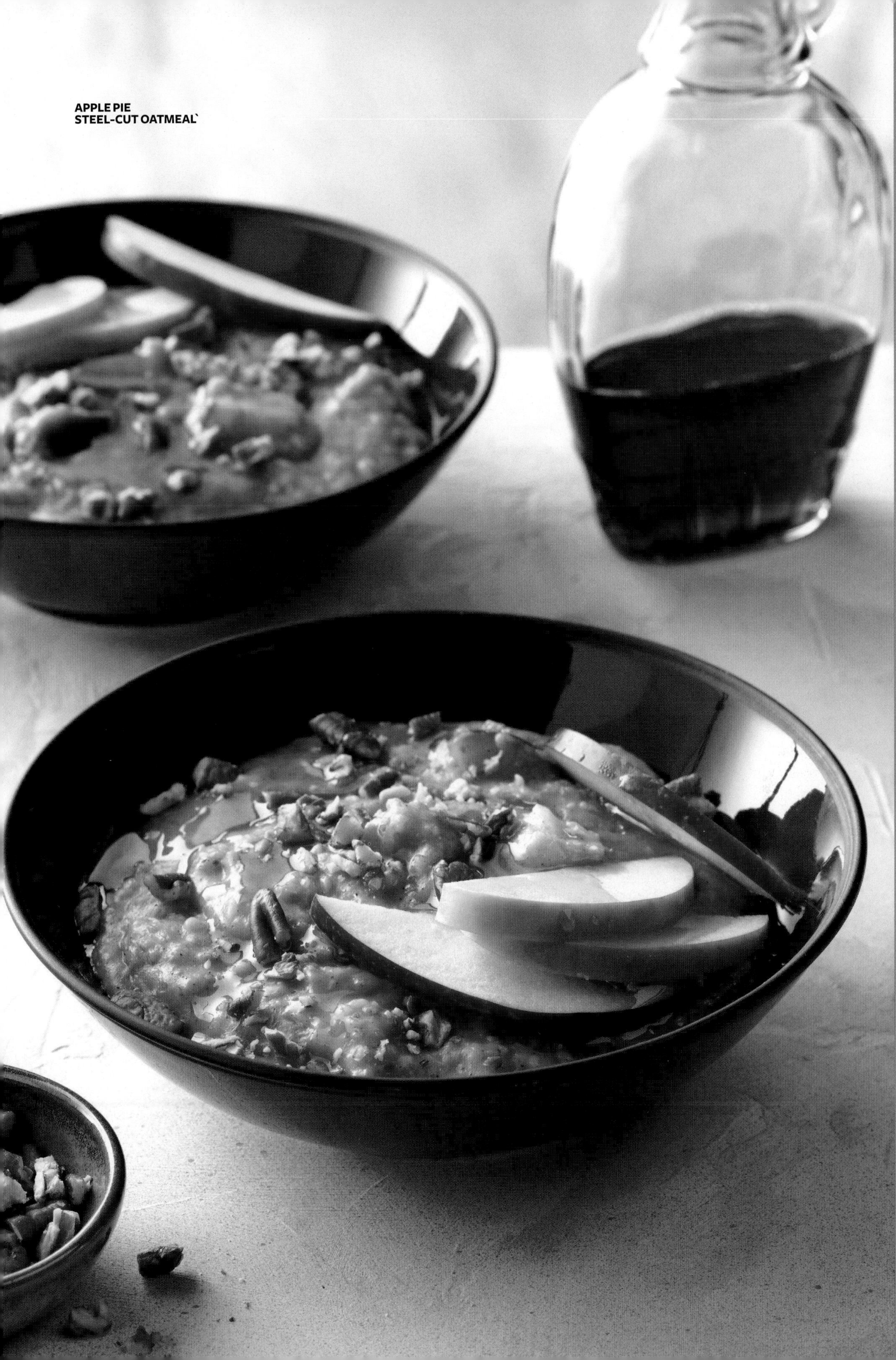

PUMPKIN PIE SMOOTHIE

I love pumpkin, and it is so good for you. I wanted a way to have my pie and eat it too—for breakfast! Add a sprinkle of granola for an extra treat.
—Alisa Christensen, Rancho Santa Margarita, CA

Takes: 10 min. • **Makes:** 2 servings

- 1 carton (5.3 oz.) fat-free plain Greek yogurt
- ½ cup 2% milk
- 2 Tbsp. maple syrup
- ¼ tsp. ground cinnamon or pumpkin pie spice
- 2 tsp. almond butter or peanut butter
- ⅔ cup canned pumpkin
- 1 cup ice cubes
- 1 Tbsp. granola

Place the first 7 ingredients in a blender; process until blended. Pour into glasses; top with granola.

1¼ cups: 197 cal., 5g fat (1g sat. fat), 5mg chol., 79mg sod., 30g carb. (21g sugars, 4g fiber), 12g pro. **Diabetic exchanges:** 2 starch, 1 fat.

BERRY PUFF PANCAKE

BERRY PUFF PANCAKE

Breakfast is my husband's favorite meal of the day. I use our homegrown blueberries in this sweet morning treat.
—Cecilia Morgan, Milwaukie, OR

Takes: 25 min. • **Makes:** 6 servings

- 1 Tbsp. butter
- 3 large eggs
- ¾ cup 2% milk
- ¾ cup all-purpose flour
- ½ tsp. salt

BERRY TOPPING
- 1 cup fresh raspberries
- 1 cup fresh blueberries
- 1 cup sliced fresh strawberries
- ⅓ cup orange marmalade
- 2 Tbsp. confectioners' sugar
  Whipped cream, optional

1. Place the butter in a 9-in. pie plate; place in a 400° oven for 4-5 minutes or until melted. Tilt pie plate to evenly coat bottom and sides with butter.

2. In a small bowl, whisk the eggs and milk. In another small bowl, combine the flour and salt; whisk in egg mixture until smooth. Pour batter into prepared pie plate. Bake until sides are crisp and golden brown, 15-20 minutes.

3. Meanwhile, in a large bowl, gently combine the berries and marmalade. Sprinkle pancake with confectioners' sugar; fill with berry mixture. Serve immediately. If desired, serve with whipped cream.

1 piece: 215 cal., 6g fat (3g sat. fat), 116mg chol., 273mg sod., 36g carb. (21g sugars, 3g fiber), 6g pro.

PUFFY APPLE OMELET

This delicious omelet recipe is such a fun way to use up fresh apples in the fall. With all the eggs our chickens produce, I could make (and we could eat) this omelet every day!
—Melissa Davenport, Campbell, MN

Takes: 30 min. • **Makes:** 2 servings

- 3 Tbsp. all-purpose flour
- ¼ tsp. baking powder
- ⅛ tsp. salt, optional
- 2 large eggs, separated
- 3 Tbsp. 2% milk
- 1 Tbsp. lemon juice
- 3 Tbsp. sugar

TOPPING
- 1 large apple, peeled if desired and thinly sliced
- 1 tsp. sugar
- ¼ tsp. ground cinnamon

1. Preheat oven to 375°. Mix flour, baking powder and, if desired, salt. In a small bowl, whisk together egg yolks, milk and lemon juice; stir into flour mixture.

2. In another bowl, beat egg whites on medium speed until foamy. Gradually add sugar, 1 Tbsp. at a time, beating on high after each addition until stiff peaks form. Fold into flour mixture.

3. Pour into a 9-in. deep-dish pie plate coated with cooking spray. Arrange apple slices over top. Mix sugar and cinnamon; sprinkle over apple.

4. Bake, uncovered, until a knife inserted in the center comes out clean, 18-20 minutes. Serve immediately.

1 piece: 253 cal., 5g fat (2g sat. fat), 188mg chol., 142mg sod., 44g carb. (32g sugars, 2g fiber), 9g pro.

* HEALTH TIP * Most puff pancakes are pretty lean but are satisfying even as breakfast for dinner. The filling often makes them unhealthy, but this recipe uses just a touch of sugar for sweetness.

PUFFY APPLE OMELET

CINNAMON BLUEBERRY
FRENCH TOAST

CINNAMON BLUEBERRY FRENCH TOAST

What's not to love about cozy French toast that cooks hands-free in the slow cooker? This is a standout dish for holidays and birthdays.
—Angela Lively, Conroe, TX

Prep: 15 min. + chilling • **Cook:** 3 hours
Makes: 6 servings

- 3 large eggs
- 2 cups 2% milk
- ¼ cup sugar
- 1 tsp. ground cinnamon
- 1 tsp. vanilla extract
- ¼ tsp. salt
- 9 cups cubed French bread (about 9 oz.)
- 1 cup fresh or frozen blueberries, thawed
  Maple syrup

1. Whisk together the first 6 ingredients. Place half of the bread in a greased 5-qt. slow cooker; top with ½ cup blueberries and half of the milk mixture. Repeat layers. Refrigerate, covered, 4 hours or overnight.
2. Cook, covered, on low until a knife inserted in the center comes out clean, 3-4 hours. Serve warm with syrup.

1 cup: 265 cal., 6g fat (2g sat. fat), 100mg chol., 430mg sod., 42g carb. (18g sugars, 2g fiber), 11g pro.

* HEALTH TIP * Swap whole wheat for white French bread to increase fiber. Or you can cube 100% whole wheat buns.

GINGERBREAD COFFEE CAKE

At our house, we love gingerbread that's not too sweet. To sweeten it a bit, just mix powdered sugar, milk and vanilla extract for drizzling on top.
—Barbara Humiston, Tampa, FL

Prep: 20 min. • **Bake:** 20 min. + cooling
Makes: 8 servings

- 1 cup all-purpose flour
- ½ cup plus 1 Tbsp. sugar, divided
- 1¾ tsp. ground cinnamon, divided
- 1 tsp. ground ginger
- ¼ tsp. salt
- ¼ tsp. ground allspice
- ¼ cup cold butter
- ¾ tsp. baking powder
- ½ tsp. baking soda
- 1 large egg, room temperature
- ½ cup buttermilk
- 2 Tbsp. molasses

1. Preheat oven to 350°. In a large bowl, mix flour, ½ cup sugar, ¾ tsp. cinnamon, ginger, salt and allspice; cut in butter until crumbly. Reserve ⅓ cup for topping.
2. Stir baking powder and baking soda into remaining flour mixture. In a small bowl, whisk egg, buttermilk and molasses. Add to the flour mixture; stir just until moistened. Transfer batter to a greased 8-in. round baking pan.
3. Add remaining sugar and cinnamon to reserved topping; sprinkle over batter. Bake 20-25 minutes or until a toothpick inserted in center comes out clean. Cool completely in pan on a wire rack.

1 slice: 195 cal., 7g fat (4g sat. fat), 39mg chol., 283mg sod., 31g carb. (19g sugars, 1g fiber), 3g pro. **Diabetic exchanges:** 2 starch, 1½ fat.
Confectioners' Sugar Icing (optional): Mix ¾ cup confectioners' sugar, 1 Tbsp. 2% milk and ½ tsp. vanilla extract. Drizzle over cooled coffee cake. Sprinkle with 2 Tbsp. finely chopped crystallized ginger.

GINGERBREAD COFFEE CAKE

APPLE CINNAMON OVERNIGHT OATS

Many folks love this oatmeal cold, but I like to heat it up a little since I'm not a big fan of it right out of the fridge. Add a handful of nuts for extra crunch, flavor and health benefits.

—Sarah Farmer, Waukesha, WI

Prep: 5 min. + chilling • **Makes:** 1 serving

½ cup old-fashioned oats
½ medium Gala or Honeycrisp apple, chopped
1 Tbsp. raisins
1 cup 2% milk
¼ tsp. ground cinnamon
Dash salt
Toasted, chopped nuts, optional

In a small container or Mason jar, combine all ingredients. Seal; refrigerate overnight.
1 serving: 349 cal., 8g fat (4g sat. fat), 20mg chol., 263mg sod., 59g carb. (28g sugars, 7g fiber), 14g pro.

CRANBERRY ORANGE ALMOND QUICK BREAD

CRANBERRY ORANGE ALMOND QUICK BREAD

You can customize this bread to your family's specific tastes. Try dried apricots and pecans, or dried blueberries and hazelnuts.

—*Taste of Home* Test Kitchen

Prep: 15 min. • **Bake:** 40 min. + cooling
Makes: 1 loaf (12 slices)

3 cups all-purpose flour
3 Tbsp. sugar
1 Tbsp. baking powder
½ tsp. salt
1 cup dried cranberries
½ cup sliced almonds, toasted
1 large egg, room temperature
1 cup fat-free milk
⅓ cup canola oil
¾ tsp. grated orange zest
¾ tsp. almond extract

1. Preheat oven to 350°. In a large bowl, whisk together first 4 ingredients; stir in cranberries and almonds. In another bowl, whisk together egg, milk, oil, zest and extract. Add to flour mixture; stir just until moistened.
2. Transfer to a 9x5-in. loaf pan coated with cooking spray. Bake until a toothpick inserted in center of loaf comes out clean, 40-50 minutes. Cool in pan 10 minutes before removing to a wire rack to cool.
1 slice: 258 cal., 9g fat (1g sat. fat), 16mg chol., 234mg sod., 40g carb. (14g sugars, 2g fiber), 5g pro.

> **TEST KITCHEN TIP**
>
> For skillet bread, prepare the batter as directed. Spoon into a greased 8-in. cast-iron skillet and bake at 350° until a toothpick comes out clean, 45-50 minutes. For muffins, spoon batter into 9 greased muffin tins and bake at 350° until a toothpick comes out clean, 25-30 minutes.

HAM MUFFINWICHES

I created this recipe when looking for something to pack for lunch. I had leftover ham but no bread, so I got creative with cornbread mix. The muffins freeze well and are handy for an on-the-go breakfast or lunch.

—Jenny Wiebe, Villa Hills, KY

....

Takes: 30 min. • **Makes:** 4 servings

- 1 large egg, room temperature, lightly beaten
- ⅓ cup 2% milk
- 1 Tbsp. canola oil
- ⅛ tsp. ground mustard
- 1 pkg. (8½ oz.) cornbread/muffin mix
- 1 cup chopped fully cooked ham
- 2 green onions, thinly sliced
- 2 Tbsp. shredded cheddar cheese

1. Preheat oven to 400°. Whisk together the first 4 ingredients. Add muffin mix; stir just until moistened. Fold in ham and green onions. Fill 8 greased or paper-lined muffin cups half full.

2. Bake until a toothpick inserted in center comes out clean, 15-20 minutes. Immediately sprinkle with cheese. Cool 5 minutes before removing from pan to a wire rack. Serve warm.

2 muffins: 186 cal., 8g fat (2g sat. fat), 37mg chol., 483mg sod., 22g carb. (7g sugars, 2g fiber), 7g pro. **Diabetic exchanges:** 1½ starch, 1 lean meat, 1 fat.

FLOWER PETAL SWEET ROLLS
(PICTURED ON P. 6)

I got the idea for these from the back of a package of frozen dinner rolls and adapted the recipe to use a homemade yeast dough. The pretty rolls make an impression on overnight guests when they come into the kitchen. You can prepare them the night before, chill, and then bake them in the morning.

—Celinda Skogsberg, Tuxedo Park, NY

....

Prep: 35 min. + rising
Bake: 20 min.
Makes: 11 petal rolls plus center roll

- ⅔ cup plain yogurt
- 1 pkg. (¼ oz.) active dry yeast
- ¼ cup warm water (110° to 115°)
- 3 Tbsp. canola oil
- 4½ tsp. sugar
- 2¼ cups all-purpose flour
- ½ tsp. baking soda
- ¼ tsp. salt

FILLING
- ¼ cup seedless raspberry jam or flavors of your choice

GLAZE
- ¼ cup confectioners' sugar
- 1½ tsp. butter, melted
- ¼ tsp. vanilla extract

1. Let yogurt stand at room temperature 15 minutes. In a large bowl, dissolve yeast in warm water. Add yogurt, oil and sugar. In another bowl, whisk flour, baking soda and salt. Add to yeast mixture; beat until smooth. Let stand 10 minutes.

2. Turn dough onto a floured surface; punch down. Divide and shape dough into 13 balls. For center of flower, combine 2 balls and place in the center of a greased pizza pan. Place remaining balls around center, allowing room for balls to rise. Cover with a kitchen towel; let rise in a warm place until doubled, about 1 hour. Preheat oven to 350°.

3. Depress centers of rolls; fill each with about 1 tsp. jam. Bake 20-25 minutes or until golden brown. Cool on pan for 5 minutes. Remove to a wire rack. Mix glaze ingredients; drizzle over rolls.

1 regular-sized roll: 151 cal., 4g fat (1g sat. fat), 3mg chol., 104mg sod., 25g carb. (8g sugars, 1g fiber), 3g pro. **Diabetic exchanges:** 1½ starch, 1 fat.

HAM MUFFINWICHES

STARTERS
& SNACKS

"Strawberries and basil are everywhere in the early summer, so get them together for a sipper that's pure sunshine. Garnish with basil leaves and sip it in the shade."
—Carolyn Turner, Reno, NV

Crumb-Topped Clams (p. 33) **Roasted Red Pepper Hummus** (p. 37) **Watermelon Tapas** (p. 43)
9-Layer Greek Dip (p. 38) **Strawberry-Basil Refresher** (p. 42) **Honey Horseradish Dip** (p. 43)

**ROASTED FRESH
PUMPKIN SEEDS**

ROASTED FRESH PUMPKIN SEEDS

I learned how to roast pumpkin seeds from my mother, who learned it from her mother. It's a wholesome, healthy snack and fun to make after you finish carving Halloween jack-o'-lanterns.
—Margaret Drye, Plainfield, NH

Prep: 20 min. + soaking
Bake: 1½ hours + cooling
Makes: 1½ cups

- 2 cups fresh pumpkin seeds
- 1 tsp. salt
- 1 Tbsp. olive oil
- ¾ tsp. kosher or fine sea salt

1. Place seeds in a 1-qt. bowl; cover with water. Stir in salt; let stand, covered, overnight.

2. Preheat oven to 200°. Drain and rinse seeds; drain again and pat dry. Transfer to a 15x10x1-in. baking pan. Toss with oil and salt; spread in a single layer.

3. Roast 1½-1¾ hours or until crisp and lightly browned, stirring occasionally. Cool completely. Store in an airtight container.

¼ cup: 115 cal., 6g fat (1g sat. fat), 0 chol., 248mg sod., 11g carb. (0 sugars, 4g fiber), 4g pro. **Diabetic exchanges:** 1 fat, ½ starch.

CRAB RANGOON

Bite into these golden appetizers and you'll find a creamy crab filling that rivals restaurant fare. Best of all, these crowd-pleasers are baked and not fried, so there's no reason to feel guilty about enjoying them.
—Taste of Home Test Kitchen

Takes: 25 min. • **Makes:** 14 appetizers

- 3 oz. reduced-fat cream cheese
- ⅛ tsp. garlic salt
- ⅛ tsp. Worcestershire sauce
- ½ cup lump crabmeat, drained
- 1 green onion, chopped
- 14 wonton wrappers
  Cooking spray

1. In a small bowl, combine the cream cheese, garlic salt and Worcestershire sauce until smooth. Stir in crab and onion. Place 2 teaspoonfuls in the center of each wonton wrapper. Moisten edges with water; bring corners to center over filling and press edges together to seal.

2. Place on a baking sheet coated with cooking spray. Lightly spray wontons with cooking spray. Bake at 425° for 8-10 minutes or until golden brown. Serve warm.

1 appetizer: 43 cal., 1g fat (1g sat. fat), 10mg chol., 117mg sod., 5g carb. (0 sugars, 0 fiber), 2g pro.

"BROCCOMOLE" DIP

For a snack that's very much like guacamole but without the avocados, which are high in fat, try this dip. I grow and freeze broccoli, so this recipe is convenient to make.
—Sue Gronholz, Beaver Dam, WI

Prep: 10 min. + chilling
Makes: 6 servings

- 2 cups chopped fresh broccoli, cooked and chilled
- ¼ cup reduced-fat sour cream
- 1 to 2 Tbsp. finely chopped onion
- 1 Tbsp. fat-free mayonnaise
- 2 to 3 Tbsp. lemon juice
- ¼ to ½ tsp. chili powder
  Assorted fresh vegetables or tortilla chips

In a food processor, combine the first 6 ingredients; cover and process until smooth. Refrigerate for several hours. Serve with vegetables or tortilla chips.

3 Tbsp.: 27 cal., 2g fat (0 sat. fat), 5mg chol., 33mg sod., 3g carb. (0 sugars, 0 fiber), 2g pro.
Diabetic exchanges: 1 vegetable.
* HEALTH TIP * This slim take on guacamole has just one-third of the calories of the popular avocado-based dip.

"BROCCOMOLE" DIP

GREEN TOMATO SALSA

I came up with this fresh salsa so I could use all the green tomatoes from the garden when it started to get cold.
—Vanessa Moon, Tucson, AZ

Prep: 20 min. + standing • **Cook:** 10 min.
Makes: 6 cups

- 1 medium green pepper
- 1 serrano pepper
- 5 medium green tomatoes or 5 large tomatillos, husks removed
- 1 medium onion, chopped
- 2 garlic cloves, minced
- ⅓ cup lime juice
- 2 Tbsp. olive oil
- 4 tsp. agave nectar
- 1 tsp. coarsely ground pepper
- ½ tsp. salt
- 3 Tbsp. fresh cilantro leaves
- 1 medium ripe avocado, peeled, pitted and quartered
  Tortilla chips

1. Preheat broiler. Place peppers on a foil-lined baking sheet. Broil 3-4 in. from heat until skins blister, about 5 minutes. With tongs, rotate peppers a quarter turn. Broil and rotate until all sides are blistered and blackened. Immediately place in a bowl; let stand, covered, 20 minutes.
2. Using tongs, place tomatoes, a few at a time, in a pot of boiling water for 5 minutes. Remove tomatoes; cool slightly. Peel and finely chop tomatoes; place in a large bowl.
3. Remove skin, stems and seeds from charred peppers. Finely chop peppers; add to tomatoes. Stir in onion and garlic.
4. Place all remaining ingredients except chips in a blender; cover and process until smooth. Add to tomato mixture, stirring to combine. Serve with chips.
Note: Wear disposable gloves when cutting hot peppers; the oils can burn skin. Avoid touching your face.
¼ cup: 27 cal., 2g fat (0 sat. fat), 0 chol., 50mg sod., 2g carb. (1g sugars, 1g fiber), 0 pro.
Diabetic exchanges: Free food.

SMOKED TROUT PATÉ

This tasty spread is easy to make in a food processor, and it's a guaranteed winner at any party. The recipe is versatile, so feel free to substitute other favorite smoked fish.
—Judy Walle, Toledo, OH

Takes: 15 min. • **Makes:** 2⅔ cups

- 1 lb. flaked smoked trout
- 3 oz. reduced-fat cream cheese
- ½ cup half-and-half cream
- 1 Tbsp. horseradish sauce
- 1 Tbsp. lemon juice
- ⅛ tsp. pepper
- 2 tsp. minced fresh parsley
  Cucumber slices
  Assorted crackers

Pulse the first 7 ingredients in a food processor until blended. Refrigerate, covered, until serving. Serve with cucumber slices and assorted crackers.

2 Tbsp.: 55 cal., 3g fat (1g sat. fat), 16mg chol., 174mg sod., 1g carb. (1g sugars, 0 fiber), 5g pro.

HOISIN MEATBALL LETTUCE WRAPS

HOISIN MEATBALL LETTUCE WRAPS

I make these tangy-sweet appetizers every year during the holidays, and it doesn't take long for them to disappear.
—Elaine Sweet, Dallas, TX

Prep: 35 min. • **Cook:** 35 min.
Makes: 3 dozen

- 2 Tbsp. cornstarch
- 2 large eggs, lightly beaten
- ¼ cup minced fresh chives
- 3 Tbsp. dry bread crumbs
- 3 Tbsp. hoisin sauce
- 4 tsp. minced fresh gingerroot
- 3 garlic cloves, minced
- ½ tsp. crushed red pepper flakes
- ¾ lb. lean ground beef (90% lean)
- ½ lb. ground pork
- 2 to 3 Tbsp. canola oil, divided

SAUCE
- ½ cup red currant jelly
- ½ cup hoisin sauce
- 2 Tbsp. mirin (sweet rice wine)
- 3 garlic cloves, minced
- 1½ tsp. Thai red chili paste

WRAPS
- 36 small Bibb or Boston lettuce leaves
- ¼ cup minced fresh cilantro

1. Place cornstarch in a shallow bowl. In a large bowl, combine the next 7 ingredients. Add beef and pork; mix lightly but thoroughly. Shape into 1-in. balls; coat with cornstarch.

2. In a large cast-iron or other heavy skillet, heat 2 Tbsp. oil over medium heat. Brown meatballs in batches, adding additional oil as needed. Remove with a slotted spoon; drain on paper towels.

3. Add sauce ingredients to skillet; cook and stir over medium heat until blended. Return meatballs to pan; bring to a boil. Reduce heat; simmer, uncovered, until meatballs are glazed and cooked through, 5-8 minutes, stirring occasionally. Serve meatballs in lettuce leaves; sprinkle with cilantro.

Note: Look for mirin in the Asian condiments section.

1 appetizer: 69 cal., 3g fat (1g sat. fat), 21mg chol., 99mg sod., 6g carb. (4g sugars, 0 fiber), 4g pro.

CHILI-LIME ROASTED CHICKPEAS

Looking for a lighter snack that's still a crowd-pleaser? You've found it! These zesty, crunchy chickpeas will have everyone happily munching.
—Julie Ruble, Charlotte, NC

Prep: 10 min. • **Bake:** 40 min. + cooling
Makes: 2 cups

- 2 cans (15 oz. each) chickpeas or garbanzo beans, rinsed, drained and patted dry
- 2 Tbsp. extra virgin olive oil
- 1 Tbsp. chili powder
- 2 tsp. ground cumin
- 1 tsp. grated lime zest
- 1 Tbsp. lime juice
- ¾ tsp. sea salt

1. Preheat oven to 400°. Line 15x10x1-in. baking sheet with foil. Spread chickpeas in a single layer over foil, removing any loose skins. Bake until very crunchy, 40-45 minutes, stirring every 15 minutes.

2. Meanwhile, whisk the remaining ingredients. Remove chickpeas from oven; let cool 5 minutes. Drizzle with oil mixture; shake pan to coat. Cool completely. Store in an airtight container.
⅓ cup: 178 cal., 8g fat (1g sat. fat), 0mg chol., 463mg sod., 23g carb. (3g sugars, 6g fiber), 6g pro.
Rosemary-Sea Salt variation: Prepare chickpeas according to step 1. Toss beans with 2 Tbsp. extra virgin olive oil, 1 Tbsp. minced fresh rosemary and ½ tsp. sea salt.
Orange-Curry variation: Prepare chickpeas according to step 1. Whisk 2 Tbsp. extra virgin olive oil, 1 tsp. grated orange zest and 1 Tbsp. curry powder. Toss with chickpeas. Cool completely.
Lemon-Pepper variation: Prepare chickpeas according to step 1. Whisk 2 Tbsp. extra virgin olive oil, 1 tsp. grated lemon zest and 2 tsp. freshly cracked pepper. Toss with chickpeas. Cool completely.

> **TEST KITCHEN TIP**
> Chickpeas are tossed with the spice mixture after baking because spices can become bitter if they burn.

GRILLED PINEAPPLE WITH LIME DIP

Serve this dish as an appetizer or a dessert—the choice is yours! If desired, the pineapple spears can be rolled in flaked coconut before grilling.
—*Taste of Home* Test Kitchen

Prep: 20 min. + marinating • **Grill:** 10 min.
Makes: 8 servings

- 1 fresh pineapple
- ¼ cup packed brown sugar
- 3 Tbsp. honey
- 2 Tbsp. lime juice

LIME DIP
- 3 oz. cream cheese, softened
- ¼ cup plain yogurt
- 2 Tbsp. honey
- 1 Tbsp. brown sugar
- 1 Tbsp. lime juice
- 1 tsp. grated lime zest

1. Peel and core the pineapple; cut vertically into 8 wedges. Cut each wedge horizontally into 2 spears. In a bowl or shallow dish, combine the brown sugar, honey and lime juice; add pineapple and turn to coat. Cover and refrigerate for 1 hour.
2. In a small bowl, beat cream cheese until smooth. Beat in the yogurt, honey, brown sugar, lime juice and zest. Cover and refrigerate until serving.
3. Coat grill rack with cooking spray before starting the grill. Drain pineapple, discarding marinade. Grill pineapple spears, covered, over medium heat for 3-4 minutes on each side or until golden brown. Serve with lime dip.
2 spears with 2 Tbsp. dip: 160 cal., 4g fat (2g sat. fat), 12mg chol., 41mg sod., 32g carb. (28g sugars, 2g fiber), 2g pro.

CHILI-LIME ROASTED CHICKPEAS

LEMON SPICED TEA

LEMON SPICED TEA

Adding cinnamon and honey really perks up the flavor of basic lemon tea. Add a splash of lemon extract to take this drink delightfully over the top.
—Adeline Russell, Hartford, WI

Takes: 10 min. • **Makes:** 8 servings

- 8 cups water
- 14 lemon-flavored tea bags
- 6 cinnamon sticks (3 in.)
- ½ cup honey
- ½ to 1 tsp. lemon extract, optional
  Lemon slices and additional cinnamon sticks

1. In a large saucepan, bring water to a boil. Remove from the heat; add tea bags and cinnamon sticks. Cover and steep for 6 minutes.
2. Discard tea bags and cinnamon sticks. Stir in honey and extract if desired. Serve warm in mugs. Garnish with lemon slices and cinnamon sticks.

1 cup: 66 cal., 0 fat (0 sat. fat), 0 chol., 8mg sod., 18g carb. (17g sugars, 0 fiber), 0 pro.
Diabetic exchanges: 1 starch.

FRUIT SALSA WITH CINNAMON CHIPS

I first made this fresh, fruity salsa for a family baby shower. Everyone wanted the recipe. Now, someone makes this juicy snack for just about every family gathering. We love it!
—Jessica Robinson, Indian Trail, NC

Takes: 30 min.
Makes: 2½ cups salsa and 80 chips

- 1 cup finely chopped fresh strawberries
- 1 medium navel orange, peeled and finely chopped
- 3 medium kiwifruit, peeled and finely chopped
- 1 can (8 oz.) unsweetened crushed pineapple, drained
- 1 Tbsp. lemon juice
- 1½ tsp. sugar

FRUIT SALSA WITH CINNAMON CHIPS

CINNAMON CHIPS
- 10 flour tortillas (8 in.)
- ¼ cup butter, melted
- ⅓ cup sugar
- 1 tsp. ground cinnamon

1. In a small bowl, combine the first 6 ingredients. Cover and refrigerate until serving.
2. For chips, brush tortillas with butter; cut each into 8 wedges. Combine sugar and cinnamon; sprinkle over wedges. Place on ungreased baking sheets.
3. Bake at 350° for 5-10 minutes or just until crisp. Serve with fruit salsa.

2 Tbsp. salsa with 4 chips: 134 cal., 4g fat (2g sat. fat), 6mg chol., 136mg sod., 22g carb. (7g sugars, 2g fiber), 2g pro.

FRESH CORN & AVOCADO DIP

MAKEOVER DEVILED EGGS

This updated version of a classic appetizer uses only half the egg yolks of the original recipe and calls for soft bread crumbs to help firm up the filling. We replaced the mayo with fat-free mayonnaise and reduced-fat sour cream.
—*Taste of Home* Test Kitchen

Takes: 10 min. • **Makes:** 16 servings

- 8 hard-boiled large eggs
- ¼ cup fat-free mayonnaise
- ¼ cup reduced-fat sour cream
- 2 Tbsp. soft bread crumbs
- 1 Tbsp. prepared mustard
- ¼ tsp. salt
     Dash white pepper
- 4 pimiento-stuffed olives, sliced
     Paprika, optional

Slice eggs in half lengthwise and remove yolks; refrigerate 8 yolk halves for another use. Set whites aside. In a small bowl, mash remaining yolks. Stir in the mayonnaise, sour cream, bread crumbs, mustard, salt and pepper. Stuff or pipe into egg whites. Garnish with olives. If desired, sprinkle with paprika.

1 filled egg half: 62 cal., 4g fat (1g sat. fat), 140mg chol., 135mg sod., 2g carb. (1g sugars, 0 fiber), 4g pro. **Diabetic exchanges:** ½ medium-fat meat.

FRESH CORN & AVOCADO DIP

I alter my sister's dip recipe by adding finely chopped jalapeno for a little heat. It's a different way to serve corn as a dip. You can make it ahead of time and chill until serving.
—Pat Roberts, Thornton, ON

Takes: 20 min. • **Makes:** 4 cups

- 2 cups fresh or frozen corn, thawed
- 1 medium ripe avocado, peeled and diced
- 1 small peach, peeled and chopped
- 1 small sweet red pepper, chopped
- 1 small red onion, chopped
- 2 Tbsp. olive oil
- 2 Tbsp. white wine vinegar
- 1 Tbsp. lime juice
- 1½ tsp. ground cumin
- 1 tsp. minced fresh oregano
- 1 garlic clove, crushed
     Salt and pepper to taste
- 1 minced and seeded jalapeno pepper, optional
     Baked tortilla chips

Combine first 11 ingredients; add salt and pepper and, if desired, jalapeno. Serve with tortilla chips.

¼ cup: 52 cal., 3g fat (0 sat. fat), 0 chol., 4mg sod., 6g carb. (2g sugars, 1g fiber), 1g pro. **Diabetic exchanges:** ½ starch, ½ fat.

CHIA SEED PROTEIN BITES

I keep these little bites on hand in my refrigerator and grab them for breakfast or to snack on when I'm in a hurry. We have a lot of food allergies in our family, and I like to keep healthy snacks around that everyone can eat. This recipe has no gluten, eggs, dairy or corn, so it's the perfect go-to treat in our house.
—Tanja Miller, Peoria, AZ

Prep: 15 min. + chilling
Makes: about 2½ dozen

1½ cups quick-cooking oats
½ cup almond butter or creamy peanut butter
½ cup chia seeds
½ cup honey
¼ cup vanilla or chocolate protein powder
¼ cup unsweetened shredded coconut
Additional unsweetened shredded coconut, optional

In a large bowl, combine the first 6 ingredients. Refrigerate 1 hour or until firm enough to roll. Shape into 1½-in. balls. Roll in additional coconut if desired. Store in the refrigerator.

1 piece: 72 cal., 4g fat (1g sat. fat), 0 chol., 14mg sod., 9g carb. (5g sugars, 2g fiber), 2g pro.

CRUMB-TOPPED CLAMS
(PICTURED ON P. 24)

In my family, it wouldn't be Christmas Eve without baked clams. They're easy to make and always a hit. Actually, these are wonderful for any occasion.
—Annmarie Lucente, Monroe, NY

Prep: 35 min. • **Broil:** 10 min.
Makes: 2 dozen

2 lbs. kosher salt
2 dozen fresh littleneck clams
½ cup dry bread crumbs
¼ cup chicken broth
1 Tbsp. minced fresh parsley
2 Tbsp. olive oil
2 garlic cloves, minced
¼ tsp. dried oregano
Dash pepper
1 Tbsp. panko (Japanese) bread crumbs
Lemon wedges

1. Spread salt into an ovenproof metal serving platter or a 15x10x1-in. baking pan. Shuck clams, leaving clams and juices in bottom shells. Arrange in prepared platter; divide juices among shells.
2. In a small bowl, mix dry bread crumbs, chicken broth, parsley, oil, garlic, oregano and pepper; spoon over clams. Sprinkle with panko bread crumbs.
3. Broil 4-6 in. from heat 6-8 minutes or until clams are firm and crumb mixture is crisp and golden brown. Serve immediately with lemon wedges.

1 clam: 31 cal., 1g fat (0 sat. fat), 5mg chol., 35mg sod., 2g carb. (0 sugars, 0 fiber), 2g pro.

CHIA SEED PROTEIN BITES

COLD-BREW COFFEE

Cold-brewing reduces the acidity of coffee, which enhances its natural sweetness and complex flavors. Even those who take hot coffee with sugar and cream might find themselves sipping cold brew plain.
—*Taste of Home* Test Kitchen

Prep: 10 min. + chilling
Makes: 8 servings

- 1 cup coarsely ground medium-roast coffee
- 1 cup hot water (205°)
- 6 to 7 cups cold water
  2% milk or half-and-half cream, optional

1. Place the coffee grounds in a clean glass container. Pour hot water over the grounds; let stand 10 minutes. Stir in cold water. Cover and refrigerate for 12-24 hours. (The longer the coffee sits, the stronger the flavor.)
2. Strain the coffee through a fine mesh sieve; discard grounds. Strain the coffee again through a coffee filter; discard grounds. Serve over ice, with milk or cream if desired. Store in the refrigerator for up to 2 weeks.

1 cup: 2 cal., 0 fat (0 sat. fat), 0 chol., 4mg sod., 0 carb. (0 sugars, 0 fiber), 0 pro.

> **TEST KITCHEN TIP**
>
> Freeze some coffee in ice cube trays. The frozen coffee cubes will chill your beverage without watering it down.

SLOW-COOKER CAPONATA

This Italian eggplant dip preps quickly and actually gets better as it stands. Serve it warm or at room temperature. Try adding a little leftover caponata to scrambled eggs for a savory breakfast.
—Nancy Beckman, Helena, MT

Prep: 20 min. • **Cook:** 5 hours
Makes: 6 cups

- 2 medium eggplants, cut into ½-in. pieces
- 1 medium onion, chopped
- 1 can (14½ oz.) diced tomatoes, undrained
- 12 garlic cloves, sliced
- ½ cup dry red wine
- 3 Tbsp. extra virgin olive oil
- 2 Tbsp. red wine vinegar
- 4 tsp. capers, undrained
- 5 bay leaves
- 1½ tsp. salt
- ¼ tsp. coarsely ground pepper
  French bread baguette slices, toasted
  Optional: Fresh basil leaves, toasted pine nuts and additional olive oil

Place first 11 ingredients in a 6-qt. slow cooker (do not stir). Cook, covered, on high for 3 hours. Stir gently; replace cover. Cook on high until vegetables are tender, about 2 hours longer. Cool slightly; discard bay leaves. Serve with toasted baguette slices. Serve with toppings as desired.

¼ cup: 34 cal., 2g fat (0 sat. fat), 0 chol., 189mg sod., 4g carb. (2g sugars, 2g fiber), 1g pro.

COLD-BREW COFFEE

SLOW-COOKER CAPONATA

ASPARAGUS BRUSCHETTA

ASPARAGUS BRUSCHETTA

I really like asparagus, so I'm always trying it in different things. Here's a delicious twist on traditional bruschetta.
—Elaine Sweet, Dallas, TX

....

Takes: 30 min. • **Makes:** 1 dozen

- 3 cups water
- ½ lb. fresh asparagus, cut into ½-in. pieces
- 2 cups grape tomatoes, halved
- ¼ cup minced fresh basil
- 3 green onions, chopped
- 3 Tbsp. lime juice
- 1 Tbsp. olive oil
- 3 garlic cloves, minced
- 1½ tsp. grated lime zest
- ¼ tsp. salt
- ¼ tsp. pepper
- 12 slices French bread baguette (½ in. thick), toasted
- ½ cup crumbled blue cheese

1. In a large saucepan, bring water to a boil. Add the asparagus; cover and boil for 2-4 minutes. Drain and immediately place asparagus in ice water. Drain and pat dry.
2. In a large bowl, combine the asparagus, tomatoes, basil, onions, lime juice, oil, garlic, lime zest, salt and pepper. Using a slotted spoon, spoon asparagus mixture onto bread. Sprinkle with blue cheese.
1 piece: 59 cal., 3g fat (1g sat. fat), 4mg chol., 165mg sod., 6g carb. (1g sugars, 1g fiber), 3g pro.

FRUIT & NUT TRAIL MIX

This mouthwatering mix is filled with nutrition and flavor. Whether you're enjoying the outdoors or headed out the door to work, you'll find that this munchable medley hits the spot.
—Mary Ann Dell, Phoenixville, PA

....

Prep: 15 min. • **Bake:** 1 hour + cooling
Makes: 4 cups

- 1 pkg. (6 oz.) dried apricots, quartered
- ¾ cup golden raisins
- ¾ cup walnut halves
- ½ cup salted cashews
- ½ cup sunflower kernels
- ⅓ cup dried cranberries
- ¼ cup sugar
- 1½ tsp. Chinese five-spice powder
- ½ tsp. salt
- ¼ tsp. ground cinnamon
- 1 large egg white
- 1 tsp. water

1. Preheat oven to 250°. Coat a foil-lined 15x10x1-in. baking pan with cooking spray; set aside. In a large bowl, combine the first 10 ingredients. In a small bowl, beat egg white and water on high speed for 1 minute or until frothy; fold into the fruit mixture.
2. Spread into prepared pan. Bake until aromatic and nuts are lightly browned, about 1 hour, stirring every 15 minutes. Cool mixture completely. Store in an airtight container.
⅓ cup: 203 cal., 10g fat (1g sat. fat), 0 chol., 173mg sod., 28g carb. (21g sugars, 3g fiber), 4g pro.

WARM SPICED NUTS

I like to set out bowls of spiced nuts at my holiday parties. Sometimes I stir in M&M's to create a sweet and salty snack.
—Jill Matson, Zimmerman, MN

....

Prep: 5 min. • **Bake:** 30 min.
Makes: 3 cups

- 1 cup pecan halves
- 1 cup unblanched almonds
- 1 cup unsalted dry roasted peanuts
- 3 Tbsp. butter, melted
- 4½ tsp. Worcestershire sauce
- 1 tsp. chili powder
- ½ tsp. garlic salt
- ¼ tsp. cayenne pepper

1. In a large bowl, combine the pecans, almonds and peanuts. Combine butter and Worcestershire sauce; pour over nuts and toss to coat.

2. Spread nuts in a single layer in an ungreased 15x10x1-in. baking pan. Bake at 300° until browned, about 30 minutes, stirring occasionally.

3. Transfer warm nuts to a bowl. Combine the chili powder, garlic salt and cayenne; sprinkle over nuts and stir to coat. Serve warm, or allow to cool before storing in an airtight container.

¼ cup: 231 cal., 22g fat (4g sat. fat), 8mg chol., 123mg sod., 7g carb. (2g sugars, 3g fiber), 6g pro.

WARM SPICED NUTS

ROASTED RED PEPPER HUMMUS

(PICTURED ON P. 25)

My son taught me how to make hummus, which is a smart alternative to many calorie-laden dips. This recipe is simply delicious. Fresh-roasted bell peppers make it really special.
—Nancy Watson-Pistole, Shawnee, KS

....

Prep: 30 min. + standing • **Makes:** 3 cups

- 2 large sweet red peppers
- 2 cans (15 oz. each) garbanzo beans or chickpeas, rinsed and drained
- ⅓ cup lemon juice
- 3 Tbsp. tahini
- 1 Tbsp. olive oil
- 2 garlic cloves, peeled
- 1¼ tsp. salt
- 1 tsp. curry powder
- ½ tsp. ground coriander
- ½ tsp. ground cumin
- ½ tsp. pepper
  Fresh vegetables, pita bread or assorted crackers, optional

1. Broil red peppers 4 in. from heat until skins blister, about 5 minutes. With tongs, rotate peppers a quarter turn. Broil and rotate until all sides are blistered and blackened. Immediately place peppers in a bowl; cover and let stand 15-20 minutes.

2. Peel off and discard charred skins. Remove stems and seeds. Place the peppers in a food processor. Add the beans, lemon juice, tahini, oil, garlic and seasonings; cover and process until blended.

3. Transfer to a serving bowl. Serve with vegetables, pita bread or crackers.

¼ cup: 113 cal., 5g fat (1g sat. fat), 0 chol., 339mg sod., 14g carb. (3g sugars, 4g fiber), 4g pro. **Diabetic exchanges:** 1 starch, 1 fat.

9-LAYER GREEK DIP
(PICTURED ON P. 24)

Instead of the same old taco dip at every potluck, try serving this light, cool, refreshing alternative. It not only looks healthy—it really is!
—Shawn Barto, Winter Garden, FL

Takes: 20 min. • **Makes:** 5½ cups

- 1 carton (10 oz.) hummus
- 1 cup refrigerated tzatziki sauce
- ½ cup chopped green pepper
- ½ cup chopped sweet red pepper
- ½ cup chopped peeled cucumber
- ½ cup chopped water-packed artichoke hearts, drained
- ½ cup chopped pitted Greek olives, optional
- ¼ cup chopped pepperoncini
- 1 cup crumbled feta cheese
  Baked pita chips

In a 9-in. deep-dish pie plate, layer the first 6 ingredients; top with olives, if desired, and pepperoncini. Sprinkle with feta cheese. Refrigerate until serving. Serve with pita chips.

¼ cup: 60 cal., 4g fat (1g sat. fat), 5mg chol., 210mg sod., 4g carb. (1g sugars, 1g fiber), 3g pro. **Diabetic exchanges:** ½ starch, ½ fat.

PEAR WALDORF PITAS

PEAR WALDORF PITAS

Here's a guaranteed table brightener for a shower, luncheon or party. Just stand back and watch these little sandwiches disappear. For an eye-catching presentation, I tuck each one into a colorful paper napkin.
—Roxann Parker, Dover, DE

Prep: 20 min. + chilling
Makes: 20 mini pitas

- 2 medium ripe pears, diced
- ½ cup thinly sliced celery
- ½ cup halved seedless red grapes
- 2 Tbsp. finely chopped walnuts
- 2 Tbsp. lemon yogurt
- 2 Tbsp. mayonnaise
- ⅛ tsp. poppy seeds
- 20 miniature pita pocket halves
  Lettuce leaves

1. In a large bowl, combine the pears, celery, grapes and walnuts. In another bowl, whisk the yogurt, mayonnaise and poppy seeds. Add to pear mixture; toss to coat. Refrigerate for 1 hour or overnight.
2. Line pita halves with lettuce; fill each with 2 Tbsp. pear mixture.

1 pita half: 67 cal., 2g fat (0 sat. fat), 0 chol., 86mg sod., 12g carb. (3g sugars, 1g fiber), 2g pro. **Diabetic exchanges:** 1 starch.

10-MINUTE SALSA

The view from our mountain home includes Pikes Peak, so we frequently dine on our wraparound porch in good weather. During family get-togethers, we often savor this zippy salsa with chips while we feast on the natural beauty all around us.
—Kim Morin, Lake George, CO

Takes: 10 min. • **Makes:** 1½ cups

- 1 can (10 oz.) diced tomatoes and green chiles, undrained
- 1 Tbsp. seeded chopped jalapeno pepper
- 1 Tbsp. chopped red onion
- 1 Tbsp. minced fresh cilantro
- 1 garlic clove, minced
- 1 Tbsp. olive oil
- Dash salt
- Dash pepper
- Tortilla chips

In a small bowl, combine the tomatoes, jalapeno, onion, cilantro, garlic, oil, salt and pepper. Refrigerate until serving. Serve with tortilla chips.

Note: Wear disposable gloves when cutting hot peppers; the oils can burn skin. Avoid touching your face.

¼ cup: 29 cal., 2g fat (0 sat. fat), 0 chol., 214mg sod., 2g carb. (0 sugars, 1g fiber), 0 pro. **Diabetic exchanges:** ½ fat.

HOT GINGER COFFEE

I like to sit by the fire and sip this coffee on chilly days. It's a delightful way to warm up when you come in from the cold, but it's the perfect pick-me-up on any morning, too.
—Audrey Thibodeau, Gilbert, AZ

Takes: 25 min. • **Makes:** 6 servings

- 6 Tbsp. ground coffee (not instant)
- 1 Tbsp. grated orange zest
- 1 Tbsp. chopped crystallized ginger
- ½ tsp. ground cinnamon
- 6 cups cold water
- Whipped cream, cinnamon sticks and/or additional orange zest, optional

1. Combine coffee, orange zest, ginger and cinnamon. Place in a coffee filter and brew with the cold water according to the manufacturer's directions.

2. Pour into mugs; if desired, garnish with whipped cream, cinnamon sticks and orange zest.

Note: Look for crystallized or candied ginger in the spice or baking section of your grocery store.

1 cup: 3 cal., 0 fat (0 sat. fat), 0 chol., 5mg sod., 5g carb. (0 sugars, 0 fiber), 0 pro.

10-MINUTE SALSA

CLASSIC SWEDISH MEATBALLS

CLASSIC SWEDISH MEATBALLS

I'm a Svenska flicka (Swedish girl) from northwest Iowa, where many Swedes settled at the turn of the century. This recipe was given to me by a Swedish friend. It's obviously a modern version of a 19th-century favorite, since back then they didn't have bouillon granules or evaporated milk! I think you'll agree that these modern-day kottbullar *are quite tasty.*
—Emily Gould, Hawarden, IA

Prep: 15 min. + chilling • **Cook:** 20 min.
Makes: 3½ dozen

- 1⅔ cups evaporated milk, divided
- ⅔ cup chopped onion
- ¼ cup fine dry bread crumbs
- ½ tsp. salt
- ½ tsp. allspice
  Dash pepper
- 1 lb. lean ground beef (90% lean)
- 2 tsp. butter
- 2 tsp. beef bouillon granules
- 1 cup boiling water
- ½ cup cold water
- 2 Tbsp. all-purpose flour
- 1 Tbsp. lemon juice
  Canned lingonberries, optional

1. Combine ⅔ cup evaporated milk with the next 5 ingredients. Add beef; mix lightly. Refrigerate until chilled.
2. With wet hands, shape meat mixture into 1-in. balls. In a large skillet, heat butter over medium heat. Brown meatballs in batches. Dissolve bouillon in boiling water. Pour over meatballs; bring to a boil. Cover; simmer 15 minutes.
3. Meanwhile, stir together cold water and flour. Remove meatballs from skillet; skim fat, reserving juices. Add the flour mixture and remaining evaporated milk to pan juices; cook, uncovered, over low heat, stirring until sauce thickens.
4. Return meatballs to skillet. Stir in lemon juice. If desired, top with lingonberries.
1 meatball: 36 cal., 2g fat (1g sat. fat), 10mg chol., 87mg sod., 2g carb. (1g sugars, 0 fiber), 3g pro.

CRESCENT SAMOSAS

CRESCENT SAMOSAS

Tender, buttery crescents are filled with a delicious potato mixture, making these appetizers a real standout. No one will guess that they're light!
—Jennifer Kemp, Grosse Pointe Park, MI

Prep: 25 min. • **Bake:** 10 min.
Makes: 16 appetizers (¾ cup sauce)

- ¾ cup reduced-fat plain yogurt
- 2 Tbsp. minced fresh cilantro
- 1 garlic clove, minced
- ½ tsp. ground cumin
  Dash pepper
  SAMOSAS
- 1 Tbsp. olive oil
- 1 can (14½ oz.) diced new potatoes, well drained, or 1¾ cups diced cooked red potatoes
- ¼ cup canned chopped green chiles
- 1 garlic clove, minced
- 1 tsp. curry powder
  Dash pepper
- 1½ tsp. lemon juice
- 1 cup frozen peas, thawed
- 2 tubes (8 oz. each) refrigerated reduced-fat crescent rolls

1. Preheat oven to 375°. For sauce, mix first 5 ingredients; refrigerate until serving.
2. In a large nonstick skillet, heat oil over medium-high heat; saute potatoes until lightly browned. Add chiles, garlic, curry powder and pepper; cook and stir 1 minute. Transfer to a bowl; add lemon juice and coarsely mash. Stir in peas.
3. Unroll crescent dough and separate into 16 triangles. Place 1 Tbsp. potato mixture on the wide end of each triangle; roll up from wide end. Place 2 in. apart on ungreased baking sheets, point side down; curve to form crescents.
4. Bake samosas until golden brown, 10-12 minutes. Serve with sauce.
1 appetizer with 2 tsp. sauce: 130 cal., 6g fat (2g sat. fat), 1mg chol., 305mg sod., 18g carb. (3g sugars, 1g fiber), 4g pro.

GARLIC BEAN DIP

GARLIC BEAN DIP

There isn't a bean that my family does not like. In fact, I serve one kind or another almost every day. This dip is one of our favorite ways to enjoy beans.
—Nancy Testin, Harrington, DE

. . . .

Takes: 10 min. • **Makes:** 6 servings

- 1 can (15 oz.) cannellini beans, rinsed and drained
- 1 Tbsp. cider vinegar
- 2 garlic cloves, minced
- ½ tsp. salt
- ½ tsp. ground cumin
- ⅓ cup reduced-fat mayonnaise
- 2 Tbsp. chopped fresh parsley
    Baked pita chips or assorted fresh vegetables

Place the first 5 ingredients in a food processor; process until almost smooth. Add mayonnaise and parsley; pulse just until blended. Serve with pita chips or fresh vegetables.

¼ cup dip: 102 cal., 5g fat (1g sat. fat), 5mg chol., 371mg sod., 11g carb. (1g sugars, 3g fiber), 3g pro. **Diabetic exchanges:** 1 starch, 1 fat.

STRAWBERRY-BASIL REFRESHER
(PICTURED ON P. 25)

Strawberries and basil are everywhere in the early summer, so get them together for a sipper that's pure sunshine. Garnish with basil leaves and enjoy it in the shade.
—Carolyn Turner, Reno, NV

. . . .

Takes: 10 min. • **Makes:** 12 servings

- ⅔ cup lemon juice
- ½ cup sugar
- 1 cup sliced fresh strawberries
    Ice cubes
- 1 to 2 Tbsp. chopped fresh basil
- 1 bottle (1 liter) club soda, chilled

1. Place lemon juice, sugar, strawberries and 1 cup ice cubes in a blender; cover and process until blended. Add basil; pulse 1 or 2 times to combine.

2. Divide strawberry mixture among 12 cocktail glasses. Fill with ice; top with club soda.

1 serving: 40 cal., 0 fat (0 sat. fat), 0 chol., 18mg sod., 10g carb. (9g sugars, 0 fiber), 0 pro. **Diabetic exchanges:** ½ starch.

WATERMELON TAPAS

I start looking forward to biting into this summery treat when snow is still on the ground! Whenever I make this for my friends, they swoon. It's also my secret for getting my kids to eat their fruit.
—Jami Geittmann, Greendale, WI

Takes: 25 min. • **Makes:** 8 servings

- ½ cup plain Greek yogurt
- 1 Tbsp. minced fresh mint
- 1 Tbsp. honey
- 8 wedges seedless watermelon, about 1 in. thick
- 1 medium kiwifruit, peeled and chopped
- 1 tangerine, sliced
- ½ cup sliced ripe mangoes
- ½ cup fresh raspberries
- ¼ cup fresh blueberries
- ¼ cup pomegranate seeds
- 2 Tbsp. pistachios, chopped
  Additional honey and mint, optional

In a bowl, combine yogurt, mint and honey. Arrange watermelon wedges on a platter; top each with yogurt mixture, fruit and pistachios. If desired, top with additional honey and mint. Serve immediately.

1 wedge: 103 cal., 2g fat (1g sat. fat), 4mg chol., 18mg sod., 21g carb. (18g sugars, 2g fiber), 2g pro. **Diabetic exchanges:** 1½ fruit.

WATERMELON TAPAS

HONEY HORSERADISH DIP
(PICTURED ON P. 25)

We love having appetizers on Friday night instead of a meal, and during the summer we enjoy cooler foods. This has just the right amount of zing when served with chilled shrimp and crisp garden peas.
—Ann Marie Eberhart, Gig Harbor, WA

Prep: 10 min. + chilling • **Makes:** 1 cup

- ½ cup fat-free plain Greek yogurt
- ¼ cup stone-ground mustard
- ¼ cup honey
- 2 Tbsp. prepared horseradish
  Cold cooked shrimp and fresh sugar snap peas

Combine yogurt, mustard, honey and horseradish; refrigerate 1 hour. Serve with shrimp and snap peas.

2 Tbsp.: 54 cal., 1g fat (0 sat. fat), 0 chol., 177mg sod., 11g carb. (10g sugars, 0 fiber), 2g pro. **Diabetic exchanges:** 1 starch.

SLOW-COOKER MARINATED MUSHROOMS

ITALIAN VEGGIE BITES

These colorful appetizers are not only tasty, but they also pack in a surprising amount of veggies! The addition of mozzarella and Parmesan cheeses is the perfect Italian touch.
—Cathy Horvath, Surrey, BC

Prep: 35 min. • **Bake:** 5 min.
Makes: 4 dozen

- 1 small eggplant, finely chopped
- 1 cup finely chopped onion
- 1 medium sweet red pepper, finely chopped
- 1 medium zucchini, finely chopped
- 2 garlic cloves, minced
- ¼ cup reduced-fat sun-dried tomato salad dressing
- 1 large tomato, finely chopped
- ¼ cup grated Parmesan cheese
- 10 flavored tortillas of your choice (10 in.)
- ¼ cup shredded part-skim mozzarella cheese

1. In a large skillet over medium heat, cook and stir the eggplant, onion, red pepper, zucchini and garlic in salad dressing for 3 minutes. Bring to a boil. Reduce heat; cover and simmer for 5-7 minutes or until vegetables are tender. Remove from heat; stir in tomato and Parmesan cheese.
2. With a 3-in. biscuit cutter, cut 48 circles from tortillas. Cut a slit halfway into each tortilla circle. Shape into a cone; place in a miniature muffin cup. Spoon 4 tsp. vegetable mixture into each cup. Sprinkle with mozzarella cheese.
3. Bake at 350° for 5-7 minutes or until tortilla cups are crisp and cheese is melted. Serve warm.

1 appetizer: 40 cal., 1g fat (0 sat. fat), 1mg chol., 63mg sod., 7g carb. (1g sugars, 1g fiber), 1g pro. **Diabetic exchanges:** ½ starch.

SLOW-COOKER MARINATED MUSHROOMS

Here's a healthy and delicious addition to any buffet spread. Mushrooms and pearl onions seasoned with herbs, balsamic and red wine are terrific on their own or alongside a tenderloin roast.
—Courtney Wilson, Fresno, CA

Prep: 15 min. • **Cook:** 6 hours
Makes: 5 cups

- 2 lbs. medium fresh mushrooms
- 1 pkg. (14.4 oz.) frozen pearl onions, thawed
- 4 garlic cloves, minced
- 2 cups reduced-sodium beef broth
- ½ cup dry red wine
- 3 Tbsp. balsamic vinegar
- 3 Tbsp. olive oil
- 1 tsp. salt
- 1 tsp. dried basil
- ½ tsp. dried thyme
- ½ tsp. pepper
- ¼ tsp. crushed red pepper flakes

Place mushrooms, onions and garlic in a 5- or 6-qt. slow cooker. In a small bowl, whisk remaining ingredients; pour over mushrooms. Cook, covered, on low until mushrooms are tender, 6-8 hours.
Freeze option: Freeze the cooled mushrooms and juices in freezer containers. To use, partially thaw in refrigerator overnight. Microwave, covered, on high in a microwave-safe dish until heated through, stirring gently and adding a little broth or water if necessary.
¼ cup: 42 cal., 2g fat (0 sat. fat), 1mg chol., 165mg sod., 4g carb. (2g sugars, 0 fiber), 1g pro.

ITALIAN VEGGIE BITES

SOUPS & SANDWICHES

"Because it looks different from traditional chili, my family was a little hesitant to try this dish at first. But thanks to full, hearty flavor, it's become a real favorite."

—Jeanette Urbom, Louisburg, KS

Lentil, Bacon & Bean Soup (p. 53) Shredded Chicken Gyros (p. 59) Golden Butternut Squash Soup (p. 61)
Turkey Sandwich with Raspberry-Mustard Spread (p. 50) Chicken Chili with Black Beans (p. 62) Lentil Sloppy Joes (p. 57)

ITALIAN BEEF ON ROLLS

This slow-cooker recipe is one of my all-time favorites! With 29 grams of protein per serving, it's a great way to meet your daily needs.
—Jami Hilker, Harrison, AR

Prep: 15 min. • **Cook:** 8 hours
Makes: 8 servings

- 1 beef sirloin tip roast (2 lbs.)
- 1 can (14½ oz.) diced tomatoes, undrained
- 1 medium green pepper, chopped
- ½ cup water
- 1 Tbsp. sesame seeds
- 1½ tsp. garlic powder
- 1 tsp. fennel seed, crushed
- ½ tsp. salt
- ½ tsp. pepper
- 8 kaiser rolls, split

1. Place the roast in a 3-qt. slow cooker. In a small bowl, combine the tomatoes, green pepper, water and seasonings; pour over roast. Cover; cook on low 8-9 hours or until meat is tender.

2. Remove roast; cool slightly. Skim fat from cooking juices; shred beef and return to the slow cooker. Serve on rolls.

1 sandwich: 333 cal., 8g fat (2g sat. fat), 72mg chol., 573mg sod., 34g carb. (3g sugars, 3g fiber), 29g pro. **Diabetic exchanges:** 2 starch, 3 lean meat.

GOLDEN BEET & PEACH SOUP WITH TARRAGON

GOLDEN BEET & PEACH SOUP WITH TARRAGON

We had a bumper crop of peaches from our two trees one summer, and I had fun experimenting with different recipes. After seeing a beet soup recipe in a cookbook, I changed it just a bit to include our homegrown golden beets and sweet peaches.
—Sue Gronholz, Beaver Dam, WI

Prep: 20 min. • **Bake:** 40 min. + chilling
Makes: 6 servings

- 2 lbs. fresh golden beets, peeled and cut into 1-in. cubes
- 1 Tbsp. olive oil
- 2 cups white grape-peach juice
- 2 Tbsp. cider vinegar
- ¼ cup plain Greek yogurt
- ¼ tsp. finely chopped fresh tarragon
- 2 medium fresh peaches, peeled and diced
  Additional fresh tarragon sprigs

1. Preheat oven to 400°. Place beets in a 15x10x1-in. baking pan. Drizzle with olive oil; toss to coat. Roast until tender, 40-45 minutes. Cool slightly.

2. Transfer beets to a blender or food processor. Add juice and vinegar; process until smooth. Refrigerate at least 1 hour. In a small bowl, combine Greek yogurt and tarragon; refrigerate.

3. To serve, divide beet mixture among individual bowls; place a spoonful of yogurt mixture into each bowl. Top with diced peaches and additional tarragon.

⅔ cup: 159 cal., 4g fat (1g sat. fat), 3mg chol., 129mg sod., 31g carb. (26g sugars, 4g fiber), 3g pro. **Diabetic exchanges:** 2 vegetable, 1 fruit, ½ fat.

TEST KITCHEN TIP

For a different taste sensation, substitute ½ tsp. of either chopped fresh basil, thyme or chives for the tarragon.

ASIAN VEGETABLE-BEEF SOUP

My husband is Korean American, and I enjoy working Asian flavors into our menus. This tasty soup was something I put together one night with what we had in our fridge. Everyone loved it!
—Mollie Lee, Rockwall, TX

Prep: 30 min. • **Cook:** 1¾ hours
Makes: 6 servings

- 1 lb. beef stew meat, cut into 1-in. cubes
- 1 Tbsp. canola oil
- 2 cups water
- 1 cup beef broth
- ¼ cup sherry or additional beef broth
- ¼ cup reduced-sodium soy sauce
- 6 green onions, chopped
- 3 Tbsp. brown sugar
- 2 garlic cloves, minced
- 1 Tbsp. minced fresh gingerroot
- 2 tsp. sesame oil
- ¼ tsp. cayenne pepper
- 1½ cups sliced fresh mushrooms
- 1½ cups julienned carrots
- 1 cup sliced bok choy
- 1½ cups uncooked long grain rice
  Chive blossoms, optional

1. In a large saucepan, brown meat in oil on all sides; drain. Add the water, broth, sherry, soy sauce, onions, brown sugar, garlic, ginger, sesame oil and cayenne. Bring to a boil. Reduce heat; cover and simmer for 1 hour.
2. Stir in the mushrooms, carrots and bok choy; cover and simmer 20-30 minutes longer or until vegetables are tender. Meanwhile, cook rice according to package directions.
3. Divide rice among 6 soup bowls, ¾ cup in each; top each with 1 cup soup. Garnish with chive blossoms if desired.

1 cup soup with ¾ cup rice: 379 cal., 10g fat (2g sat. fat), 47mg chol., 621mg sod., 50g carb. (9g sugars, 2g fiber), 20g pro.

ASIAN VEGETABLE-BEEF SOUP

COLORFUL THREE-BEAN SOUP

When I was growing up, my mother prepared many different soups, each seasoned just right. She often made this colorful combination that's chock-full of harvest-fresh goodness. It showcases an appealing assortment of beans, potatoes, carrots and spinach.
—Valerie Lee, Snellville, GA

Prep: 20 min. • **Cook:** 15 min.
Makes: 12 servings (about 3 qt.)

- 1 medium onion, chopped
- 1 Tbsp. canola oil
- 3 small potatoes, peeled and cubed
- 2 medium carrots, sliced
- 3 cans (14½ oz. each) chicken or vegetable broth
- 3 cups water
- 2 Tbsp. dried parsley flakes
- 2 tsp. dried basil
- 1 tsp. dried oregano
- 1 garlic clove, minced
- ½ tsp. pepper
- 1 can (15½ oz.) great northern beans, rinsed and drained
- 1 can (15 oz.) pinto beans, rinsed and drained
- 1 can (15 oz.) garbanzo beans or chickpeas, rinsed and drained
- 3 cups chopped fresh spinach

In a Dutch oven, saute onion in oil. Add next 9 ingredients. Simmer, uncovered, until vegetables are tender. Add beans and spinach; heat through.

1 cup: 158 cal., 2g fat (0 sat. fat), 2mg chol., 604mg sod., 28g carb. (3g sugars, 6g fiber), 7g pro. **Diabetic exchanges:** 2 starch, 1½ meat.

FIRE-ROASTED
TOMATO MINESTRONE

TURKEY SANDWICH WITH RASPBERRY-MUSTARD SPREAD

My hearty sandwich has different yet complementary flavors and textures. It is filled with flavor and nutrients, without all the unhealthy fats, sodium and added sugar many other sandwiches have. And it's absolutely delicious!
—Sarah Savage, Buena Vista, VA

Takes: 25 min. • **Makes:** 2 servings

- 1 Tbsp. honey
- 1 Tbsp. spicy brown mustard
- 1 tsp. red raspberry preserves
- ¼ tsp. mustard seed
- 1 Tbsp. olive oil
- 4 oz. fresh mushrooms, thinly sliced
- 1 cup fresh baby spinach, coarsely chopped
- 1 garlic clove, minced
- ½ tsp. chili powder
- 4 slices multigrain bread, toasted
- 6 oz. sliced cooked turkey breast
- ½ medium ripe avocado, sliced

1. Combine the honey, mustard, preserves and mustard seed; set aside. In a large skillet, heat oil over medium-high heat. Add mushrooms; cook and stir until tender, 4-5 minutes. Add spinach, garlic and chili powder; cook and stir until spinach is wilted, 3-4 minutes.
2. Spread half of the mustard mixture over 2 slices of toast. Layer with turkey, mushroom mixture and avocado. Spread remaining mustard mixture over remaining toast; place over top.

1 sandwich: 449 cal., 16g fat (3g sat. fat), 68mg chol., 392mg sod., 40g carb. (14g sugars, 7g fiber), 35g pro.

> **TEST KITCHEN TIP**
>
> If you don't have spicy brown mustard handy, use stone-ground mustard instead. Apricot or strawberry preserves may be used in place of raspberry.

FIRE-ROASTED TOMATO MINESTRONE

This soup was created to accommodate special Christmas dinner guests who are vegetarians. It was so good, we all enjoyed it. This can also be cooked on the stove for two hours at a low simmer.
—Donna-Marie Ryan, Topsfield, MA

Prep: 20 min. • **Cook:** 4½ hours
Makes: 8 servings (about 3 qt.)

- 1 medium sweet onion, chopped
- 1 cup cut fresh green beans
- 1 small zucchini, cubed
- 1 medium carrot, chopped
- 1 celery rib, chopped
- 2 garlic cloves, minced
- 2 Tbsp. olive oil
- ¼ tsp. salt
- ¼ tsp. pepper
- 2 cans (14½ oz. each) fire-roasted diced tomatoes
- 1 can (15 oz.) cannellini beans, rinsed and drained
- 1 carton (32 oz.) vegetable broth
- 1 cup uncooked small pasta shells
- 1 cup chopped fresh spinach
  Shredded Parmesan cheese, optional

1. In a 5-qt. slow cooker, combine the first 9 ingredients. Add tomatoes and beans; pour in broth. Cook, covered, on low until vegetables are tender, 4-6 hours.
2. Stir in pasta; cook, covered, on low until pasta is tender, 30-40 minutes. Stir in spinach before serving. If desired, top with shredded Parmesan.

1⅓ cups: 175 cal., 4g fat (1g sat. fat), 0 chol., 767mg sod., 29g carb. (7g sugars, 5g fiber), 6g pro.

TURKEY SANDWICH WITH
RASPBERRY-MUSTARD SPREAD

BEEFY SWEET
POTATO SOUP

BEEFY SWEET POTATO SOUP

I hate being cold, but one of the best remedies for that is a comforting bowl of warm soup. I revised my mother's water-based vegetable soup recipe to make the flavors richer. The meat and veggies in my version are the perfect cure for a chilly night and a hungry family.
—Lisa Cooper, Leander, TX

Prep: 20 min. • **Cook:** 1½ hours
Makes: 12 servings (4 qt.)

- ¼ cup olive oil, divided
- 2 lbs. beef sirloin tip roast, cut into ½-in. cubes
- 2 tsp. kosher salt
- 1 tsp. coarsely ground pepper
- 2 cups finely chopped sweet onion
- 2 medium sweet potatoes, cut into 1-in. pieces
- 2 cans (14½ oz. each) Italian stewed tomatoes, undrained
- 3 fresh thyme sprigs
- 2 fresh rosemary sprigs
- 1 carton (32 oz.) beef broth
- 4 cups fresh green beans, trimmed and cut into 2-in. pieces
- 2 cups (about 10 oz.) frozen corn
- 2 oz. bittersweet chocolate, chopped
- 3 Tbsp. strong brewed coffee
  Additional salt and pepper, optional

1. In a Dutch oven or stockpot, heat 2 Tbsp. oil over medium-high heat. Season beef with salt and pepper; brown in batches, adding oil as needed. Remove with a slotted spoon. Add onion and sweet potatoes to pan. Cook, stirring occasionally, until onion is translucent and light golden brown.

2. Meanwhile, puree tomatoes and their juices in a blender or food processor. Place thyme and rosemary sprigs on a double thickness of cheesecloth. Gather corners of cloth to enclose herbs; tie securely with string.

3. Return beef to pan; add herb bag, tomatoes and broth. Bring to a boil. Reduce the heat; simmer, covered, until meat and potatoes are almost tender, about 20 minutes. Add green beans. Cook until meat, potatoes and green beans are tender, about 20 more minutes.

4. Add corn, chocolate and coffee, stirring until well blended. Discard herb bag. If desired, season with salt and pepper to taste.

1⅓ cups: 260 cal., 10g fat (3g sat. fat), 48mg chol., 792mg sod., 22g carb. (9g sugars, 4g fiber), 19g pro. **Diabetic exchanges:** 2 lean meat, 1 starch, 1 vegetable, 1 fat.

LEMONY MUSHROOM-ORZO SOUP FOR TWO

Here's a versatile soup that's great as a first course or alongside a sandwich. It's loaded with mushrooms and orzo pasta, with a hint of lemon to brighten the flavor.
—Edrie O'Brien, Denver, CO

Takes: 30 min. • **Makes:** 2 servings

2½ cups sliced fresh mushrooms
2 green onions, chopped
1 Tbsp. olive oil
1 garlic clove, minced
1½ cups reduced-sodium chicken broth
1½ tsp. minced fresh parsley
¼ tsp. dried thyme
⅛ tsp. pepper
¼ cup uncooked orzo pasta
1½ tsp. lemon juice
⅛ tsp. grated lemon zest

1. In a small saucepan, saute mushrooms and onions in oil until tender. Add garlic; cook 1 minute longer. Stir in the broth, parsley, thyme and pepper.
2. Bring to a boil. Stir in the orzo, lemon juice and zest. Cook until pasta is tender, 5-6 minutes.

1 cup: 191 cal., 8g fat (1g sat. fat), 0 chol., 437mg sod., 24g carb. (4g sugars, 2g fiber), 9g pro. **Diabetic exchanges:** 1½ fat, 1 starch, 1 vegetable.

LENTIL, BACON & BEAN SOUP

(PICTURED ON P. 46)

This quick soup feels extra cozy with lots of lentils and a touch of smoky, bacony goodness. You might want to cook up extra—I think it's even better the next day!
—Janie Zirbser, Mullica Hill, NJ

Prep: 15 min. • **Cook:** 30 min.
Makes: 8 servings (2 qt.)

4 bacon strips, chopped
6 medium carrots, chopped
2 small onions, diced
2 Tbsp. tomato paste
2 garlic cloves, minced
1 tsp. minced fresh thyme
½ tsp. pepper
5 cups chicken stock
1 cup dry white wine or additional chicken stock
2 cans (15 to 16 oz. each) butter beans, rinsed and drained
2 cans (15 oz. each) lentils, rinsed and drained
Fresh thyme sprigs, optional

1. In a Dutch oven, cook the bacon over medium heat until crisp, stirring occasionally. Remove with a slotted spoon; drain on paper towels. Cook and stir carrots and onions in drippings until crisp-tender, 3-4 minutes. Add tomato paste, garlic, thyme and pepper; cook 1 minute longer.
2. Add stock and wine; increase heat to medium-high. Cook 2 minutes, stirring to loosen browned bits from pan. Stir in butter beans, lentils and bacon. Bring to a boil. Reduce heat; simmer, covered, 5 minutes. Uncover; continue simmering until vegetables are tender, 15-20 minutes. Garnish with thyme sprigs, if desired.

1 cup: 252 cal., 6g fat (2g sat. fat), 9mg chol., 793mg sod., 38g carb. (7g sugars, 13g fiber), 17g pro. **Diabetic exchanges:** 2½ starch, 1 medium-fat meat.

> **TEST KITCHEN TIP**
>
> Top each serving with a dollop of sour cream to create a cool flavor contrast.

LEMONY MUSHROOM-ORZO SOUP FOR TWO

HOMEMADE BONE BROTH

Bone broth is excellent in place of stocks or broth called for in recipes. It's also great on its own or as a base for soup.
—*Taste of Home* Test Kitchen

Prep: 25 min. • **Cook:** 5½ hours
Makes: 10 servings (about 2½ qt.)

- 4 lbs. meaty beef soup bones (beef shanks or short ribs)
- 2 medium onions, quartered
- 3 chopped medium carrots, optional
- ½ cup warm water (110° to 115°)
- 3 bay leaves
- 3 garlic cloves, peeled
- 8 to 10 whole peppercorns
  Cold water

1. Place bones in a large stockpot or Dutch oven; add enough water to cover. Bring to a boil over medium-high heat; reduce heat and simmer 15 minutes. Drain, discarding liquid. Rinse bones; drain.
2. Meanwhile, preheat oven to 450°. In a large roasting pan, roast boiled bones, uncovered, 30 minutes. Add onions and, if desired, carrots. Roast until bones and vegetables are dark brown, 30-45 minutes longer; drain fat.
3. Transfer bones and vegetables to a large stockpot. Add ½ cup warm water to roasting pan; stir to loosen browned bits. Transfer pan juices to pot. Add seasonings and enough cold water to cover. Slowly bring to a boil; this should take about 30 minutes. Reduce the heat; simmer, covered, with lid slightly ajar, 8-24 hours, skimming foam occasionally. If necessary, add water to keep ingredients covered.
4. Remove beef bones; cool. Strain broth through a cheesecloth-lined colander, discarding vegetables and seasonings. If using immediately, skim fat. Or, refrigerate 8 hours or overnight; remove fat from surface of broth.

1 cup: 30 cal., 0 fat (0 sat. fat), 0 chol., 75mg sod., 0 carb. (0 sugars, 0 fiber), 6g pro.

TEST KITCHEN TIP

If you want a clear broth it's important to not let the mixture boil rapidly. Use the lowest setting you can get while maintaining a gentle bubble. Bone broth can be covered and refrigerated up to 3 days or frozen for 4-6 months.

TANDOORI CHICKEN PANINI

TANDOORI CHICKEN PANINI

The tandoori-style spices in this chicken sandwich give it a bold flavor that's so hard to resist. It tastes incredible tucked between pieces of naan, then grilled to make an Indian-inspired panini.
—Yasmin Arif, Manassas, VA

Prep: 25 min. • **Cook:** 3 hours
Makes: 6 servings

- 1½ lbs. boneless skinless chicken breasts
- ¼ cup reduced-sodium chicken broth
- 2 garlic cloves, minced
- 2 tsp. minced fresh gingerroot
- 1 tsp. paprika
- ¼ tsp. salt
- ¼ to ½ tsp. cayenne pepper
- ¼ tsp. ground turmeric
- 6 green onions, chopped
- 6 Tbsp. chutney
- 6 naan flatbreads

1. Place the first 8 ingredients in a 3-qt. slow cooker. Cook, covered, on low until chicken is tender, 3-4 hours.
2. Shred chicken breasts with 2 forks. Stir in green onions.
3. Spread chutney over 1 side of each naan. Top chutney side of 3 naan with chicken mixture; top with remaining naan, chutney side down.
4. Cook sandwiches on a panini maker or an indoor grill until golden brown, 6-8 minutes. To serve, cut each sandwich in half.

½ sandwich: 351 cal., 6g fat (2g sat. fat), 68mg chol., 830mg sod., 44g carb. (12g sugars, 2g fiber), 27g pro. **Diabetic exchanges:** 3 starch, 3 lean meat.

PASTA FAGIOLI SOUP

My husband enjoys my version of this dish so much that he doesn't even order it at restaurants anymore. With fresh spinach, pasta and sausage, it makes a hearty meal. And I can get it to the table in no time.
—Brenda Thomas, Springfield, MO

Takes: 30 min. • **Makes:** 5 servings

- ½ lb. Italian turkey sausage links, casings removed, crumbled
- 1 small onion, chopped
- 1½ tsp. canola oil
- 1 garlic clove, minced
- 2 cups water
- 1 can (15½ oz.) great northern beans, rinsed and drained
- 1 can (14½ oz.) diced tomatoes, undrained
- 1 can (14½ oz.) reduced-sodium chicken broth
- ¾ cup uncooked elbow macaroni
- ¼ tsp. pepper
- 1 cup fresh spinach leaves, cut as desired
- 5 tsp. shredded Parmesan cheese

1. In a large saucepan, cook sausage over medium heat until no longer pink; drain, remove from pan and set aside. In the same pan, saute onion in oil until tender. Add garlic; saute 1 minute longer.
2. Add the water, beans, tomatoes, broth, macaroni and pepper; bring to a boil. Cook, uncovered, until macaroni is tender, 8-10 minutes.
3. Reduce heat to low; stir in sausage and spinach. Cook until spinach is wilted, 2-3 minutes. Garnish with cheese.

1⅓ cups: 228 cal., 7g fat (1g sat. fat), 29mg chol., 841mg sod., 27g carb. (4g sugars, 6g fiber), 16g pro.

AMISH CHICKEN CORN SOUP

Cream-style corn and butter make my chicken noodle soup homey and rich. The recipe makes a big batch, but the soup freezes well for future meals.
—Beverly Hoffman, Sandy Lake, PA

Prep: 15 min. • **Cook:** 50 min.
Makes: 12 servings (about 4 qt.)

- 1 medium onion, chopped
- 2 celery ribs, chopped
- 1 cup shredded carrots
- 2 lbs. boneless skinless chicken breasts, cubed
- 3 chicken bouillon cubes
- 1 tsp. salt
- ¼ tsp. pepper
- 12 cups water
- 2 cups uncooked egg noodles
- 2 cans (14¾ oz. each) cream-style corn
- ¼ cup butter

1. Place first 8 ingredients in a Dutch oven; bring slowly to a boil. Reduce heat; simmer, uncovered, until chicken is no longer pink and vegetables are tender, about 30 minutes.
2. Stir in noodles, corn and butter. Cook, uncovered, until noodles are tender, about 10 minutes, stirring occasionally.

1⅓ cups: 201 cal., 6g fat (3g sat. fat), 57mg chol., 697mg sod., 19g carb. (3g sugars, 2g fiber), 18g pro. **Diabetic exchanges:** 2 lean meat, 1 starch, 1 fat.

PASTA FAGIOLI SOUP

ARBORIO RICE &
WHITE BEAN SOUP

ARBORIO RICE & WHITE BEAN SOUP

Soup is the ultimate comfort food, and this hearty, satisfying one is low in fat and comes together in just 30 minutes.
—Deanna McDonald, Muskegon, MI

Takes: 30 min.
Makes: 4 servings

- 1 Tbsp. olive oil
- 3 garlic cloves, minced
- ¾ cup uncooked arborio rice
- 1 carton (32 oz.) vegetable broth
- ¾ tsp. dried basil
- ½ tsp. dried thyme
- ¼ tsp. dried oregano
- 1 pkg. (16 oz.) frozen broccoli-cauliflower blend
- 1 can (15 oz.) cannellini beans, rinsed and drained
- 2 cups fresh baby spinach
  Lemon wedges, optional

1. In a large saucepan, heat oil over medium heat; saute garlic 1 minute. Add rice; cook and stir 2 minutes. Stir in broth and herbs; bring to a boil. Reduce heat; simmer, covered, until rice is al dente, about 10 minutes.
2. Stir in frozen vegetables and cannellini beans; cook, covered, over medium heat until heated through and rice is tender, 8-10 minutes, stirring occasionally. Stir in spinach until wilted. If desired, serve with lemon wedges.

1¾ cups: 303 cal., 4g fat (1g sat. fat), 0 chol., 861mg sod., 52g carb. (2g sugars, 6g fiber), 9g pro.

* HEALTH TIP * Neutral flavor and tender skin make white beans a versatile addition to any soup or stew. They add almost 4 grams of fiber to each serving in this recipe. If you want to cut sodium, use reduced-sodium broth.

> **TEST KITCHEN TIP**
>
> A combination of fresh and frozen veggies makes this soup easy to throw together. The pieces of broccoli and cauliflower are large, but cut easily with your spoon if you find them to be too big.

LENTIL SLOPPY JOES

LENTIL SLOPPY JOES

When I experimented with making more vegetarian-friendly recipes, this was one of my biggest hits—we still eat it weekly! My now-preschooler will always eat all of these tangy lentil joes.
—Christina Rock, Covington, WA

Prep: 30 min. • **Cook:** 35 min.
Makes: 14 servings

- 2 Tbsp. olive oil
- 1 large sweet onion, chopped
- 1 medium green pepper, chopped
- ½ medium sweet red pepper, chopped
- 1 medium carrot, shredded
- 6 garlic cloves, minced
- 2½ cups reduced-sodium vegetable broth
- 1 cup dried red lentils, rinsed
- 5 plum tomatoes, chopped
- 1 can (8 oz.) tomato sauce
- 2 Tbsp. chili powder
- 2 Tbsp. yellow mustard
- 4½ tsp. cider vinegar
- 2 tsp. vegan Worcestershire sauce
- 2 tsp. honey
- 1½ tsp. tomato paste
- ¼ tsp. salt
- ⅛ tsp. pepper
- 14 whole wheat hamburger buns, split and toasted

1. In a large skillet, heat oil over medium-high heat. Add onion, peppers and carrot; cook and stir until crisp-tender, 6-8 minutes. Add garlic; cook 1 minute longer.
2. Add broth and lentils; bring to a boil. Reduce heat; simmer, uncovered until lentils are tender, about 15 minutes, stirring occasionally. Stir in chopped tomatoes, tomato sauce, chili powder, mustard, cider vinegar, Worcestershire sauce, honey, tomato paste, salt and pepper. Bring to a boil. Reduce heat; simmer until thickened, about 10 minutes. Serve on buns.

1 sandwich: 215 cal., 5g fat (1g sat. fat), 0 chol., 438mg sod., 38g carb. (8g sugars, 7g fiber), 8g pro. **Diabetic exchanges:** 2½ starch, 1 fat.

WHITE TURKEY CHILI

Cut the fat and calories while savoring all the comfort, heartiness and flavor you love. This recipe makes it easy!
—Tina Barrett, Houston, TX

Prep: 10 min. • **Cook:** 35 min.
Makes: 6 servings (1½ qt.)

- 2 cans (15 oz. each) cannellini beans, rinsed and drained
- 1 can (10¾ oz.) reduced-fat reduced-sodium condensed cream of chicken soup, undiluted
- 2 cups cubed cooked turkey breast
- 1⅓ cups fat-free milk
- 1 can (4 oz.) chopped green chiles, drained
- 1 Tbsp. minced fresh cilantro
- 1 Tbsp. dried minced onion
- 1 tsp. garlic powder
- 1 tsp. ground cumin
- 1 tsp. dried oregano
- 6 Tbsp. fat-free sour cream

In a large saucepan, combine the first 10 ingredients; bring to a boil, stirring occasionally. Reduce heat; simmer, covered, 25-30 minutes or until heated through. Top servings with sour cream.

1 cup with 1 Tbsp. sour cream: 255 cal., 3g fat (1g sat. fat), 41mg chol., 508mg sod., 31g carb. (7g sugars, 6g fiber), 24g pro. **Diabetic exchanges:** 3 lean meat, 2 starch.

CHICKPEA TORTILLA SOUP

CHICKPEA TORTILLA SOUP

This vegan tortilla soup recipe is healthy, filling and family-friendly! We love how hearty and flavorful it is. We like to play around with the different toppings we add each time it's served.
—Julie Peterson, Crofton, MD

Takes: 30 min. • **Makes:** 8 servings (3 qt.)

- 1 Tbsp. olive oil
- 1 medium red onion, chopped
- 4 garlic cloves, minced
- 1 to 2 jalapeno peppers, seeded and chopped, optional
- ¼ tsp. pepper
- 8 cups vegetable broth
- 1 cup red quinoa, rinsed
- 2 cans (15 oz. each) no-salt-added chickpeas or garbanzo beans, rinsed and drained
- 1 can (15 oz.) no-salt-added black beans, rinsed and drained
- 3 medium tomatoes, chopped
- 1 cup fresh or frozen corn
- ⅓ cup minced fresh cilantro
  Optional ingredients: Crushed tortilla chips, cubed avocado, lime wedges and additional chopped cilantro

Heat oil in a Dutch oven over medium-high heat. Add the red onion, garlic, jalapeno if desired, and pepper; cook and stir until tender, 3-5 minutes. Add vegetable broth and quinoa. Bring to a boil; reduce heat. Simmer, uncovered, until quinoa is tender, about 10 minutes. Add chickpeas, beans, tomatoes, corn and cilantro; heat through. If desired, serve with optional ingredients.

1½ cups: 289 cal., 5g fat (0 sat. fat), 0 chol., 702mg sod., 48g carb. (5g sugars, 9g fiber), 13g pro.

TEST KITCHEN TIP

Don't skip the lime wedges—the little bit of acid really perks up the flavor of the soup.

SHREDDED CHICKEN GYROS

Our family has no links to Greece of any kind, but we always have a great time at Salt Lake City's annual Greek Festival. One of my favorite parts, of course, is the awesome food. This meal is a good way to mix up our menu, and my kids are big fans.
—Camille Beckstrand, Layton, UT

Prep: 20 min. • **Cook:** 3 hours
Makes: 8 servings

- 2 medium onions, chopped
- 6 garlic cloves, minced
- 1 tsp. lemon-pepper seasoning
- 1 tsp. dried oregano
- ½ tsp. ground allspice
- ½ cup water
- ½ cup lemon juice
- ¼ cup red wine vinegar
- 2 Tbsp. olive oil
- 2 lbs. boneless skinless chicken breasts
- 8 whole pita breads
  Optional toppings: Tzatziki sauce, torn romaine and sliced tomato, cucumber and onion

1. In a 3-qt. slow cooker, combine the first 9 ingredients; add chicken breasts. Cook, covered, on low 3-4 hours or until chicken is tender (a thermometer should read at least 165°).

2. Remove chicken from slow cooker. Shred with 2 forks; return to slow cooker. Using tongs, place chicken mixture on pita breads. Serve with toppings.

1 gyro: 337 cal., 7g fat (1g sat. fat), 63mg chol., 418mg sod., 38g carb. (2g sugars, 2g fiber), 29g pro. **Diabetic exchanges:** 3 lean meat, 2½ starch, ½ fat.

CABBAGE & BEEF SOUP

Back when I was a little girl, I helped my parents work in the fields of our small farm. Lunchtime was always a treat when my mother picked fresh vegetables from her garden and simmered them in a big soup pot. We loved making this delicious soup—and eating it.
—Ethel Ledbetter, Canton, NC

Prep: 10 min. • **Cook:** 70 min.
Makes: 12 servings (3 qt.)

- 1 lb. lean ground beef (90% lean)
- ½ tsp. garlic salt
- ¼ tsp. garlic powder
- ¼ tsp. pepper
- 2 celery ribs, chopped
- 1 can (16 oz.) kidney beans, rinsed and drained
- ½ medium head cabbage, chopped
- 1 can (28 oz.) diced tomatoes, undrained
- 3½ cups water
- 4 tsp. beef bouillon granules
  Minced fresh parsley

1. In a Dutch oven, cook beef over medium heat until no longer pink; drain. Stir in the remaining ingredients except minced parsley.

2. Bring to a boil. Reduce heat; cover and simmer for 1 hour. Garnish with parsley.

1 cup: 116 cal., 3g fat (1g sat. fat), 19mg chol., 582mg sod., 11g carb. (3g sugars, 3g fiber), 11g pro. **Diabetic exchanges:** 1 starch, 1 lean meat.

SHREDDED CHICKEN GYROS

BEEF LENTIL SOUP

You can prepare this soup as the main course in a hearty lunch or dinner. On cold winter evenings here in New England, I've often poured a steaming mugful to enjoy in front of our fireplace as well.
—Guy Turnbull, Arlington, MA

Prep: 15 min. • **Cook:** 70 min.
Makes: 6 servings

- 1 lb. lean ground beef (90% lean)
- 1 can (46 oz.) tomato or V8 juice
- 4 cups water
- 1 cup dried lentils, rinsed
- 2 cups chopped cabbage
- 1 cup sliced carrots
- 1 cup sliced celery
- 1 cup chopped onion
- ½ cup diced green pepper
- ½ tsp. pepper
- ½ tsp. dried thyme
- 1 bay leaf
- 1 pkg. (10 oz.) frozen chopped spinach, thawed

1. In a large stockpot, cook beef over medium heat until no longer pink; drain. Add the tomato juice, water, lentils, cabbage, carrots, celery, onion, green pepper, pepper, thyme and bay leaf.
2. Bring to a boil. Reduce heat; simmer, uncovered, for 1-1½ hours or until the lentils and vegetables are tender. Add chopped spinach and heat through. Remove bay leaf.

1 cup: 314 cal., 8g fat (3g sat. fat), 47mg chol., 661mg sod., 37g carb. (10g sugars, 8g fiber), 27g pro. **Diabetic exchanges:** 2 lean meat, 2 vegetable, 1½ starch.

ENGLISH PUB SPLIT PEA SOUP

ENGLISH PUB SPLIT PEA SOUP

This family favorite has a history—it's the same recipe my grandmother used. Now, with the magic of the slow cooker, I can spend 15 minutes putting it together and walk away for five hours. When I come back, soup's on. Finish it with more milk if you like your soup a bit thinner.
—Judy Batson, Tampa, FL

Prep: 15 min. • **Cook:** 5 hours
Makes: 8 servings (2 qt.)

- 1 meaty ham bone
- 1⅓ cups dried green split peas, rinsed
- 2 celery ribs, chopped
- 1 large carrot, chopped
- 1 sweet onion, chopped
- 4 cups water
- 1 bottle (12 oz.) light beer
- 1 Tbsp. prepared English mustard
- ½ cup 2% milk
- ¼ cup minced fresh parsley
- ½ tsp. salt
- ¼ tsp. pepper
- ¼ tsp. ground nutmeg
  Minced fresh parsley, optional

1. Place ham bone in a 4-qt. slow cooker. Add peas, celery, carrot and onion. Combine water, beer and mustard; pour over vegetables. Cook, covered, on high 5-6 hours or until peas are tender.
2. Remove ham bone from soup. Cool slightly, trim away fat and remove meat from bone; discard fat and bone. Cut the meat into bite-sized pieces; return to slow cooker. Stir in remaining ingredients. If desired, top with minced parsley.

1 cup: 141 cal., 1g fat (0 sat. fat), 1mg chol., 193mg sod., 25g carb. (6g sugars, 9g fiber), 9g pro. **Diabetic exchanges:** 1½ starch, 1 lean meat.

TEST KITCHEN TIP

For a less chunky soup, puree in batches in a blender or food processor.

GOLDEN BUTTERNUT SQUASH SOUP

I created this soup for my vegan relatives for Christmas Eve, but the rest of us loved it, too! It's so creamy and delicious.
—Susan Sabia, Windsor, CA

Prep: 20 min. • **Cook:** 20 min.
Makes: 6 servings

- 2 Tbsp. olive oil
- 2 cups cubed peeled butternut squash
- 2 medium carrots, chopped
- 1 medium sweet red or yellow pepper, chopped
- 1 medium Gala apple, peeled and chopped
- 1 small onion, chopped
- 2 cups water
- 2 tsp. vegetable base
- ½ tsp. salt
- ½ tsp. dried oregano
- ¼ tsp. ground nutmeg
- ¼ tsp. pepper
- 1½ cups unsweetened almond milk

1. In a large saucepan, heat olive oil over medium heat. Add squash, carrots, red pepper, apple and onion; cook and stir until crisp-tender, 8-10 minutes. Stir in water, vegetable base and seasonings. Bring to a boil; reduce heat. Simmer, uncovered, until vegetables are tender, 8-10 minutes. Stir in almond milk.
2. Puree the soup using an immersion blender. Or, cool soup slightly and puree in batches in a blender; return to pan and heat through.

1 cup: 110 cal., 6g fat (1g sat. fat), 0 chol., 486mg sod., 15g carb. (6g sugars, 3g fiber), 2g pro. **Diabetic exchanges:** 1 starch, 1 fat.

GOLDEN BUTTERNUT SQUASH SOUP

PEANUT BUTTER, HONEY & PEAR OPEN-FACED SANDWICHES

After working a 12-hour night shift at a hospital, I don't feel like cooking a big breakfast when I get home in the morning. These sandwiches are perfect because they're quick and versatile; sometimes I use apples instead of pears, or choose different cheeses, such as Brie or some grated Parmesan.
—L.J. Washington, Carpinteria, CA

Takes: 10 min. • **Makes:** 4 servings

- ¼ cup chunky peanut butter
- 4 slices honey whole wheat bread, toasted
- 1 medium pear, thinly sliced
- ¼ tsp. salt
- 4 tsp. honey
- ½ cup shredded cheddar cheese

Spread peanut butter over toast. Top with pear slices, salt, honey and cheese. Place on a microwave-safe plate; microwave on high until cheese is melted, 20-25 seconds.

1 open-faced sandwich: 268 cal., 14g fat (4g sat. fat), 14mg chol., 446mg sod., 28g carb. (13g sugars, 4g fiber), 11g pro.

OVEN-FRIED GREEN TOMATO BLT

CHICKEN CHILI WITH BLACK BEANS

Because it looks different from traditional chili, my family was a little hesitant to try this dish at first. But thanks to full, hearty flavor, it's become a real favorite.
—Jeanette Urbom, Louisburg, KS

Prep: 10 min. • **Cook:** 25 min.
Makes: 10 servings (3 qt.)

- 1¾ lbs. boneless skinless chicken breasts, cubed
- 2 medium sweet red peppers, chopped
- 1 large onion, chopped
- 3 Tbsp. olive oil
- 1 can (4 oz.) chopped green chiles
- 4 garlic cloves, minced
- 2 Tbsp. chili powder
- 2 tsp. ground cumin
- 1 tsp. ground coriander
- 2 cans (15 oz. each) black beans, rinsed and drained
- 1 can (28 oz.) Italian stewed tomatoes, cut up
- 1 cup chicken broth or beer
- ½ to 1 cup water

In a Dutch oven, saute the chicken, red peppers and onion in oil until chicken is no longer pink, about 5 minutes . Add the green chiles, garlic, chili powder, cumin and coriander; cook 1 minute longer. Stir in the beans, tomatoes, broth and ½ cup water; bring to a boil. Reduce heat and simmer, uncovered, for 15 minutes, stirring often and adding water as necessary.

1¼ cups: 236 cal., 6g fat (1g sat. fat), 44mg chol., 561mg sod., 21g carb. (5g sugars, 6g fiber), 22g pro. **Diabetic exchanges:** 2 lean meat, 1½ starch, 1 fat.

OVEN-FRIED GREEN TOMATO BLT

I had used this frying method on eggplant slices for years and decided to try it on my green tomatoes. It worked! The whole family loves them in BLTs.
—Jolene Martinelli, Fremont, NH

Takes: 25 min. • **Makes:** 4 servings

- 1 large green tomato (about 8 oz.)
- 1 large egg, beaten
- 1 cup panko (Japanese) bread crumbs
- ¼ tsp. salt
- ¼ cup reduced-fat mayonnaise
- 2 green onions, thinly sliced
- 1 tsp. snipped fresh dill or ¼ tsp. dill weed
- 8 slices whole wheat bread, toasted
- 8 cooked center-cut bacon strips
- 4 Bibb or Boston lettuce leaves

1. Preheat broiler. Cut tomato into 8 slices, each about ¼ in. thick. Place egg and bread crumbs in separate shallow bowls; mix salt into bread crumbs. Dip tomato slices in egg, then in bread crumb mixture, patting to help adhere.

2. Place tomato slices on a wire rack set in a 15x10x1-in. baking pan; broil 4-5 in. from heat until golden brown, 30-45 seconds per side.

3. Mix mayonnaise, green onions and dill. Layer each of 4 slices of bread with 2 bacon strips, 1 lettuce leaf and 2 tomato slices. Spread mayonnaise mixture over remaining slices of bread; place over top layer.

1 sandwich: 313 cal., 12g fat (2g sat. fat), 55mg chol., 744mg sod., 36g carb. (5g sugars, 4g fiber), 16g pro. **Diabetic exchanges:** 2 starch, 2 high-fat meat, 1 fat.

TEST KITCHEN TIP

Bacon can be included in a healthy diet; just reach for the center-cut variety. It has far less fat and more lean meat.

CHICKEN CHILI
WITH BLACK BEANS

MARKET BASKET SOUP

MARKET BASKET SOUP

I use kohlrabi in this soothing veggie soup. The vegetable has a mellow broccoli-cabbage flavor and can be served raw, but this is my favorite way to eat it.
—Kellie Foglio, Salem, WI

Prep: 25 min. • **Cook:** 40 min.
Makes: 11 servings (2¾ qt.)

- 1   Tbsp. olive oil
- 1   large kohlrabi bulb, peeled and chopped
- 4   celery ribs, chopped
- 2   medium onions, chopped
- 2   medium carrots, chopped
- 3   garlic cloves, minced
- 1   tsp. salt
- 1   tsp. coarsely ground pepper
- 6   cups vegetable stock or water
- 2   cans (15½ oz. each) great northern beans, rinsed and drained
- 2   bay leaves
- 2   medium tomatoes, chopped
- 2   Tbsp. minced fresh parsley
- 2   Tbsp. minced fresh tarragon or ¾ tsp. dried tarragon
- 2   Tbsp. minced fresh thyme or ¾ tsp. dried thyme

1. In a stockpot, heat oil over medium-high heat. Stir in kohlrabi, celery, onions and carrots; cook 5 minutes or until onions are softened. Add garlic, salt and pepper; cook and stir 5 minutes.
2. Stir in stock, beans and bay leaves. Bring to a boil over medium-high heat. Reduce heat; simmer, covered, until vegetables are tender, 20-25 minutes. Add remaining ingredients; simmer for 5 minutes more. Discard bay leaves.
1 cup: 110 cal., 2g fat (0 sat. fat), 0 chol., 664mg sod., 19g carb. (3g sugars, 6g fiber), 5g pro. **Diabetic exchanges:** 1 starch, 1 vegetable.

CHICKEN WILD RICE SOUP WITH SPINACH

I stir together this creamy chicken soup whenever we're craving something warm and comforting. The reduced-fat and reduced-sodium ingredients make it a healthier option.
—Deborah Williams, Peoria, AZ

Prep: 10 min. • **Cook:** 5¼ hours
Makes: 6 servings (about 2 qt.)

- 3   cups water
- 1   can (14½ oz.) reduced-sodium chicken broth
- 1   can (10¾ oz.) reduced-fat reduced-sodium condensed cream of chicken soup, undiluted
- ⅔   cup uncooked wild rice
- 1   garlic clove, minced
- ½   tsp. dried thyme
- ½   tsp. pepper
- ¼   tsp. salt
- 3   cups cubed cooked chicken breast
- 2   cups fresh baby spinach

1. In a 3-qt. slow cooker, combine first 8 ingredients. Cook, covered, on low for 5-7 hours or until rice is tender.
2. Stir in chicken and spinach. Cook, covered, on low until heated through, about 15 minutes longer.
1¼ cups: 212 cal., 3g fat (1g sat. fat), 56mg chol., 523mg sod., 19g carb. (4g sugars, 2g fiber), 25g pro. **Diabetic exchanges:** 3 lean meat, 1 starch.

GREENS & BEANS TURKEY SOUP

On winter evenings, we like nothing better than a piping hot bowl of soup. This one uses the turkey carcass to make a flavorful stock for the soup.
—Susan Albert, Jonesburg, MO

Prep: 15 min. • **Cook:** 2½ hours
Makes: 10 servings (2½ qt.)

- 1 leftover turkey carcass (from a 12-lb. turkey)
- 9 cups water
- 2 celery ribs, cut into ½-in. pieces
- 1 medium onion, cut into chunks
- 1 can (15½ oz.) great northern beans, rinsed and drained
- 1 pkg. (10 oz.) frozen chopped spinach, thawed and squeezed dry
- 3 Tbsp. chopped onion
- 2 tsp. chicken bouillon granules
- 1 tsp. salt
- ¼ tsp. pepper

1. Place turkey carcass in a stockpot; add water, celery and onion. Slowly bring to a boil. Reduce heat; simmer, covered, for 2 hours.
2. Remove carcass and cool. Strain broth through a cheesecloth-lined colander; discard vegetables. Skim fat. Remove meat from bones and cut into bite-sized pieces; discard bones. Return broth and meat to the pot.
3. Add beans, spinach, chopped onion, bouillon, salt and pepper. Bring to a boil. Reduce heat; simmer, covered, for 10 minutes.

1 cup: 105 cal., 2g fat (0 sat. fat), 22mg chol., 568mg sod., 10g carb. (1g sugars, 3g fiber), 10g pro. **Diabetic exchanges:** 1 lean meat, ½ starch.

HERBED TUNA SANDWICHES

A delightful combination of herbs and reduced-fat cheese makes this simple tuna sandwich a standout.
—Marie Connor, Virginia Beach, VA

Takes: 20 min. • **Makes:** 4 servings

- 1 can (12 oz.) light tuna in water, drained and flaked
- 2 hard-boiled large eggs, chopped
- ⅓ cup reduced-fat mayonnaise
- ¼ cup minced chives
- 2 tsp. minced fresh parsley
- ½ tsp. dried basil
- ¼ tsp. onion powder
- 8 slices whole wheat bread, toasted
- ½ cup shredded reduced-fat cheddar cheese

1. Preheat broiler. Combine the first 7 ingredients. Place 4 slices of toast on an ungreased baking sheet; top with tuna mixture and sprinkle with cheese.
2. Broil 3-4 in. from the heat until cheese is melted, 1-2 minutes. Top with remaining toast slices.

1 sandwich: 367 cal., 15g fat (4g sat. fat), 141mg chol., 718mg sod., 27g carb. (4g sugars, 4g fiber), 31g pro. **Diabetic exchanges:** 4 lean meat, 2 starch, 2 fat.

GREENS & BEANS TURKEY SOUP

SALADS

"This refreshing cold salad is wonderful on hot days. It has a nice crunch and a delicious balance of sweet and spicy flavors."
—Kristina Segarra, Yonkers, NY

Strawberry-Turkey Spinach Salad (p. 84) **Red Potato Salad with Lemony Vinaigrette** (p. 68) **Balsamic Asparagus Salad** (p. 74)
Cranberry & Roasted Beet Salad (p. 83) **Kohlrabi, Cucumber & Tomato Salad** (p. 71) **Spring Pea & Radish Salad** (p. 77)

TASTY MARINATED TOMATOES

TASTY MARINATED TOMATOES

My niece introduced me to this colorful recipe some time ago. Now I make it for buffets or large gatherings because it can be prepared hours ahead. This is a great way to use a bumper crop of tomatoes.

—Myrtle Matthews, Marietta, GA

Prep: 10 min. + marinating
Makes: 8 servings

- 3 large or 5 medium fresh tomatoes, thickly sliced
- ⅓ cup olive oil
- ¼ cup red wine vinegar
- 1 tsp. salt, optional
- ¼ tsp. pepper
- ½ garlic clove, minced
- 2 Tbsp. chopped onion
- 1 Tbsp. minced fresh parsley
- 1 Tbsp. minced fresh basil or 1 tsp. dried basil

Arrange tomatoes in a large shallow dish. Combine remaining ingredients in a jar; cover tightly and shake well. Pour over tomato slices. Cover and refrigerate for several hours.

1 serving: 93 cal., 9g fat (1g sat. fat), 0 chol., 4mg sod., 4g carb. (2g sugars, 1g fiber), 1g pro.
Diabetic exchanges: 2 fat, 1 vegetable.

RED POTATO SALAD WITH LEMONY VINAIGRETTE
(PICTURED ON P. 66)

At our house, a red potato salad with red onion, Greek olives and a lemony vinaigrette is a zippy improvement on the usual mayo-based salads.

—Elizabeth Dehart, West Jordan, UT

Prep: 15 min. • **Cook:** 20 min. + chilling
Makes: 12 servings

- 3 lbs. red potatoes, cubed (about 10 cups)
- ⅓ cup olive oil
- 2 Tbsp. lemon juice
- 2 Tbsp. red wine vinegar
- 1½ tsp. salt
- ¼ tsp. pepper
- 2 Tbsp. minced fresh parsley
- 1 garlic clove, minced
- ½ tsp. dried oregano
- ½ cup pitted Greek olives, chopped
- ⅓ cup chopped red onion
- ½ cup shredded Parmesan cheese

1. Place potatoes in a 6-qt. stockpot; add water to cover. Bring to a boil. Reduce heat; cook, uncovered, 10-15 minutes or until tender. Drain potatoes; transfer to a large bowl.
2. In a small bowl, whisk oil, lemon juice, vinegar, salt and pepper until blended; stir in parsley, garlic and oregano. Drizzle over potatoes; toss to coat. Gently stir in olives and onion. Refrigerate, covered, at least 2 hours before serving.
3. Just before serving, stir in cheese.
¾ cup: 168 cal., 9g fat (2g sat. fat), 2mg chol., 451mg sod., 20g carb. (1g sugars, 2g fiber), 4g pro. **Diabetic exchanges:** 2 fat, 1½ starch.

CHOPPED GREEK SALAD

While living in San Diego during college, I had a favorite Greek casual dining spot. Now that I'm back in my hometown, I've re-created some dishes from the Greek diner and it takes me right back.
—Jenn Tidwell, Fair Oaks, CA

Takes: 20 min. • **Makes:** 4 servings

- 4 cups chopped romaine
- 1 can (15 oz.) garbanzo beans or chickpeas, rinsed and drained
- 2 celery ribs, sliced
- 1 medium tomato, chopped
- ⅓ cup sliced Greek olives
- ⅓ cup crumbled feta cheese
- ¼ cup finely chopped pepperoncini

DRESSING

- 2 Tbsp. minced fresh basil
- 2 Tbsp. pepperoncini juice
- 2 Tbsp. extra virgin olive oil
- 1 Tbsp. lemon juice
- ¼ tsp. salt
- ¼ tsp. pepper

Place first 7 ingredients in a large bowl. In a small bowl, whisk together dressing ingredients. Drizzle over salad; toss to combine. Serve immediately.

1½ cups: 235 cal., 14g fat (2g sat. fat), 5mg chol., 617mg sod., 22g carb. (4g sugars, 6g fiber), 7g pro. **Diabetic exchanges:** 2 fat, 1½ starch, 1 lean meat, 1 vegetable.

* HEALTH TIP * Replace the feta cheese with toasted pine nuts to make this a healthy vegan salad.

> **TEST KITCHEN TIP**
>
> Kalamatas are the most widely known Greek olives. They are almond-shaped and deep purple-black in color.

FAST MACARONI SALAD

Chopped veggies provide crunch, and cherry tomatoes add vibrant color to this refreshing and creamy pasta salad.
—Frankiee Bush, Freedom, IN

Prep: 20 min. + chilling
Makes: 2 servings

- ½ cup uncooked elbow macaroni
- ½ cup quartered cherry tomatoes
- 3 Tbsp. chopped celery
- 3 Tbsp. chopped carrot
- 3 Tbsp. chopped peeled cucumber
- 2 Tbsp. chopped radishes
- ¼ cup fat-free mayonnaise
- ⅛ tsp. salt
- ⅛ tsp. pepper

1. Cook macaroni according to package directions; drain and rinse in cold water. In a small bowl, combine the macaroni and vegetables.
2. In another bowl, combine the mayonnaise, salt and pepper. Pour over salad and toss to coat. Cover and refrigerate until chilled. Stir before serving.

¾ cup: 107 cal., 2g fat (0 sat. fat), 3mg chol., 408mg sod., 22g carb. (5g sugars, 2g fiber), 3g pro. **Diabetic exchanges:** 1 starch, 1 vegetable.

CHOPPED GREEK SALAD

EASY ORANGE & RED ONION SALAD

Here's an unusual salad that's easy to prepare when holiday obligations have you short on time. The combination of red onions and oranges may seem unusual, but it's surprisingly delightful.
—Edie DeSpain, Logan, UT

Takes: 20 min. • **Makes:** 10 servings

- 6 Tbsp. canola oil
- 2 Tbsp. white wine vinegar
- ½ tsp. grated orange zest
- 2 Tbsp. orange juice
- 1 Tbsp. sugar
- ⅛ tsp. ground cloves
  Dash salt
  Dash pepper
- 6 medium navel oranges, peeled and sliced
- 1 medium red onion, thinly sliced and separated into rings

For dressing, whisk together the first 8 ingredients. Place oranges and onion in a large bowl; toss gently with dressing. Refrigerate, covered, until serving.

¾ cup: 127 cal., 9g fat (1g sat. fat), 0 chol., 148mg sod., 13g carb. (9g sugars, 2g fiber), 1g pro. **Diabetic exchanges:** 1½ fat, ½ fruit.

SAVORY PORK SALAD

SAVORY PORK SALAD

You can make an easy meal in a bowl by tossing together healthful veggies, pork tenderloin, fresh herbs and spices with a warm soy dressing.
—*Taste of Home* Test Kitchen

Takes: 25 min. • **Makes:** 2 servings

- 1 garlic clove, minced
- ½ tsp. minced fresh gingerroot
- 2 tsp. olive oil
- ½ lb. pork tenderloin, thinly sliced
- 2 tsp. brown sugar
- 2 tsp. minced fresh basil
- 2 tsp. reduced-sodium soy sauce
- 1½ tsp. lime juice
- 1½ tsp. water
- 1 tsp. minced fresh oregano
- 3 cups torn mixed salad greens
- ½ cup grape tomatoes
- ½ small red onion, sliced and separated into rings
- ½ small sweet yellow pepper, cut into strips

1. In a large skillet, cook garlic and ginger in oil over medium heat for 30 seconds. Add pork; cook and stir until meat is no longer pink. Remove and keep warm.

2. In the same skillet, combine the brown sugar, basil, soy sauce, lime juice, water and oregano. Bring to a boil. Remove from the heat.

3. In a salad bowl, combine the greens, tomatoes, onion, yellow pepper and pork. Drizzle with warm dressing and toss to coat; serve immediately.

1 serving: 229 cal., 9g fat (2g sat. fat), 63mg chol., 274mg sod., 13g carb. (8g sugars, 3g fiber), 25g pro. **Diabetic exchanges:** 3 lean meat, 2 vegetable.

CHICKEN QUINOA SALAD

We pile our favorite gyro fixin's into nutritious quinoa bowls. Our local gyro guy has a cool but spicy sauce that really transforms his sandwiches. It's a must here, too.

—Leah Lyon, Ada, OK

Takes: 25 min. • **Makes:** 4 servings

- 1½ cups plus 2 Tbsp. water, divided
- ¾ cup quinoa, rinsed
- 2 Tbsp. reduced-fat plain yogurt
- 1 Tbsp. reduced-fat mayonnaise
- 1 tsp. Sriracha chili sauce
- ¼ cup crumbled reduced-fat feta cheese
- 1 medium cucumber, seeded and diced
- ¾ cup finely chopped fresh parsley
- 2 green onions, chopped
- ¼ cup extra virgin olive oil
- 3 Tbsp. lemon juice
- ¾ tsp. Greek seasoning
- 1 pkg. (6 oz.) ready-to-use grilled chicken breast strips
- 1 medium tomato, finely chopped

1. In a small saucepan, bring 1½ cups water to a boil. Add quinoa. Reduce heat; simmer, covered, until liquid is absorbed, 12-15 minutes.
2. For dressing, place remaining water, yogurt, mayonnaise, chili sauce and cheese in a small food processor or blender. Cover; process until blended.
3. In a fine-mesh strainer, rinse cooked quinoa with cold water; drain well. In a bowl, toss quinoa with cucumber, parsley, green onions, oil, lemon juice and Greek seasoning. Top with chicken, tomato and dressing.

1 serving: 341 cal., 19g fat (3g sat. fat), 30mg chol., 590mg sod., 27g carb. (3g sugars, 4g fiber), 19g pro. **Diabetic exchanges:** 3 fat, 2 starch, 2 lean meat.

KOHLRABI, CUCUMBER & TOMATO SALAD

(PICTURED ON P. 67)

This refreshing cold salad is wonderful on hot days. It has a nice crunch and a delicious balance of sweet and spicy flavors.

—Kristina Segarra, Yonkers, NY

Prep: 30 min. + chilling
Makes: 6 servings

- 2 Tbsp. olive oil
- 1 medium red onion, finely chopped
- 2 pickled hot cherry peppers, seeded and finely chopped
- 2 garlic cloves, minced
- 2 Tbsp. cider vinegar
- 1 tsp. salt
- 1 kohlrabi, peeled and cut into ½-in. pieces
- 2 large yellow tomatoes, seeded and chopped
- 2 mini cucumbers, cut into ½-in. pieces
- 2 Tbsp. minced fresh cilantro

1. In a small skillet, heat oil over medium-high heat. Add the onion; cook and stir 2-3 minutes or until crisp-tender. Add peppers and garlic; cook 2 minutes longer. Stir in vinegar and salt; remove from heat.
2. In a large bowl, combine the kohlrabi, tomatoes and cucumbers. Pour in the onion mixture; gently toss to coat. Chill for 1 hour. Sprinkle with cilantro just before serving.

¾ cup: 59 cal., 4g fat (1g sat. fat), 0 chol., 372mg sod., 6g carb. (2g sugars, 2g fiber), 2g pro. **Diabetic exchanges:** 1 vegetable, ½ fat.

> **TEST KITCHEN TIP**
>
> The peppers in this recipe aren't terribly hot, but if you're sensitive to heat, you can cut back or eliminate them altogether.

CHICKEN QUINOA SALAD

ASPARAGUS NICOISE SALAD

ASPARAGUS NICOISE SALAD

I've used this Nicoise as an appetizer or a main-dish salad, and it's a winner every time I put it on the table. Here's to a colorful, do-ahead sure thing.
—Jan Meyer, St. Paul, MN

Takes: 20 min. • **Makes:** 4 servings

- 1 lb. small red potatoes (about 10), halved
- 1 lb. fresh asparagus, trimmed and halved crosswise
- 3 pouches (2½ oz. each) albacore white tuna in water
- ½ cup pitted Greek olives, halved, optional
- ½ cup zesty Italian salad dressing

1. Place potatoes in a large saucepan; add water to cover by 2 in. Bring to a boil. Reduce heat; cook, uncovered, until tender, 10-12 minutes, adding asparagus during the last 2-4 minutes of cooking. Drain potatoes and asparagus; immediately drop into ice water.
2. To serve, drain the potatoes and asparagus; pat dry and divide among 4 plates. Add tuna and, if desired, olives. Drizzle with dressing.

1 serving: 233 cal., 8g fat (0 sat. fat), 22mg chol., 583mg sod., 23g carb. (4g sugars, 3g fiber), 16g pro. **Diabetic exchanges:** 2 lean meat, 1½ starch, 1½ fat, 1 vegetable.

GINGER-CASHEW CHICKEN SALAD

I revamped an Asian-style chicken salad recipe to create this gingery, crunchy salad. Now it's a huge success when I serve it at luncheons.
—Shelly Gramer, Long Beach, CA

Prep: 20 min. + marinating • **Broil:** 10 min.
Makes: 8 servings

- ½ cup cider vinegar
- ½ cup molasses
- ⅓ cup canola oil
- 2 Tbsp. minced fresh gingerroot
- 2 tsp. reduced-sodium soy sauce
- 1 tsp. salt
- ⅛ tsp. cayenne pepper
- 4 boneless skinless chicken breast halves (6 oz. each)

GINGER-CASHEW CHICKEN SALAD

SALAD
- 8 oz. fresh baby spinach (about 10 cups)
- 1 can (11 oz.) mandarin oranges, drained
- 1 cup shredded red cabbage
- 2 medium carrots, shredded
- 3 green onions, thinly sliced
- 2 cups chow mein noodles
- ¾ cup salted cashews, toasted
- 2 Tbsp. sesame seeds, toasted

1. In a small bowl, whisk the first 7 ingredients until blended. Pour ¾ cup marinade into a large shallow dish. Add chicken; turn to coat. Cover and refrigerate at least 3 hours. Cover and refrigerate remaining marinade.

2. Preheat broiler. Drain the chicken, discarding marinade in dish. Place chicken in a 15x10x1-in. baking pan. Broil 4-6 in. from heat 4-6 minutes on each side or until a thermometer reads 165°. Cut chicken into strips.
3. Place spinach on a serving platter. Arrange chicken, oranges, cabbage, carrots and green onions on top. Sprinkle with chow mein noodles, cashews and sesame seeds. Stir reserved molasses mixture; drizzle over salad and toss to coat. Serve immediately.

Note: To toast nuts, bake in a shallow pan in a 350° oven for 5-10 minutes or cook in a skillet over low heat until lightly browned, stirring occasionally.

1½ cups: 379 cal., 18g fat (3g sat. fat), 47mg chol., 533mg sod., 33g carb. (16g sugars, 3g fiber), 23g pro. **Diabetic exchanges:** 2½ fat, 2 lean meat, 1½ starch, 1 vegetable.

BALSAMIC ASPARAGUS SALAD

(PICTURED ON P. 67)

Allow enough time to let the flavors blend for at least an hour when making this salad; that's one of the secrets to why it tastes so delicious. If you're short on time, use ½ cup prepared balsamic vinaigrette instead of making it from scratch.

—Dolores Brigham, Inglewood, CA

Prep: 20 min. + chilling
Makes: 6 servings

- 2 lbs. fresh asparagus, trimmed and cut into 1-in. pieces
- ⅓ cup thinly sliced red onion
- ½ cup chopped sweet red pepper
- ¼ cup dried cranberries
- 3 Tbsp. olive oil
- 3 Tbsp. balsamic vinegar
- 1 Tbsp. lemon juice
- 1 Tbsp. Dijon mustard
  Dash salt and pepper
- 3 Tbsp. slivered almonds, toasted
- 3 Tbsp. chopped cooked bacon or bacon bits

1. In a large saucepan, bring 1 in. of water to a boil. Add asparagus; cover and boil for 3-4 minutes or until crisp-tender. Drain and immediately place asparagus in ice water. Drain and pat dry. Transfer to a large bowl; add the onion, red pepper and cranberries.

2. In a jar with a tight-fitting lid, combine the oil, vinegar, lemon juice, mustard, salt and pepper; shake well. Pour over asparagus mixture; toss to coat. Cover and refrigerate for at least 1 hour. Just before serving, stir in almonds and bacon.

¾ cup: 139 cal., 9g fat (1g sat. fat), 3mg chol., 208mg sod., 12g carb. (7g sugars, 2g fiber), 4g pro. **Diabetic exchanges:** 2 vegetable, 2 fat.

TEST KITCHEN TIP

If you need to make the salad more than a day ahead of time, don't add the dressing. Keep separately in the refrigerator up to 2 days. Toss them together an hour before you're ready to serve.

TWISTED EGGS BENEDICT SALAD

TWISTED EGGS BENEDICT SALAD

Salad for breakfast? Absolutely. You can prepare everything but the dressing and the eggs and chill overnight. In the morning, simply dress the salad and poach the eggs.

—Noelle Myers, Grand Forks, ND

Prep: 20 min. • **Cook:** 20 min.
Makes: 8 servings

- 4 Tbsp. olive oil, divided
- 1½ lbs. fresh asparagus, trimmed and chopped
- 1⅓ cups chopped fennel bulb
- 8 oz. diced deli ham or Canadian bacon
- 6 cups baby kale salad blend (about 4 oz.)
- 1 cup chopped roasted sweet red peppers
- 3 Tbsp. chopped green onion tops
- 3 Tbsp. Dijon mustard
- 2 Tbsp. cider vinegar
- ¼ tsp. salt
- ¼ tsp. pepper
- 2 qt. water
- 8 large eggs

1. In a large nonstick skillet, heat 1 Tbsp. olive oil over medium heat. Add asparagus, fennel and ham; saute until vegetables are crisp-tender, about 8 minutes. Cool for 3 minutes.

2. Toss vegetable mixture with salad blend, peppers and green onions. Whisk together mustard, vinegar, salt, pepper and remaining oil until smooth.

3. In a large saucepan, bring water to a boil; reduce heat to a gentle simmer. Break eggs, 1 at a time, into a small bowl; slip eggs into water. Poach, uncovered, until whites are completely set and yolks begin to thicken, 3-5 minutes.

4. Meanwhile, toss salad with dressing. Divide salad among 8 plates. Using a slotted spoon, remove eggs from water; place 1 on top of each salad.

1 cup salad with 1 egg: 199 cal., 13g fat (3g sat. fat), 200mg chol., 710mg sod., 5g carb. (3g sugars, 2g fiber), 14g pro. **Diabetic exchanges:** 2 lean meat, 2 fat, 1 vegetable.

MINTED BEET SALAD

We have neighbors who share vegetables from their garden, and every year my husband and I look forward to their beets. My interest in Mediterranean food inspired this recipe. The sweetness of the beets is toned down by the vinegar and oil dressing with fresh mint. Kalamata olives add a salty touch.

—Barbara Estabrook, Appleton, WI

Prep: 20 min. • **Cook:** 15 min. + chilling
Makes: 6 servings

- 5 medium fresh beets (about 2 lbs.)
- 2 Tbsp. water
- 2 Tbsp. champagne vinegar or rice vinegar
- 2 Tbsp. olive oil
- ½ tsp. salt
- ¼ tsp. coarsely ground pepper
- ¼ cup pitted kalamata olives, quartered
- 2 Tbsp. thinly sliced fresh mint, divided

1. Scrub beets; trim tops to 1 in. Place in a single layer in a large microwave-safe dish. Drizzle with water. Microwave, covered, on high 14-15 minutes or until easily pierced with a fork, turning once; let stand 5 minutes.

2. When cool enough to handle, peel and cut beets into ¾-in. pieces. In a bowl, whisk vinegar, oil, salt and pepper until blended. Add olives, beets and 1 Tbsp. mint; toss to coat. Refrigerate, covered, at least 1 hour or until cold. Top with remaining mint.

½ cup: 123 cal., 6g fat (1g sat. fat), 0 chol., 406mg sod., 16g carb. (12g sugars, 3g fiber), 3g pro. **Diabetic exchanges:** 1 vegetable, 1 fat.

ORZO WITH FETA & ARUGULA

My family enjoys this orzo salad because it is such a good blend of flavors. It's a good choice for picnics because there is no mayonnaise, so it can sit out longer. This may be served either warm or cool.

—Laura Adamsky, Decatur, AL

Takes: 30 min. • **Makes:** 6 servings

- 1 cup uncooked orzo pasta
- 6 cups fresh arugula
- ½ cup crumbled feta cheese
- ½ cup sliced almonds, toasted
- ½ cup dried cherries or dried cranberries
- 2 Tbsp. extra virgin olive oil
- ¼ tsp. salt
- ⅛ tsp. pepper
  Lemon wedges, optional

Cook pasta according to package directions for al dente. Drain orzo; rinse with cold water and drain well. In a large bowl, combine arugula, feta, almonds, cherries, oil, salt and pepper. Add the orzo; toss to coat. If desired, serve with lemon wedges.

1 cup: 279 cal., 11g fat (2g sat. fat), 5mg chol., 198mg sod., 38g carb. (11g sugars, 3g fiber), 8g pro.

MINTED BEET SALAD

WATERMELON TOMATO SALAD

Watermelon and tomatoes may seem an unlikely pair, but they team up to make a winning combination in this juicy salad.
—Matthew Denton, Seattle, WA

Takes: 25 min. • **Makes:** 18 servings

- 10 cups cubed seedless watermelon
- 2 pints yellow grape or pear tomatoes, halved
- 1 medium red onion, chopped
- ½ cup minced fresh parsley
- ½ cup minced fresh basil
- ¼ cup lime juice

In a large bowl, combine the watermelon, tomatoes and onion. In a small bowl, combine the parsley, basil and lime juice. Pour over watermelon mixture and toss to coat. Refrigerate until serving.

¾ cup: 33 cal., 0 fat (0 sat. fat), 0 chol., 7mg sod., 10g carb. (8g sugars, 1g fiber), 1g pro. **Diabetic exchanges:** ½ fruit.

CRUNCHY LEMON-PESTO GARDEN SALAD

CRUNCHY LEMON-PESTO GARDEN SALAD

I love using vegetables straight from the garden in preparing this salad. If I pick the squash and cucumbers early enough, their skins are so tender that there's no need to remove them! Best of all, it's easily adaptable—any fresh veggie from the garden can be swapped in with delicious results!
—Carmell Childs, Clawson, UT

Takes: 25 min. • **Makes:** 6 servings

- 5 Tbsp. prepared pesto
- 1 Tbsp. lemon juice
- 2 tsp. grated lemon zest
- 1½ tsp. Dijon mustard
- ¼ tsp. garlic salt
- ¼ tsp. pepper
- 2½ cups thinly sliced yellow summer squash
- 1¾ cups thinly slice mini cucumbers
- ¾ cup fresh peas
- ½ cup shredded Parmesan cheese
- ¼ cup thinly sliced green onions
- 5 thick-sliced bacon strips, cooked and crumbled

In a bowl, whisk together the first 6 ingredients until blended. In another bowl, combine squash, cucumber, peas, Parmesan and green onions. Pour dressing over salad; toss to coat. Top with bacon to serve.

¾ cup: 159 cal., 11g fat (3g sat. fat), 13mg chol., 586mg sod., 8g carb. (4g sugars, 2g fiber), 8g pro. **Diabetic exchanges:** 2 fat, 1 vegetable.

SHRIMP SCAMPI SPINACH SALAD

My husband and I really enjoy both shrimp scampi and fresh spinach salad, so I put the two together. My oldest son loves it, too, and he's only 3!
—Jamie Porter, Garnett, KS

....

Takes: 20 min. • **Makes:** 4 servings

- 2 Tbsp. butter
- 1 lb. uncooked shrimp (31-40 per lb.), peeled and deveined
- 3 garlic cloves, minced
- 2 Tbsp. chopped fresh parsley
- 6 oz. fresh baby spinach (about 8 cups)
- 1 cup cherry tomatoes, halved
  Lemon halves
- ⅛ tsp. salt
- ⅛ tsp. coarsely ground pepper
- ¼ cup sliced almonds, toasted
  Shredded Parmesan cheese, optional

1. In a large skillet, heat butter over medium heat; saute shrimp and garlic until shrimp turn pink, 3-4 minutes. Stir in parsley; remove from heat.

2. To serve, place spinach and tomatoes in a serving dish; top with shrimp mixture. Squeeze lemon juice over salad; sprinkle with salt and pepper. Sprinkle with almonds and, if desired, cheese.

Note: To toast nuts, cook in a skillet over low heat until lightly browned, stirring occasionally.

1 serving: 201 cal., 10g fat (4g sat. fat), 153mg chol., 291mg sod., 6g carb. (1g sugars, 2g fiber), 21g pro. **Diabetic exchanges:** 3 lean meat, 1½ fat, 1 vegetable.

SPRING PEA & RADISH SALAD

(PICTURED ON P. 67)

Winters can be very long here in New Hampshire. I always look forward to the first veggies of spring and making some lighter dishes like this fresh salad.
—Jolene Martinelli, Fremont, NH

....

Takes: 20 min. • **Makes:** 6 servings

- ½ lb. fresh wax or green beans
- ½ lb. fresh sugar snap peas
- 2 cups water
- 6 large radishes, thinly sliced
- 2 Tbsp. honey
- 1 tsp. dried tarragon
- ¼ tsp. kosher salt
- ¼ tsp. coarsely ground pepper

1. Snip ends off beans and sugar snap peas; remove strings from snap peas. In a large saucepan, bring water to a boil over high heat. Add beans and reduce heat; simmer, covered, 4-5 minutes. Add sugar snap peas; simmer, covered, until both beans and peas are crisp-tender, another 2-3 minutes. Drain.

2. Toss beans and peas with radishes. Stir together honey, tarragon, salt and pepper. Drizzle over vegetables.

⅔ cup: 50 cal., 0 fat (0 sat. fat), 0 chol., 86mg sod., 11g carb. (8g sugars, 2g fiber), 2g pro. **Diabetic exchanges:** 1 vegetable, ½ starch.

SHRIMP SCAMPI SPINACH SALAD

SALMON & SPINACH SALAD WITH AVOCADO

We eat a power salad packed with salmon and spinach at least once a week. It's a cinch to make, even after a hard day's work.
—Jenny Dawson, Fond du Lac, WI

Takes: 25 min. • **Makes:** 2 servings

- 2 salmon fillets (4 oz. each)
- ¼ tsp. salt
- ⅛ tsp. pepper
- 1 tsp. canola oil
- 4 cups fresh baby spinach
- 2 Tbsp. balsamic vinaigrette
- ½ medium ripe avocado, peeled and cubed
- 2 Tbsp. dried cranberries
- 2 Tbsp. sunflower kernels or pepitas (salted pumpkin seeds)
- 2 Tbsp. chopped walnuts, toasted, optional

1. Sprinkle salmon with salt and pepper. In a large nonstick skillet, heat oil over medium heat. Add fillets, skin side up; cook until fish just begins to flake easily with a fork, 4-5 minutes on each side.
2. In a large bowl, toss spinach with vinaigrette; divide between 2 plates. Place salmon over spinach; top with remaining ingredients. Serve immediately.
Note: To toast nuts, bake in a shallow pan in a 350° oven for 5-10 minutes or cook in a skillet over low heat until lightly browned, stirring occasionally.
1 serving: 386 cal., 27g fat (4g sat. fat), 57mg chol., 614mg sod., 15g carb. (7g sugars, 5g fiber), 23g pro. **Diabetic exchanges:** 3 lean meat, 3 fat, 2 vegetable.

SPICY MONGOLIAN BEEF SALAD

SPICY MONGOLIAN BEEF SALAD

This light and loaded beef salad even satisfies my meat-loving husband.
—Marla Clark, Albuquerque, NM

Takes: 30 min. • **Makes:** 4 servings

- ¼ cup olive oil
- 2 Tbsp. rice vinegar
- 1 Tbsp. reduced-sodium soy sauce
- 1 Tbsp. sesame oil
- 2 tsp. minced fresh gingerroot
- 1 small garlic clove, minced
- 1 tsp. sugar

BEEF
- 1 Tbsp. reduced-sodium soy sauce
- 2 garlic cloves, minced
- 2 tsp. sugar
- 1 to 2 tsp. crushed red pepper flakes
- 1 tsp. sesame oil
- 1 beef top sirloin steak (1 lb.), cut into ¼-in. strips
- 1 Tbsp. olive oil

SALAD
- 8 cups torn mixed salad greens
- 1 cup shredded carrots
- ½ cup thinly sliced cucumber
- 4 radishes, thinly sliced

1. For dressing, whisk together first 7 ingredients.
2. Mix first 5 beef ingredients; toss with beef strips. In a large cast-iron or other heavy skillet, heat olive oil over medium-high heat; stir-fry beef mixture until browned, 2-3 minutes. Remove from pan.
3. Combine salad ingredients; divide among 4 plates. Top with beef. Drizzle with dressing.
1 serving: 396 cal., 26g fat (5g sat. fat), 46mg chol., 550mg sod., 15g carb. (7g sugars, 3g fiber), 27g pro.

GINGER GREEN BEANS

The bright gingery sauce on these green beans is delicious and so simple to whip up. It's perfection on either hot or cold green beans. I also really love the dressing tossed with cooked shrimp.
—Marina Castle Kelley, Canyon Country, CA

Takes: 30 minutes • **Makes:** 8 servings

- 1½ lbs. fresh green beans, trimmed
- 1 tangerine, peeled, segmented, seeds removed
- ¼ cup chopped green onions
- ¼ cup soy sauce
- 1 Tbsp. lemon juice
- 1 Tbsp. olive oil
- 1 Tbsp. minced fresh gingerroot
- 1 garlic clove, peeled and halved
- 1 tsp. packed brown sugar
- ½ tsp. salt
- ¼ tsp. pepper
- ¼ tsp. white vinegar

In a 6-qt. stockpot, bring 12 cups water to a boil. Add green beans; cook, uncovered, 2-3 minutes or just until crisp-tender and bright green. Quickly remove beans and immediately drop into ice water. Drain and pat dry. In a blender or food processor, combine remaining ingredients; process until well blended. Pour dressing mixture over beans; toss to coat. Refrigerate until serving.

¾ cup: 59 cal., 2g fat (0 sat. fat), 0 chol., 614mg sod., 9g carb. (4g sugars, 3g fiber), 3g pro. **Diabetic exchanges:** 1 vegetable, ½ fat.

SIMPLE WALDORF SALAD

This is my go-to salad when I need a quick little something for a meal. When I want a sweeter taste I use whipped cream instead of yogurt.
—Wendy Masters, East Garafraxa, ON

Takes: 10 min. • **Makes:** 6 servings

- 2 large Gala or Honeycrisp apples, unpeeled and chopped (about 3 cups)
- 2 cups chopped celery
- ¼ cup raisins
- ¼ cup chopped walnuts, toasted
- ⅓ cup reduced-fat mayonnaise
- ⅓ cup plain yogurt

Combine apples, celery, raisins and walnuts. Add mayonnaise and yogurt; toss to coat. Refrigerate, covered, until serving. **Note:** To toast nuts, bake in a shallow pan in a 350° oven for 5-10 minutes or cook in a skillet over low heat until lightly browned, stirring occasionally.

¾ cup: 140 cal., 8g fat (1g sat. fat), 6mg chol., 119mg sod., 17g carb. (12g sugars, 3g fiber), 2g pro. **Diabetic exchanges:** 1½ fat, 1 fruit.

GINGER GREEN BEANS

TURKEY & APPLE ARUGULA SALAD

This satisfying salad proves that turkey can be enjoyed outside of the holidays. Peppery salad greens, sweet grapes and rich walnuts combine to create a flavor sensation.

—Nancy Heishman, Las Vegas, NV

Takes: 20 minutes • **Makes:** 6 servings

½ cup orange juice
3 Tbsp. red wine vinegar
3 Tbsp. sesame oil
2 Tbsp. minced fresh chives
¼ tsp. salt
¼ tsp. coarsely ground pepper
SALAD
4 cups cubed cooked turkey
4 tsp. curry powder
½ tsp. freshly ground pepper
¼ tsp. salt
1 large apple, chopped
1 cup green grapes, halved
3 cups fresh arugula or baby spinach
1 can (11 oz.) mandarin oranges, drained
½ cup chopped walnuts
½ cup pomegranate seeds

1. For dressing, whisk together the first 6 ingredients.
2. Place turkey in a large bowl; sprinkle with seasonings and toss to combine. Stir in apple and grapes. Add arugula and mandarin oranges. Drizzle with dressing; toss lightly to combine.
3. Sprinkle with walnuts and pomegranate seeds. Serve immediately.
1½ cups: 354 cal., 17g fat (3g sat. fat), 94mg chol., 301mg sod., 22g carb. (17g sugars, 3g fiber), 30g pro.

CHICKPEA MINT TABBOULEH

You'll love this salad warm or chilled. For variety, add feta cheese or use this as a filling for stuffed tomatoes or mushrooms.

—Bryan Kennedy, Kaneohe, HI

Takes: 30 min. • **Makes:** 4 servings

1 cup bulgur
2 cups water
1 cup fresh or frozen peas (about 5 oz.), thawed
1 can (15 oz.) chickpeas or garbanzo beans, rinsed and drained
½ cup minced fresh parsley
¼ cup minced fresh mint
¼ cup olive oil
2 Tbsp. julienned soft sun-dried tomatoes (not packed in oil)
2 Tbsp. lemon juice
½ tsp. salt
¼ tsp. pepper

1. In a large saucepan, combine bulgur and water; bring to a boil. Reduce heat; simmer, covered, 10 minutes. Stir in fresh or frozen peas; cook, covered, until bulgur and peas are tender, about 5 minutes.
2. Transfer to a large bowl. Stir in the remaining ingredients. Serve warm, or refrigerate and serve cold.
Note: This recipe was tested with soft sun-dried tomatoes that do not need to be soaked before use.
1 cup: 380 cal., 16g fat (2g sat. fat), 0 chol., 450mg sod., 51g carb. (6g sugars, 11g fiber), 11g pro. **Diabetic exchanges:** 3 starch, 3 fat, 1 lean meat.

* HEALTH TIP * Bulgur is made from whole wheat kernels that are boiled, dried and cracked. Since it's made from the whole kernel, bulgur is always a whole grain. It has more fiber than quinoa, oats and corn.

TARRAGON TUNA SALAD

It's surprising how a few herbs brighten up tuna salad. Made with reduced-fat mayonnaise, it gets its zip from mustard. This salad makes a terrific light lunch or Sunday brunch dish.
—Billie Moss, Walnut Creek, CA

Takes: 10 min. • **Makes:** 4 servings

- 2 cans (6 oz. each) light water-packed tuna, drained and flaked
- 1 cup chopped celery
- ¼ cup chopped sweet onion
- ⅓ cup reduced-fat mayonnaise
- 2 Tbsp. minced fresh parsley
- 1 Tbsp. lemon juice
- 1 tsp. minced fresh tarragon or ¼ tsp. dried tarragon
- ½ tsp. Dijon mustard
- ¼ tsp. white pepper
  Lettuce leaves, optional

In a small bowl, combine the tuna, celery and onion. Combine the mayonnaise, parsley, lemon juice, tarragon, mustard and pepper. Stir into tuna mixture. Serve on lettuce leaves if desired.

⅔ cup: 151 cal., 7g fat (1g sat. fat), 38mg chol., 373mg sod., 4g carb. (2g sugars, 1g fiber), 17g pro. **Diabetic exchanges:** 2 lean meat, 1½ fat.

ZUCCHINI & SUMMER SQUASH SALAD

ZUCCHINI & SUMMER SQUASH SALAD

I came up with this colorful and tasty slaw years ago for a recipe contest and was delighted when I won honorable mention! The recipe easily doubles and is the perfect dish to take to potlucks or family gatherings.
—Paula Wharton, El Paso, TX

Prep: 25 min. + chilling
Makes: 12 servings

- 4 medium zucchini
- 2 yellow summer squash
- 1 medium sweet red pepper
- 1 medium red onion
- 1 cup fresh sugar snap peas, trimmed and halved
- ⅓ cup olive oil
- ¼ cup balsamic vinegar
- 2 Tbsp. reduced-fat mayonnaise
- 4 tsp. fresh sage or 1 tsp. dried sage leaves
- 2 tsp. honey
- 1 tsp. garlic powder
- 1 tsp. celery seed
- 1 tsp. dill weed
- ½ tsp. salt
- ½ tsp. pepper

Thinly slice zucchini, squash, red pepper and onion; place in a large bowl. Add snap peas. In a small bowl, whisk remaining ingredients until blended. Pour over vegetables; toss to coat. Refrigerate, covered, at least 3 hours.

¾ cup: 101 cal., 7g fat (1g sat. fat), 1mg chol., 124mg sod., 8g carb. (6g sugars, 2g fiber), 2g pro. **Diabetic exchanges:** 1½ fat, 1 vegetable.

> **TEST KITCHEN TIP**
>
> This salad is really versatile. Mix and match your favorite veggies—you'll need about 9 cups total—for a custom salad.

HEARTY SPINACH SALAD WITH HOT BACON DRESSING

This warm, hearty spinach and bacon salad offers cold-weather comfort at any meal. The glossy dressing features a hint of celery seed for a special touch.
—*Taste of Home* Test Kitchen

Takes: 30 min. • **Makes:** 6 servings

- 8 cups torn fresh spinach
- 3 bacon strips, diced
- ½ cup chopped red onion
- 2 Tbsp. brown sugar
- 2 Tbsp. cider vinegar
- ¼ tsp. salt
- ¼ tsp. ground mustard
- ⅛ tsp. celery seed
- ⅛ tsp. pepper
- 1 tsp. cornstarch
- ⅓ cup cold water

1. Place spinach in a large salad bowl; set aside. In a small nonstick skillet, cook bacon over medium heat until crisp. Using a slotted spoon, remove to paper towels to drain.
2. In the drippings, saute onion until tender. Stir in the brown sugar, vinegar, salt, mustard, celery seed and pepper. Combine cornstarch and water until smooth; stir into skillet. Bring to a boil; cook and stir until thickened, 1-2 minutes.
3. Remove from the heat; pour over spinach and toss to coat. Sprinkle with bacon. Serve immediately.

¾ cup: 97 cal., 7g fat (2g sat. fat), 8mg chol., 215mg sod., 8g carb. (6g sugars, 1g fiber), 2g pro. **Diabetic exchanges:** 1½ fat, 1 vegetable.

CRANBERRY & ROASTED BEET SALAD
(PICTURED ON P. 66)

I created this as a healthy, tasty side dish to complement Christmas dinner. An enticing substitute for cranberry relish, it goes well with turkey. Even the children loved it! Serve it alone or on a bed of salad greens.
—Brianna St. Clair, Worland, WY

Prep: 15 min. + chilling
Bake: 45 min. + cooling
Makes: 6 servings

- 5 medium fresh beets (about 1½ lbs.)
- 1 medium pear, chopped
- ¼ cup dried cranberries
- 2 Tbsp. olive oil
- 2 Tbsp. balsamic vinegar
- 2 Tbsp. cranberry juice
- 1 Tbsp. orange juice
- ¼ tsp. salt
- 4 oz. crumbled goat cheese
- ¼ cup sliced almonds
- 2 Tbsp. minced fresh parsley
  Fresh arugula or spring mix salad greens, optional

1. Preheat oven to 425°. Scrub beets and trim tops to 1 in. Wrap in foil; place on a baking sheet. Bake until tender, 45-50 minutes. Remove foil; cool completely. Peel beets and cut into ½-in. cubes; transfer to a large bowl. Add pear and cranberries.
2. In a small bowl, whisk oil, vinegar, juices and salt; drizzle over beet mixture. Refrigerate, covered, overnight. Remove from refrigerator 20 minutes before serving. Toss to coat. Top with goat cheese, almonds and parsley. If desired, serve with arugula.

⅔ cup: 212 cal., 11g fat (4g sat. fat), 24mg chol., 278mg sod., 25g carb. (19g sugars, 5g fiber), 6g pro. **Diabetic exchanges:** 2 fat, 1 starch, 1 vegetable.

HEARTY SPINACH SALAD WITH HOT BACON DRESSING

JAMBALAYA RICE SALAD

JAMBALAYA RICE SALAD

*My cold rice salad has a hint of spice
for a classic jambalaya-style kick. Shrimp,
tomatoes, ham and peppers give it holiday
colors and a delightful texture.*
—Karen Rahn, Hixon, TN

Prep: 20 min. • **Cook:** 15 min. + chilling
Makes: 8 servings

- 1⅓ cups uncooked long grain rice
- 2 Tbsp. olive oil
- 2 cups cubed fully cooked ham
- ⅓ cup chopped onion
- 2 garlic cloves, minced
- 1 tsp. dried oregano
- 1 tsp. dried thyme
- ½ to 1 tsp. salt
- ¼ to ½ tsp. cayenne pepper
- ¼ tsp. pepper
- ⅓ cup red wine vinegar
- 1½ lbs. peeled and deveined cooked shrimp (31-40 per lb.)
- 2 celery ribs, thinly sliced
- 1 small green pepper, julienned
- 1 small sweet red pepper, julienned
- 1 pint cherry tomatoes, halved
- 2 green onions, sliced

1. Prepare rice according to package directions; cool. In a large skillet, heat oil over medium heat. Add ham and onion; cook and stir until onion is tender, about 5 minutes. Add next 6 ingredients; cook and stir 2 minutes. Remove from heat; stir in vinegar.

2. Combine rice, ham mixture, shrimp, celery and peppers. Refrigerate, covered, at least 2 hours. Add tomatoes; toss to combine. Sprinkle with onions.

1¼ cups: 309 cal., 7g fat (1g sat. fat), 150mg chol., 709mg sod., 32g carb. (2g sugars, 2g fiber), 28g pro. **Diabetic exchanges:** 4 lean meat, 2 starch, 1 vegetable, 1 fat.

STRAWBERRY-TURKEY SPINACH SALAD

(PICTURED ON P. 66)

*This light, refreshing salad is a true
showstopper, visually and nutritionally,
with fresh strawberries and yellow pepper
strips tossed with fresh baby spinach.
Serve with warm whole wheat rolls or
flax or bran muffins.*
—Taste of Home Test Kitchen

Takes: 20 min. • **Makes:** 4 servings

- 5 oz. fresh baby spinach (about 6 cups)
- 2 cups julienned cooked turkey breast
- 2 cups sliced fresh strawberries
- 1 small sweet yellow pepper, julienned
- 4 green onions, sliced

DRESSING

- ¼ cup red wine vinegar
- 3 Tbsp. olive oil
- 2 Tbsp. water
- 4 tsp. honey
- ½ tsp. dried minced onion
- ½ tsp. salt
- ¼ tsp. pepper

Place the first 5 ingredients in a large bowl. Place dressing ingredients in a jar with a tight-fitting lid; shake well. Drizzle over salad; toss to combine. Serve immediately.

1¾ cups: 260 cal., 12g fat (2g sat. fat), 56mg chol., 397mg sod., 17g carb. (11g sugars, 3g fiber), 23g pro. **Diabetic exchanges:** 3 lean meat, 1 vegetable, ½ fruit, 2 fat.

CRAN-ORANGE COUSCOUS SALAD

I often create salads for summer using a variety of healthy, filling grains. This version with tender couscous is amped up by the bright flavors of oranges, cranberries, basil and a touch of fennel.

—Kristen Heigl, Staten Island, NY

Prep: 25 min. • **Cook:** 15 min.
Makes: 12 servings

- 3 cups uncooked pearl (Israeli) couscous
- 2 cans (14 oz. each) garbanzo beans or chickpeas, rinsed and drained
- 2 large navel oranges, peeled and chopped
- 2 cups fresh baby spinach
- 1 cup crumbled goat cheese
- 1 small red onion, chopped
- ¾ cup dried cranberries
- ½ cup fennel bulb, thinly sliced, fronds reserved
- ½ cup chopped pecans, toasted
- 8 fresh basil leaves, chopped, plus more for garnish

VINAIGRETTE
- ½ cup olive oil
- ¼ cup orange juice
- ¼ cup balsamic vinegar
- 1 Tbsp. grated orange zest
- 2 tsp. honey
- 1 tsp. salt
- ½ tsp. pepper

Prepare couscous according to package directions. Fluff with a fork; cool. In a bowl, combine couscous and the next 9 ingredients. In a small bowl, whisk together vinaigrette ingredients until blended. Pour over salad; toss to coat. Garnish with additional chopped basil and reserved fennel fronds.

¾ cup: 403 cal., 16g fat (3g sat. fat), 12mg chol., 335mg sod., 57g carb. (15g sugars, 5g fiber), 10g pro.

THAI-STYLE COBB SALAD

This dish is like a mix of Cobb salad and my favorite Thai summer rolls. When you toss in rotisserie chicken, it makes a satisfying hot-weather meal.

—Elisabeth Larsen, Pleasant Grove, UT

Takes: 15 min.
Makes: 6 servings (¾ cup dressing)

- 1 bunch romaine, torn
- 2 cups shredded rotisserie chicken
- 3 hard-boiled large eggs, coarsely chopped
- 1 medium ripe avocado, peeled and thinly sliced
- 1 medium carrot, shredded
- 1 medium sweet red pepper, julienned
- 1 cup fresh snow peas, halved
- ½ cup unsalted peanuts
- ¼ cup fresh cilantro leaves
- ¾ cup Asian toasted sesame salad dressing
- 2 Tbsp. creamy peanut butter

1. Place romaine on a large serving platter. Arrange chicken, eggs, avocado, vegetables and peanuts over romaine; sprinkle with cilantro.

2. In a small bowl, whisk salad dressing and peanut butter until smooth. Serve with salad.

1 serving: 382 cal., 25g fat (5g sat. fat), 135mg chol., 472mg sod., 18g carb. (10g sugars, 5g fiber), 23g pro.

CRAN-ORANGE COUSCOUS SALAD

SIDES

"Here's a very easy way to have homemade bread for dinner tonight. Don't worry if you're new to baking. Anyone who can stir can make this a success!"
—Heather Chambers, Largo, FL

Peas with Shallots (p. 101) Apple Stuffing Balls (p. 104) Cilantro-Lime Rice (p. 93)
Twice-Baked Red Potatoes (p. 98) One-Dish No-Knead Bread (p. 108) Vegetable Barley Saute (p. 103)

ROASTED ARTICHOKES WITH LEMON AIOLI

Petals of savory artichoke leaves are so delicious dipped into a creamy lemon aioli. It may seem intimidating to roast whole artichokes, but the steps couldn't be simpler—and the earthy, comforting flavor is a definite payoff.
—*Taste of Home* Test Kitchen

Prep: 20 min. • **Bake:** 50 min.
Makes: 4 servings

- 4 medium artichokes
- 2 Tbsp. olive oil
- ½ medium lemon
- ½ tsp. salt
- ¼ tsp. pepper

AIOLI
- ¼ cup mayonnaise
- ¼ cup plain Greek yogurt
- ½ tsp. minced fresh garlic
- ¼ tsp. grated lemon zest
  Dash pepper

1. Preheat oven to 400°. Using a sharp knife, cut 1 in. from top of each artichoke. Using kitchen scissors, cut off tips of outer leaves. Cut each artichoke lengthwise in half. With a spoon, carefully scrape and remove fuzzy center of artichokes.
2. Drizzle oil into a 15x10x1-in. baking pan. Rub cut surfaces of artichokes with lemon half; sprinkle with salt and pepper. Place in pan, cut side down. Squeeze lemon juice over artichokes. Cover pan with foil; bake on a lower oven rack until tender and a leaf near the center pulls out easily, 50-55 minutes.
3. Meanwhile, mix aioli ingredients; chill until serving. Serve with artichokes.

2 halves with 2 Tbsp. aioli: 233 cal., 19g fat (3g sat. fat), 5mg chol., 446mg sod., 16g carb. (2g sugars, 7g fiber), 4g pro.

TEST KITCHEN TIP

The edible parts of an artichoke are the bases of the petals, the center core of the stem, and the heart. The fuzzy choke at the center is not edible.

PARTYTIME BEANS

PARTYTIME BEANS

A friend brought this colorful bean dish to my house for a church circle potluck dinner. As soon as I tasted the slightly sweet slow-cooked beans, I knew I had to have the recipe. I've served the beans and shared the recipe many times since.
—Jean Cantner, Boston, VA

Prep: 10 min. • **Cook:** 5 hours
Makes: 16 servings (½ cup each)

- 1½ cups ketchup
- 1 medium onion, chopped
- 1 medium green pepper, chopped
- 1 medium sweet red pepper, chopped
- ½ cup water
- ½ cup packed brown sugar
- 2 bay leaves
- 2 to 3 tsp. cider vinegar
- 1 tsp. ground mustard
- ⅛ tsp. pepper
- 1 can (16 oz.) kidney beans, rinsed and drained
- 1 can (15½ oz.) great northern beans, rinsed and drained
- 1 can (15¼ oz.) lima beans
- 1 can (15 oz.) black beans, rinsed and drained
- 1 can (15½ oz.) black-eyed peas, rinsed and drained

In a 5-qt. slow cooker, combine the first 10 ingredients. Stir in the beans and peas. Cover and cook on low for 5-7 hours or until onion and peppers are tender. Discard bay leaves before serving.

½ cup: 166 cal., 0 fat (0 sat. fat), 0 chol., 528mg sod., 34g carb. (15g sugars, 7g fiber), 6g pro.

STEWED ZUCCHINI & TOMATOES

Zucchini, tomatoes and green peppers star in this dish that offers a fresh take on traditional vegetable sides. Bubbly cheddar cheese adds a down-home feel.
—Barbara Smith, Salem, OR

Prep: 20 min. • **Cook:** 3½ hours
Makes: 6 servings

- 3 medium zucchini, cut into ¼-in. slices
- 1 tsp. salt, divided
- ½ tsp. pepper, divided
- 1 medium onion, thinly sliced
- 1 medium green pepper, thinly sliced
- 3 medium tomatoes, sliced
- ⅔ cup condensed tomato soup, undiluted
- 1 tsp. dried basil
- 1 cup shredded cheddar cheese
  Minced fresh basil, optional

1. Place zucchini in a greased 3-qt. slow cooker. Sprinkle with ½ tsp. salt and ¼ tsp. pepper. Layer with onion, green pepper and tomatoes. In a small bowl, combine the soup, basil and remaining salt and pepper; spread over tomatoes.
2. Cover and cook on low for 3-4 hours or until vegetables are tender. Sprinkle with cheese. Cover and cook 30 minutes longer or until cheese is melted. If desired, top with fresh basil.

¾ cup: 126 cal., 6g fat (4g sat. fat), 20mg chol., 678mg sod., 14g carb. (8g sugars, 3g fiber), 7g pro. **Diabetic exchanges:** 1 vegetable, 1 fat, ½ starch.

LEMON-SESAME GREEN BEANS

There's a kabob shop in Charlottesville, Virginia, called Sticks that serves terrific sides, including sesame green beans. I love them so much that I had to make my own version. You can use fresh or frozen green beans; haricots verts (French green beans) work well, too. This dish only gets better as it sits, so it's great (and convenient!) to make a day or two in advance.
—Dyan Carlson, Kents Store, VA

Takes: 20 min. • **Makes:** 6 servings

- 1½ lbs. fresh green beans, trimmed and cut into 1-in. pieces
- 3 Tbsp. sesame oil
- 1 Tbsp. lemon juice
- 3 Tbsp. sesame seeds, toasted
- 3 tsp. grated lemon zest
- 2 garlic cloves, minced
- ½ tsp. salt
- ⅛ to ¼ tsp. crushed red pepper flakes
- ⅛ tsp. pepper

1. In a large saucepan, bring 4 cups water to a boil. Add the green beans; cook, uncovered, 3-4 minutes or just until crisp-tender. Remove beans; drain well.
2. Whisk the remaining ingredients until blended. Pour over green beans; toss to coat. Serve hot or at room temperature.

⅔ cup: 124 cal., 9g fat (1g sat. fat), 0 chol., 204mg sod., 10g carb. (3g sugars, 5g fiber), 3g pro. **Diabetic exchanges:** 2 fat, 1 vegetable.

STEWED ZUCCHINI & TOMATOES

BEST-EVER BREADSTICKS

Serve these breadsticks with an Italian favorite like lasagna or spaghetti. They're an attractive addition to the dinner table.
—Carol Wolfer, Lebanon, OR

Prep: 20 min. + rising
Bake: 10 min. + cooling
Makes: 2 dozen

- 3 to 3¼ cups all-purpose flour
- 1 pkg. (¼ oz.) quick-rise yeast
- 1 Tbsp. sugar
- 1 tsp. salt
- ¾ cup whole milk
- ¼ cup plus 1 Tbsp. water, divided
- 1 Tbsp. butter
- 1 large egg white
  Coarse salt

1. Combine 1½ cups flour, yeast, sugar and salt. In a small saucepan, heat milk, ¼ cup water and butter to 120°-130°. Add to dry ingredients; beat on medium speed just until moistened. Stir in enough remaining flour to form a stiff dough.
2. Turn dough onto a lightly floured surface; knead until smooth and elastic, 6-8 minutes. Place in a greased bowl, turning once to grease top. Cover and let rise in a warm place until doubled, about 30 minutes.
3. Punch down dough. Pinch off golf ball-size pieces. On a lightly floured surface, shape each into a 6-in. rope. Place on greased baking sheets 1 in. apart. Cover and let rise for 15 minutes.
4. Preheat oven to 400°. Beat the egg white and remaining water; brush over breadsticks. Sprinkle with coarse salt. Bake until golden, about 10 minutes. Remove from pans to wire racks to cool.

1 breadstick: 69 cal., 1g fat (0 sat. fat), 2mg chol., 108mg sod., 13g carb. (1g sugars, 1g fiber), 2g pro. **Diabetic exchanges:** 1 starch.

MISO-BUTTERED SUCCOTASH

The miso paste used in this simple recipe gives depth and a hint of savoriness to vegetables. To brighten the flavor even more, add a splash of white wine.
—William Milton III, Clemson, SC

Takes: 20 min. • **Makes:** 6 servings

- 2 tsp. canola oil
- 1 small red onion, chopped

MISO-BUTTERED SUCCOTASH

- 2 cans (15¼ oz. each) whole kernel corn, drained
- 1½ cups frozen shelled edamame, thawed
- ½ medium sweet red pepper, chopped (about ½ cup)
- 2 Tbsp. unsalted butter, softened
- 1 tsp. white miso paste
- 3 green onions, thinly sliced
  Coarsely ground pepper

1. In a large skillet, heat oil over medium-high heat. Add red onion; cook and stir until crisp-tender, about 2-3 minutes. Add corn, edamame and red pepper. Cook until vegetables reach desired tenderness, 4-6 minutes longer.
2. In a small bowl, mix butter and miso paste until combined; stir into pan until melted. Sprinkle with green onions and pepper before serving.

¾ cup: 193 cal., 9g fat (3g sat. fat), 10mg chol., 464mg sod., 20g carb. (11g sugars, 6g fiber), 8g pro.

> **TEST KITCHEN TIP**
>
> A little miso paste is delicious in soups! Try blending a bit of leftover miso paste into cold spreads—mixed with mayonnaise, cream cheese or sour cream—to boost flavor. Miso can give salad dressings and marinades a lift, too.

COLORFUL COUSCOUS

We love it when side dishes pop with color, like the pepper accents you'll see in this light and fluffy couscous. It's a scrumptious and welcome switch from baked potatoes or rice.
—*Taste of Home* Test Kitchen

Takes: 25 min. • **Makes:** 6 servings

- 2 Tbsp. olive oil
- 5 miniature sweet peppers, julienned
- ⅓ cup finely chopped onion
- 2 garlic cloves, minced
- 1 can (14½ oz.) chicken broth
- ¼ cup water
- ½ tsp. salt
- ¼ tsp. pepper
- 1 pkg. (10 oz.) couscous

In a large saucepan, heat oil over medium-high heat; saute peppers, onion and garlic until tender, 2-3 minutes. Stir in broth, water, salt and pepper; bring to a boil. Stir in couscous. Remove from heat; let stand, covered, 5 minutes. Fluff with a fork.

¾ cup: 220 cal., 5g fat (1g sat. fat), 2mg chol., 498mg sod., 37g carb. (2g sugars, 2g fiber), 7g pro.

BLUE-RIBBON HERB ROLLS

BLUE-RIBBON HERB ROLLS

These rolls have been a favorite of ours for nearly 25 years. I even baked them in an old wood stove when we lived on a farm. I developed the recipe using techniques I learned while studying the art of bread making. The recipe won a blue ribbon at our county fair.
—Mary Ann Evans, Tarpon Springs, FL

Prep: 40 min. + rising • **Bake:** 15 min.
Makes: 4 dozen

- 2 pkg. (¼ oz. each) active dry yeast
- 2¾ cups warm water (110° to 115°), divided
- ⅓ cup canola oil
- ¼ cup honey or molasses
- 1 Tbsp. salt
- 2 tsp. dill weed
- 2 tsp. dried thyme
- 2 tsp. dried basil
- 1 tsp. onion powder
- 1 large egg, room temperature, beaten
- 4 cups whole wheat flour
- 4 to 4½ cups all-purpose flour

1. In a large bowl, dissolve yeast in ½ cup warm water. Add the oil, honey, salt, seasonings, egg, whole wheat flour and remaining water. Beat until smooth. Stir in enough all-purpose flour to form a soft dough.

2. Turn onto a floured surface; knead until smooth and elastic, 6-8 minutes. Place in a greased bowl, turning once to grease top. Cover and let rise in a warm place until doubled, about 1 hour.

3. Punch dough down. Turn onto a lightly floured surface; divide into 6 portions. Divide each into 24 pieces. Shape each into a 1-in. ball; place 3 balls in each greased muffin cup. Cover and let rise until doubled, 30-40 minutes.

4. Bake at 375° for 12-15 minutes or until tops are golden brown. Remove from pans to wire racks.

1 roll: 94 cal., 2g fat (0 sat. fat), 4mg chol., 150mg sod., 17g carb. (2g sugars, 2g fiber), 3g pro. **Diabetic exchanges:** 1 starch, ½ fat.

FENNEL SPINACH SAUTE

Spinach and fennel are two of my favorite veggies, so I'm always looking for new ways to use them. This is an amazing side dish, but if you slice the fennel a bit smaller, it also makes a terrific stuffing for chicken breasts or beef tenderloin.
—Noelle Myers, Grand Forks, ND

Takes: 25 min. • **Makes:** 4 servings

- 2 tsp. olive oil
- 2 tsp. butter
- 1 cup thinly sliced fennel bulb
- ¼ cup thinly sliced red onion
- 1 garlic clove, minced
- 6 cups fresh baby spinach
- ¼ cup minced fresh basil
- ¼ tsp. salt
- ¼ tsp. pepper

In a large cast-iron or other heavy skillet, heat oil and butter over medium-high heat. Add fennel and onion; cook and stir until tender. Add garlic; cook 1 minute longer. Add remaining ingredients; cook and stir just until the spinach is wilted, 4-5 minutes.

½ cup: 60 cal., 4g fat (2g sat. fat), 5mg chol., 209mg sod., 5g carb. (1g sugars, 2g fiber), 2g pro. **Diabetic exchanges:** 1 vegetable, 1 fat.

CILANTRO-LIME RICE

(PICTURED ON P. 87)

My family's favorite Mexican restaurant serves a similar rice dish. I threw this together when I was making fajitas and everyone loved it! It's so simple and it pairs well with kabobs on the grill, too.
—Robin Baskette, Lexington, KY

Takes: 20 min. • **Makes:** 3 cups

- 1 cup uncooked jasmine rice
- 2 cups reduced-sodium chicken broth
- 2 Tbsp. lime juice
- 2 Tbsp. minced fresh cilantro
- ⅛ tsp. ground nutmeg

In a small saucepan, combine rice and broth; bring to a boil. Reduce heat; simmer, covered, until liquid is absorbed and rice is tender, 12-15 minutes. Add lime juice, cilantro and nutmeg; fluff with a fork.

½ cup: 130 cal., 0 fat (0 sat. fat), 0 chol., 191mg sod., 28g carb. (0 sugars, 0 fiber), 4g pro. **Diabetic exchanges:** 2 starch.

FENNEL SPINACH SAUTE

SPAGHETTI SQUASH WITH TOMATOES & OLIVES

This squash is outstanding as a side dish, but you can also top it with canned tuna to create a simple, healthy main dish. It's easy and so tasty! I use my own canned tomatoes for the best flavor.
—Carol Chase, Sioux City, IA

Prep: 15 min. • **Cook:** 5¼ hours
Makes: 10 servings

- 1 medium spaghetti squash, halved, seeds removed
- 1 can (14 oz.) diced tomatoes
- ¼ cup sliced green olives with pimientos, drained
- 1 tsp. dried oregano
- ½ tsp. salt
- ½ tsp. pepper
- ½ cup shredded cheddar cheese
- ¼ cup chopped fresh basil

1. Place squash in 6- or 7-qt. slow cooker, overlapping as needed to fit. Cook, covered, on low until tender, 5-7 hours.
2. Remove squash from slow cooker; drain any cooking liquid from slow cooker. Using a fork, separate squash into strands resembling spaghetti, discarding the skin. Return squash to slow cooker. Stir in tomatoes, olives, oregano, salt and pepper; cook on low until heated through, about 15 minutes. Top with cheese and basil to serve.

¾ cup: 92 cal., 3g fat (1g sat. fat), 6mg chol., 296mg sod., 15g carb. (1g sugars, 4g fiber), 3g pro. **Diabetic exchanges:** 1 starch, ½ fat.

TEST KITCHEN TIP

If you like melted cheesy goodness, top the squash mixture with cheese during the last 15 minutes of cooking, giving it time to get melty.

MEDITERRANEAN CAULIFLOWER

MEDITERRANEAN CAULIFLOWER

I adapted a recipe I received from a friend to make this delicious—and deliciously different—cauliflower dish. It's prepared quickly in a skillet and it uses only a handful of ingredients. What an appealing way to take cauliflower to a whole new level!
—Valerie G. Smith, Aston, PA

Takes: 25 min. • **Makes:** 10 servings

- 1 large head cauliflower, broken into florets
- 2 cans (14½ oz. each) diced tomatoes with basil, oregano and garlic, drained
- ½ cup sliced green olives with pimientos
- 4 green onions, sliced
- ½ tsp. pepper
- ¼ tsp. salt
- 1 cup crumbled feta cheese

1. In a 6-qt. stockpot, place a steamer basket over 1 in. of water. Place cauliflower in basket. Bring to a boil. Reduce heat; steam, covered, until crisp-tender, 4-6 minutes. Drain and return to pan.
2. Stir in tomatoes, olives, onions, pepper and salt. Bring to a boil. Reduce heat; simmer, uncovered, until cauliflower is tender and tomatoes are heated through, 3-5 minutes. Sprinkle with feta cheese before serving.

¾ cup: 86 cal., 3g fat (1g sat. fat), 6mg chol., 548mg sod., 10g carb. (4g sugars, 4g fiber), 4g pro. **Diabetic exchanges:** 1 vegetable, ½ fat.

SEASONED BROWN RICE PILAF

For those of us who are white-rice lovers at heart, this recipe makes brown rice taste terrific! Everyone takes seconds— it's just that good. It is so easy to prepare. To convert for vegetarians, substitute vegetable broth for the beef broth. Any leftovers are just as delicious the next day.
—Amy Berry, Poland, ME

Prep: 10 min. • **Cook:** 55 min.
Makes: 10 servings

- 1 Tbsp. olive oil
- 2 cups uncooked brown rice
- 1 small onion, finely chopped
- 5 cups reduced-sodium beef broth
- 1 Tbsp. dried parsley flakes
- 1 tsp. garlic powder
- 1 tsp. seasoned salt
- ½ tsp. onion powder
- ½ tsp. ground turmeric
- ½ tsp. pepper
- ½ cup uncooked whole wheat orzo pasta

In a Dutch oven, heat oil over medium heat. Add rice and onion; saute until rice is lightly browned, 8-10 minutes. Add broth; stir in the next 6 ingredients. Bring to a boil. Reduce heat; simmer, covered, for 35 minutes. Add orzo. Cook, covered, until orzo is tender, 10-15 minutes longer.
⅔ cup: 190 cal., 3g fat (0 sat. fat), 3mg chol., 380mg sod., 36g carb. (1g sugars, 4g fiber), 5g pro. **Diabetic exchanges:** 2½ starch, ½ fat.

ROASTED CARROTS WITH CILANTRO-WALNUT PESTO

Lightly baked and lightly flavored, this unusual carrot dish uses cilantro, walnuts, olive oil, garlic, parsley, Parmesan cheese and basil.
—Aysha Schurman, Ammon, ID

Prep: 15 min. • **Bake:** 20 min.
Makes: 4 servings

- 2 Tbsp. chopped walnuts
- 2 Tbsp. fresh cilantro leaves
- 1 Tbsp. grated Parmesan cheese
- 1 garlic clove, chopped
- 1 tsp. fresh parsley leaves
- 1 tsp. chopped fresh basil
- ¼ cup olive oil
- 1 lb. medium carrots, halved lengthwise

1. Preheat oven to 400°. Pulse the first 6 ingredients in a small food processor until finely chopped. Continue processing, gradually adding oil in a steady stream.
2. Drizzle carrots with herb mixture; toss to coat. Transfer to a greased 15x10x1-in. baking pan. Roast, stirring occasionally, until tender, 20-25 minutes.
1 serving: 196 cal., 17g fat (2g sat. fat), 1mg chol., 102mg sod., 12g carb. (5g sugars, 3g fiber), 2g pro.

SEASONED BROWN RICE PILAF

SLOW-COOKER CHICKPEA TAGINE

GARLIC-ROSEMARY BRUSSELS SPROUTS

This is my go-to side dish for Thanksgiving. It's healthy, easy and it doesn't take much time to make. I usually include rosemary for my turkey so this lets me use up some of the leftover herbs!
—Elisabeth Larsen, Pleasant Grove, UT

Prep: 15 min. • **Bake:** 25 min.
Makes: 8 servings

- ¼ cup olive oil
- 4 garlic cloves, minced
- 1 tsp. salt
- ½ tsp. pepper
- 2 lbs. Brussels sprouts (about 8 cups), trimmed and halved
- 1 cup panko (Japanese) bread crumbs
- 1 to 2 Tbsp. minced fresh rosemary

1. Preheat oven to 425°. Place first 4 ingredients in a small microwave-safe bowl; microwave on high 30 seconds.
2. Place Brussels sprouts in a 15x10x1-in. pan; toss with 3 Tbsp. oil mixture. Roast 10 minutes.
3. Toss bread crumbs with rosemary and remaining oil mixture; sprinkle over sprouts. Bake until crumbs are browned and sprouts are tender, 12-15 minutes. Serve immediately.

¾ cup: 134 cal., 7g fat (1g sat. fat), 0 chol., 342mg sod., 15g carb. (3g sugars, 4g fiber), 5g pro. **Diabetic exchanges:** 1½ fat, 1 vegetable, ½ starch.

> **TEST KITCHEN TIP**
>
> If you don't have fresh rosemary, use 1-2 tsp. dried rosemary that's been crushed with a mortar and pestle or in a dish with the back of a spoon.

SLOW-COOKER CHICKPEA TAGINE

While traveling through Morocco, my wife and I fell in love with the complex flavors of the many tagines we tried. Resist the urge to stir this dish too much, as it will break down the veggies. Add shredded cooked chicken in the last 10 minutes to make a main dish, or serve this as a side with grilled fish.
—Raymond Wyatt, West St. Paul, MN

Prep: 20 min. • **Cook:** 4 hours
Makes: 12 servings

- 1 small butternut squash (about 2 lbs.), peeled and cut into ½-in. cubes
- 2 medium zucchini, cut into ½-in. pieces
- 1 medium sweet red pepper, coarsely chopped
- 1 medium onion, coarsely chopped
- 1 can (15 oz.) chickpeas or garbanzo beans, rinsed and drained
- 12 dried apricots, halved
- 2 Tbsp. olive oil
- 2 garlic cloves, minced
- 2 tsp. paprika
- 1 tsp. ground ginger
- 1 tsp. ground cumin
- ½ tsp. salt
- ¼ tsp. pepper
- ¼ tsp. ground cinnamon
- 1 can (14.5 oz.) crushed tomatoes
- 2 to 3 tsp. harissa chili paste
- 2 tsp. honey
- ¼ cup chopped fresh mint leaves
  Plain Greek yogurt, optional
  Optional: Additional olive oil, honey and fresh mint

1. Place the first 6 ingredients in a 5- or 6-qt. slow cooker.
2. In a skillet, heat oil over medium heat. Add garlic, paprika, ginger, cumin, salt, pepper and cinnamon; cook and stir until fragrant, about 1 minute. Add tomatoes, harissa and honey; bring to a boil. Pour tomato mixture over vegetables; stir to combine. Cook, covered, on low until vegetables are tender and sauce has thickened, 4-5 hours. Stir in mint.
3. If desired, top with yogurt, and additional mint, olive oil and honey to serve.

¾ cup: 127 cal., 3g fat (0 sat. fat), 0 chol., 224mg sod., 23g carb. (9g sugars, 6g fiber), 4g pro. **Diabetic exchanges:** 1½ starch, ½ fat.

Photo caption: **SLOW-COOKER CHICKPEA TAGINE**

GARLIC-ROSEMARY
BRUSSELS SPROUTS

**OKRA ROASTED WITH
SMOKED PAPRIKA**

OKRA ROASTED WITH SMOKED PAPRIKA

When you want to cook okra without frying it, roast it with lemon juice for a lighter version. The smoked paprika gives it a rich, unique flavor.
—Lee Evans, Queen Creek, AZ

....

Prep: 5 min. • **Cook:** 30 min.
Makes: 12 servings

- 3 lbs. fresh okra pods
- 3 Tbsp. olive oil
- 3 Tbsp. lemon juice
- 1½ tsp. smoked paprika
- ¼ tsp. garlic powder
- ¾ tsp. salt
- ½ tsp. pepper

Preheat oven to 400°. Toss together all ingredients. Arrange in a 15x10x1-in. baking pan; roast until okra is tender and lightly browned, 30-35 minutes.
⅔ cup: 57 cal., 4g fat (1g sat. fat), 0 chol., 155mg sod., 6g carb. (3g sugars, 3g fiber), 2g pro. **Diabetic exchanges:** 1 vegetable, ½ fat.

TWICE-BAKED RED POTATOES
(PICTURED ON P. 86)

Before my baby was born, I was in nesting mode and made lots of freezable recipes like these creamy red potatoes. The yogurt is a healthy swap for sour cream.
—Valerie Cox, Secretary, MD

....

Prep: 30 min. • **Bake:** 25 min.
Makes: 1 dozen

- 6 large red potatoes (about 10 oz. each)
- ½ cup 1% milk
- ½ cup fat-free plain yogurt
- 3 Tbsp. butter, softened
- 1½ tsp. dried parsley flakes
- 1½ tsp. garlic-herb seasoning blend
- 1 tsp. salt
- ¼ tsp. coarsely ground pepper
- 1 cup shredded Monterey Jack cheese

1. Preheat oven to 350°. Scrub potatoes; pierce each several times with a fork. Microwave, uncovered, on high until just tender, 10-12 minutes, turning once.

2. When potatoes are cool enough to handle, cut each lengthwise in half. Scoop out pulp, leaving ¼-in.-thick shells. Mash pulp with all ingredients except cheese.
3. Spoon into potato shells. Top with cheese. Bake until heated through, 25-30 minutes. If desired, broil for 2-3 minutes until the cheese is light golden brown.
½ stuffed potato: 211 cal., 6g fat (4g sat. fat), 17mg chol., 322mg sod., 34g carb. (3g sugars, 4g fiber), 7g pro. **Diabetic exchanges:** 2 starch, 1 fat.

READER REVIEW

"Looking for a side to serve one, and healthy for me, I found this recipe. It's easy to cut down using just one potato. I loved the new flavors, and I know I will make this again and again. I give Valerie's recipe five stars."

—BEEMA, TASTEOFHOME.COM

SOUR CREAM-LEEK BISCUITS

These biscuits are a wonderful pairing for soups. I've made them with whole grain flour as well as all-purpose white, and both work equally well.

—Bonnie Appleton, Canterbury, CT

....

Takes: 30 min. • **Makes:** about 1 dozen

⅓ cup cold unsalted butter, divided
1½ cups finely chopped leeks (white portion only)
2 cups white whole wheat flour
2½ tsp. baking powder
½ tsp. salt
¼ tsp. baking soda
¾ cup reduced-fat sour cream
¼ cup water

1. Preheat the oven to 400°. In a small skillet over medium heat, melt 1 Tbsp. butter. Add leeks and cook until tender, 6-7 minutes. Cool.
2. Whisk together flour, baking powder, salt and baking soda. Cut in remaining butter until mixture resembles coarse crumbs. Stir in leeks, sour cream and water just until moistened. Turn onto a lightly floured surface; knead 8-10 times.
3. Pat or roll out to ½-in. thickness; cut with a floured 2½-in. biscuit cutter. Place biscuits 2 in. apart on an ungreased baking sheet; bake until golden brown, 12-16 minutes. Serve warm.

1 biscuit: 166 cal., 7g fat (4g sat. fat), 20mg chol., 241mg sod., 20g carb. (2g sugars, 3g fiber), 4g pro. **Diabetic exchanges:** 1½ fat, 1 starch.

SOUR CREAM-LEEK BISCUITS

UNFRIED REFRIED BEANS

Refried beans were a staple in our home when I was growing up, but the dish my dad made called for both crisp bacon and bacon fat. Being health-conscious, I lightened up the recipe and found that it remained as tasty as I remember from my childhood.

—Michele Martinez, Albany, NY

....

Prep: 20 min. + standing • **Cook:** 2 hours
Makes: 5 servings

8 oz. dried pinto beans, sorted and rinsed
2 qt. water
2 Tbsp. chili powder
2 garlic cloves, lightly crushed
2 tsp. ground cumin, divided
1 tsp. pepper
1 tsp. salt, divided
⅛ to ¼ tsp. crushed red pepper flakes

1. Place beans in a soup kettle or Dutch oven; add water to cover by 2 in. Bring to a boil; boil for 2 minutes. Remove from the heat; cover and let stand for 1 hour. Drain and rinse beans, discarding liquid.
2. Return beans to Dutch oven; add the 2 qt. water. Add the chili powder, garlic, 1¾ tsp. cumin, pepper, ¾ tsp. salt and pepper flakes. Bring to a boil. Reduce heat; cover and simmer for 2-3 hours or until beans are tender.
3. Drain beans, reserving ¾ cup liquid. Place bean mixture in a bowl; coarsely mash. Gradually stir in reserved cooking liquid until mixture reaches desired consistency. Stir in the remaining cumin and salt.

½ cup: 172 cal., 1g fat (0 sat. fat), 0 chol., 572mg sod., 31g carb. (1g sugars, 9g fiber), 10g pro. **Diabetic exchanges:** 2 starch, 1 lean meat.

BLACK-EYED PEAS WITH COLLARD GREENS

This dish has special meaning on New Year's Day, when Southerners eat greens for future wealth and black-eyed peas for prosperity.
—Athena Russell, Greenville, SC

Takes: 25 min. • **Makes:** 6 servings

- 2 Tbsp. olive oil
- 1 garlic clove, minced
- 8 cups chopped collard greens
- ½ tsp. salt
- ¼ tsp. cayenne pepper
- 2 cans (15½ oz. each) black-eyed peas, rinsed and drained
- 4 plum tomatoes, seeded and chopped
- ¼ cup lemon juice
- 2 Tbsp. grated Parmesan cheese

In a Dutch oven, heat oil over medium heat. Add garlic; cook and stir 1 minute. Add collard greens, salt and cayenne; cook and stir 6-8 minutes or until greens are tender. Add peas, tomatoes and lemon juice; heat through. Sprinkle servings with cheese.

¾ cup: 177 cal., 5g fat (1g sat. fat), 1mg chol., 412mg sod., 24g carb. (3g sugars, 6g fiber), 9g pro.

FETA & CHIVE MUFFINS

FETA & CHIVE MUFFINS

This is a spring variation on a savory muffin my husband has made for years. It has a light texture, almost like a popover. These muffins taste best eaten hot right from the oven.
—Angela Buchanan, Boulder, CO

Prep: 15 min. • **Bake:** 20 min.
Makes: 1 dozen

- 1½ cups all-purpose flour
- 3 tsp. baking powder
- ¼ tsp. salt
- 2 large eggs, room temperature
- 1 cup fat-free milk
- 2 Tbsp. butter, melted
- ½ cup crumbled feta cheese
- 3 Tbsp. minced chives

1. In a large bowl, combine the flour, baking powder and salt. In another bowl, combine the eggs, milk and butter; stir into dry ingredients just until moistened. Fold in the feta cheese and chives.

2. Fill 12 greased or paper-lined muffin cups two-thirds full. Bake at 400° until a toothpick inserted in the center comes out clean, 18-22 minutes. Cool for 5 minutes before removing from pan to a wire rack. Serve warm. Refrigerate leftover muffins.

1 muffin: 105 cal., 4g fat (2g sat. fat), 43mg chol., 235mg sod., 13g carb. (1g sugars, 1g fiber), 4g pro. **Diabetic exchanges:** 1 starch, ½ fat.

BALSAMIC-GLAZED ZUCCHINI

I am a member of an organic Community Supported Agriculture (CSA) farm in Pennington, New Jersey. Every Sunday I get a bushel-size box of whatever is ready for harvest. Recently, I received the most delicious fresh garlic I've ever tasted, along with super fresh zucchini. I came up with a great way to infuse the zucchini with a robust garlic and balsamic taste.
—Joe Cherry, Metuchen, NJ

Takes: 15 min. • **Makes:** 4 servings

- 1 Tbsp. olive oil
- 3 medium zucchini, cut into ½-in. slices
- 2 garlic cloves, minced
- ¼ tsp. salt
- ¼ cup balsamic vinegar

1. In a large skillet, heat oil over medium-high heat. Add zucchini; cook and stir until tender, 5-7 minutes. Add garlic and salt; cook 1 minute longer. Remove from pan.
2. Add vinegar to same pan; bring to a boil. Cook until reduced by half. Add the zucchini; toss to coat.

⅔ cup: 65 cal., 4g fat (1g sat. fat), 0 chol., 166mg sod., 8g carb. (5g sugars, 2g fiber), 2g pro. **Diabetic exchanges:** 1 vegetable, 1 fat.

PEAS WITH SHALLOTS

(PICTURED ON P. 86)

I first served this dish at an Easter dinner. Delicious! My guests suggested I use even more shallots next time. It's so easy, nutritious and always a hit!
—Rosemary Schirm, Avondale, PA

Takes: 15 min. • **Makes:** 4 servings

- 1 Tbsp. butter
- ½ lb. fresh sugar snap peas, trimmed
- 1 cup frozen peas
- 2 shallots, thinly sliced
- ½ tsp. salt
- ¼ tsp. pepper

In a large cast-iron or other heavy skillet, heat butter over medium-high heat. Add snap peas, frozen peas and shallots; cook and stir until crisp-tender, 5-6 minutes. Stir in salt and pepper.

¾ cup: 91 cal., 3g fat (2g sat. fat), 8mg chol., 360mg sod., 12g carb. (4g sugars, 3g fiber), 4g pro. **Diabetic exchanges:** 1 vegetable, 1 fat, ½ starch.

BALSAMIC-GLAZED ZUCCHINI

BAKED SWEET POTATO FRIES

BAKED SWEET POTATO FRIES

I can never get enough of these baked fries! Even though my grocery store sells them in the frozen foods section, I still love to pull sweet potatoes out of my garden and cut them up fresh!
—Amber Massey, Argyle, TX

Prep: 10 min. • **Bake:** 35 min.
Makes: 4 servings

- 2 large sweet potatoes, cut into thin strips
- 2 Tbsp. canola oil
- 1 tsp. garlic powder
- 1 tsp. paprika
- 1 tsp. kosher salt
- ¼ tsp. cayenne pepper

Preheat the oven to 425°. Combine all ingredients; toss to coat. Spread fries in a single layer on 2 baking sheets. Bake until crisp, 35-40 minutes. Serve immediately.

1 serving: 243 cal., 7g fat (1g sat. fat), 0 chol., 498mg sod., 43g carb. (17g sugars, 5g fiber), 3g pro.

VEGETABLE BARLEY SAUTE
(PICTURED ON P. 87)

This wonderful side dish can easily be turned into a hearty entree by adding cooked chicken.
—Taste of Home Test Kitchen

Takes: 30 min. • **Makes:** 4 servings

- ½ cup quick-cooking barley
- ⅓ cup water
- 3 Tbsp. reduced-sodium soy sauce
- 2 tsp. cornstarch
- 1 garlic clove, minced
- 1 Tbsp. canola oil
- 2 carrots, thinly sliced
- 1 cup cut fresh green beans (2-in. pieces)
- 2 green onions, sliced
- ½ cup unsalted cashews, optional

1. Prepare barley according to package directions. In a small bowl, combine, water, soy sauce and cornstarch until smooth; set aside.

2. In a large skillet or wok, saute garlic in oil for 15 seconds. Add carrots and beans; stir-fry for 2 minutes. Add onions; stir-fry 1 minute longer. Stir soy sauce mixture; stir into skillet. Bring to a boil; cook and stir until thickened, about 1 minute. Add barley; heat through. If desired, stir in cashews.

⅔ cup: 148 cal., 4g fat (1g sat. fat), 0 chol., 458mg sod., 24g carb. (3g sugars, 6g fiber), 5g pro. **Diabetic exchanges:** 1½ starch, 1 fat.

FRIED CABBAGE

When I was young, my family grew our own cabbage. It was fun to put them to use in the kitchen, just as I did with this comforting side. It's so good with potatoes, deviled eggs and cornbread.
—Bernice Morris, Marshfield, MO

Takes: 20 min. • **Makes:** 6 servings

- 2 Tbsp. butter
- 1 tsp. sugar
- ½ tsp. salt
- ¼ tsp. crushed red pepper flakes
- ⅛ tsp. pepper
- 6 cups coarsely chopped cabbage
- 1 Tbsp. water

In a large skillet, melt butter over medium heat. Stir in the sugar, salt, pepper flakes and pepper. Add the cabbage and water. Cook for 5-6 minutes or until tender, stirring occasionally.

1 cup: 59 cal., 4g fat (2g sat. fat), 10mg chol., 251mg sod., 6g carb. (3g sugars, 2g fiber), 1g pro. **Diabetic exchanges:** 1 vegetable, 1 fat.

**GARDEN VEGETABLE
CORNBREAD**

GARDEN VEGETABLE
CORNBREAD

*When I was a kid, my parents would make
cornbread for my siblings and me. We'd
slather butter and maple syrup over the
warm bread—it was delicious. Today, I
experiment a lot with recipes,
just as my grandma and mom did,
and that's how my healthier version
of their easy cornbread recipe was born!*
—Kim Moyes, Kenosha, WI

....

Prep: 20 min. • **Bake:** 20 min.
Makes: 9 servings

- 1 cup yellow cornmeal
- ¾ cup whole wheat flour
- 2½ tsp. baking powder
- 2 tsp. minced fresh chives
- ¾ tsp. salt
- 2 large eggs, room temperature
- 1 cup 2% milk
- 2 Tbsp. honey
- ¾ cup shredded carrots (about
  1½ carrots)
- ¼ cup finely chopped sweet red pepper
- ¼ cup finely chopped seeded fresh
  poblano pepper

1. Preheat oven to 400°. Whisk together
the first 5 ingredients. In another bowl,
whisk eggs, milk and honey until blended.
Add to cornmeal mixture; stir just until
moistened. Fold in carrots and peppers.
2. Transfer to a greased 8-in. square
baking pan. Bake until a toothpick inserted
in center comes out clean, 20-25 minutes.
Serve warm.
1 piece: 149 cal., 2g fat (1g sat. fat), 44mg
chol., 367mg sod., 28g carb. (6g sugars, 2g
fiber), 5g pro. **Diabetic exchanges:** 2 starch.

APPLE STUFFING BALLS
(PICTURED ON P. 86)

*I served these fun appetizers for the first
time on Thanksgiving. My family asked
me to make them several times afterward,
so the tasty little bites appeared on my
Christmas spread that year, too. They're
now a holiday tradition.*
—Tracy Burdo, Burlington, VT

....

Prep: 15 min. • **Bake:** 30 min.
Makes: 18 stuffing balls

- ¼ cup butter, cubed
- 1 large onion, finely chopped
- 2 celery ribs, finely chopped
- 3 large eggs, beaten
- ¼ cup minced fresh parsley
- ¾ tsp. salt
- ½ tsp. dried thyme
- ¼ tsp. pepper
- 9 cups soft bread crumbs
- 2 medium apples, peeled and finely
  chopped

1. Preheat oven to 350°. In a large skillet,
heat butter over medium heat. Add onion
and celery; cook and stir 4-6 minutes or
just until tender.
2. In a large bowl, mix eggs, parsley, salt,
thyme and pepper. Stir in bread crumbs,
apples and the onion mixture. Shape into
2-in. balls. Place in a foil-lined 15x10x1-in.
baking pan. Bake 30-35 minutes or until
golden brown.
1 stuffing ball: 106 cal., 4g fat (2g sat. fat),
38mg chol., 245mg sod., 14g carb. (3g sugars,
1g fiber), 3g pro. **Diabetic exchanges:**
1 starch, 1 fat.

BUTTERNUT SQUASH WITH MAPLE SYRUP

Loaded with flavor, this roasted butternut squash is wonderful hot or cold.
—Marie Willette, Bellows Falls, VT

Prep: 25 min. • **Bake:** 35 min.
Makes: 10 servings

- 1 medium butternut squash, peeled and cut into 1-in. cubes (about 12 cups)
- 4 Tbsp. olive oil, divided
- ¾ tsp. salt
- ¼ tsp. pepper
- 2 Tbsp. minced fresh gingerroot
- 3 garlic cloves, minced
- ¼ tsp. crushed red pepper flakes, optional
- 2 medium leeks (white portion only) or ½ large sweet onion, finely chopped
- ⅓ cup maple syrup
- 1 cup jarred roasted sweet red peppers, coarsely chopped

1. Preheat oven to 425°. In a large bowl, toss squash with 2 Tbsp. oil, salt and pepper; divide between 2 ungreased 15x10x1-in. baking pans. Roast for 35-45 minutes or until tender, stirring occasionally and switching position of pans halfway through baking.

2. In a skillet, heat remaining oil over medium heat. Add ginger, garlic and, if desired, pepper flakes; cook and stir 1 minute. Add leeks; cook and stir for 3-4 minutes longer or until tender. Stir in maple syrup; bring to a boil. Reduce heat; simmer, uncovered, 2-3 minutes or until syrup is slightly reduced.

3. Place squash in a large bowl. Add red peppers and leek mixture; toss to combine.

¾ cup: 178 cal., 6g fat (1g sat. fat), 0 chol., 279mg sod., 32g carb. (14g sugars, 7g fiber), 2g pro. **Diabetic exchanges:** 2 starch, 1 fat.

GNOCCHI WITH MUSHROOMS & ONION

Tender gnocchi is so delicious with sauteed mushrooms and onions. It's a family favorite.
—Kris Berezansky, Clymer, PA

Takes: 20 min. • **Makes:** 5 servings

- 1 pkg. (16 oz.) potato gnocchi
- ½ lb. sliced fresh mushrooms
- ¾ cup chopped sweet onion
- ¼ cup butter, cubed
- ¼ tsp. salt
- ¼ tsp. Italian seasoning
- ¼ tsp. crushed red pepper flakes
   Grated Parmesan cheese

1. Cook gnocchi according to package directions. Meanwhile, in a large skillet, saute mushrooms and onion in butter until tender.

2. Drain gnocchi. Add gnocchi, salt, Italian seasoning and pepper flakes to the skillet; heat through. Sprinkle with cheese.

Note: Look for potato gnocchi in the pasta or frozen foods section.

¾ cup: 287 cal., 11g fat (6g sat. fat), 31mg chol., 583mg sod., 41g carb. (7g sugars, 3g fiber), 8g pro.

> **TEST KITCHEN TIP**
>
> The crushed red pepper flakes add a pleasant hit of heat. Skip them if your family prefers mild flavors.

BUTTERNUT SQUASH WITH MAPLE SYRUP

DILL & CHIVE PEAS

Growing my own herbs helps keep things fresh in the kitchen. I use fresh peas from the garden when I have them.

—Tanna Richard, Cedar Rapids, IA

Takes: 10 min. • **Makes:** 4 servings

- 1 pkg. (16 oz.) frozen peas
- ¼ cup snipped fresh dill
- 2 Tbsp. minced fresh chives
- 1 Tbsp. butter
- 1 tsp. lemon-pepper seasoning
- ¼ tsp. kosher salt

Cook peas according to the package directions. Stir in remaining ingredients; serve immediately.

¾ cup: 113 cal., 3g fat (2g sat. fat), 8mg chol., 346mg sod., 16g carb. (6g sugars, 5g fiber), 6g pro. **Diabetic exchanges:** 1 starch, ½ fat.

CARROT, PARSNIP & POTATO GRATIN

CARROT, PARSNIP & POTATO GRATIN

Thanks to a challenge in the TOH community a few years back, my husband and I tried parsnips and discovered that we liked them! In fact, I started growing them in my garden and have been trying new things with them. This recipe is one of my experiments, and it turned out to be something we really enjoy!

—Sue Gronholz, Beaver Dam, WI

Prep: 20 min. • **Bake:** 50 min.
Makes: 8 servings

- 1 lb. medium carrots, thinly sliced
- ½ lb. medium parsnips, peeled and thinly sliced
- ½ lb. Yukon Gold potatoes, peeled and thinly sliced
- 1 small onion, halved and sliced
- 2 garlic cloves, minced
- 1½ tsp. minced fresh rosemary
- ½ tsp. salt
- ½ tsp. ground nutmeg
- 1 cup half-and-half cream
- ¼ cup heavy whipping cream

Preheat oven to 400°. In a large bowl, combine all the ingredients. Transfer to a greased 3-qt. baking dish. Cover and bake until vegetables are tender, 40-45 minutes. Uncover and bake until cream thickens and is beginning to turn golden brown, 10-15 minutes longer. Let stand 5-10 minutes before serving.

¾ cup: 141 cal., 6g fat (4g sat. fat), 23mg chol., 208mg sod., 19g carb. (6g sugars, 3g fiber), 3g pro.

BROCCOLI CAULIFLOWER COMBO

Shallots, basil and broth rev up the taste of this nutritious vegetable medley. The bright color and fresh flavors will dress up your plate!
—Clara Coulson Minney,
Washington Court House, OH

Takes: 25 min. • **Makes:** 6 servings

    4   cups fresh broccoli florets
    2   cups fresh cauliflowerets
    3   shallots, chopped
    ½   cup reduced-sodium chicken broth
        or vegetable broth
    1   tsp. dried basil
    ½   tsp. seasoned salt
    ⅛   tsp. pepper

In a large cast-iron or other heavy skillet, combine all ingredients. Cover and cook over medium heat until vegetables are crisp-tender, 6-8 minutes, stirring occasionally.
¾ cup: 38 cal., 0 fat (0 sat. fat), 0 chol., 204mg sod., 8g carb. (2g sugars, 2g fiber), 3g pro. **Diabetic exchanges:** 2 vegetable.

ROASTED ASPARAGUS

Since asparagus is so abundant here in spring, I like to put it to great use with this recipe. We all look forward to this side dish each year.
—Vikki Rebholz, West Chester, OH

Takes: 25 min. • **Makes:** 12 servings

    4   lbs. fresh asparagus, trimmed
    ¼   cup olive oil
    ½   tsp. salt
    ¼   tsp. pepper
    ¼   cup sesame seeds, toasted

Arrange asparagus in a single layer in 2 foil-lined 15x10x1-in. baking pans. Drizzle with oil. Sprinkle with salt and pepper. Bake, uncovered, at 400° for 12-15 minutes or until crisp-tender, turning once. Sprinkle with sesame seeds.
1 serving: 73 cal., 6g fat (1g sat. fat), 0 chol., 122mg sod., 4g carb. (1g sugars, 2g fiber), 2g pro. **Diabetic exchanges:** 1 vegetable, 1 fat.

BROCCOLI CAULIFLOWER COMBO

ONE-DISH NO-KNEAD BREAD

(PICTURED ON P. 87)

Here's a very easy way to have homemade bread for dinner tonight. Don't worry if you're new to baking. Anyone who can stir can make this a success!
—Heather Chambers, Largo, FL

Prep: 15 min. + rising • **Bake:** 40 min.
Makes: 1 loaf (12 slices)

- 1 tsp. active dry yeast
- 1½ cups warm water (110° to 115°)
- 2¾ cups all-purpose flour
- 2 Tbsp. sugar
- 2 Tbsp. olive oil
- 1½ tsp. salt

1. In a large bowl, dissolve yeast in warm water. Stir in the remaining ingredients to form a wet dough; transfer to a greased 2½-qt. baking dish. Cover; let stand in a warm place 1 hour.
2. Stir down dough. Cover; let stand 1 hour. Preheat oven to 425°.
3. Bake 20 minutes. Reduce oven setting to 350°. Bake until top is golden brown and a thermometer reads 210°, about 20 minutes longer.
4. Remove bread from baking dish to a wire rack to cool. Serve warm.

1 slice: 133 cal., 3g fat (0 sat. fat), 0 chol., 296mg sod., 24g carb. (2g sugars, 1g fiber), 3g pro. **Diabetic exchanges:** 1½ starch, ½ fat.

* HEALTH TIP *Some packaged breads have more than 20 ingredients! This loaf contains just 6 easy-to-pronounce ones.

> **TEST KITCHEN TIP**
>
> Salt plays many roles in yeast bread. It slows the yeast's growth, allowing the dough to develop more complex flavors and a stronger structure. It also contributes to the finished bread's flavor and shelf life.

TASTY TURNIPS & GREENS

TASTY TURNIPS & GREENS

This savory dish is a hit at every church dinner. Adjust the seasonings as you please to make the recipe your own.
—Amy Inman, Hiddenite, NC

Prep: 20 min. • **Cook:** 5 hours
Makes: 14 servings

- 2¾ lbs. turnips, peeled and cut into ½-in. cubes
- 1 bunch fresh turnip greens (about 12 oz.), chopped
- 8 oz. cubed fully cooked country ham or 2 smoked ham hocks (about 1½ lbs.)
- 1 medium onion, chopped
- 3 Tbsp. sugar
- 1½ tsp. coarsely ground pepper
- 1¼ tsp. salt
- 2 cartons (32 oz. each) chicken broth

In a greased 6- or 7-qt. slow cooker, combine all ingredients. Cook, covered, on low until vegetables are tender, 5-6 hours, stirring once. If using ham hocks, remove meat from bones when cool enough to handle; cut ham into small pieces and return to slow cooker. Serve using a slotted spoon.

¾ cup: 58 cal., 1g fat (0 sat. fat), 9mg chol., 514mg sod., 9g carb. (6g sugars, 2g fiber), 5g pro. **Diabetic exchanges:** 1 lean meat, 1 vegetable.

MOM'S APPLE CORNBREAD STUFFING

My speedy recipe is the be-all and end-all stuffing in our family. Not surprisingly, we never have leftovers.
—Marie Forte, Raritan, NJ

Prep: 15 min. • **Bake:** 35 min.
Makes: 16 servings

- 6 large Granny Smith apples, peeled and chopped
- 1 pkg. (14 oz.) crushed cornbread stuffing
- ½ cup butter, melted
- 1 can (14½ oz.) chicken broth

1. Preheat oven to 350°. Combine apples, stuffing and melted butter. Add the broth; mix well.
2. Transfer stuffing to a greased 13x9-in. baking dish. Bake until golden brown, 35-40 minutes.

¾ cup: 183 cal., 7g fat (4g sat. fat), 16mg chol., 434mg sod., 28g carb. (8g sugars, 2g fiber), 3g pro. **Diabetic exchanges:** 2 starch, 1½ fat.

OLIVE OIL MASHED POTATOES WITH PANCETTA

Classic American mashed potatoes take a trip to Italy with the flavors of olive oil, garlic and pancetta.
—Bryan Kennedy, Kaneohe, HI

Prep: 20 min. • **Cook:** 20 min.
Makes: 8 servings

- 3 lbs. Yukon Gold potatoes, peeled and cubed
- 3 slices pancetta or bacon, chopped
- 1 Tbsp. plus ¼ cup olive oil, divided
- 4 garlic cloves, minced
- ⅓ cup minced fresh parsley
- ½ tsp. salt
- ½ tsp. pepper

1. Place potatoes in a large saucepan and cover with water. Bring to a boil. Reduce heat; cover and simmer until tender, 15-20 minutes.
2. Meanwhile, in a large skillet, cook pancetta in 1 Tbsp. oil over medium heat until crisp. Add garlic; cook for 1 minute longer. Remove from the heat.
3. Drain potatoes and transfer to a large bowl. Mash potatoes with remaining oil. Stir in the parsley, pancetta mixture, salt and pepper.

⅔ cup: 206 cal., 11g fat (2g sat. fat), 7mg chol., 313mg sod., 23g carb. (2g sugars, 2g fiber), 4g pro. **Diabetic exchanges:** 2 fat, 1½ starch.

MOM'S APPLE CORNBREAD STUFFING

STOVETOP MAINS

"These tasty steaks are quick enough for everyday dinners, but they feel special, too. We enjoy the mushroom-topped filets with crusty French bread, mixed salad and a light lemon dessert."
—Christel Stein, Tampa, FL

Sunshine Chicken (p. 141) **Tex-Mex Pork Chops** (p. 120) **Shrimp with Warm German-Style Coleslaw** (p. 119)
Saucy Mediterranean Chicken with Rice (p. 136) **Beef Filets with Portobello Sauce** (p. 114) **Curried Squash & Sausage** (p. 113)

SWEET ONION & SAUSAGE SPAGHETTI

This wholesome pasta dish gets tossed with light cream, basil and tomatoes for a quick, fresh-tasting meal in minutes.
—Mary Relyea, Canastota, NY

Takes: 30 min. • **Makes:** 4 servings

- 6 oz. uncooked whole wheat spaghetti
- ¾ lb. Italian turkey sausage links, casings removed
- 2 tsp. olive oil
- 1 sweet onion, thinly sliced
- 1 pint cherry tomatoes, halved
- ½ cup loosely packed fresh basil leaves, thinly sliced
- ½ cup half-and-half cream
  Shaved Parmesan cheese, optional

1. Cook spaghetti according to package directions. Meanwhile, in a large nonstick skillet over medium heat, cook sausage in oil for 5 minutes. Add onion; cook until meat is no longer pink and onion is tender, 8-10 minutes longer.
2. Stir in the tomatoes and basil; heat through. Add cream; bring to a boil. Drain spaghetti; toss with the sausage mixture. Garnish with cheese if desired.

1½ cups: 334 cal., 12g fat (4g sat. fat), 46mg chol., 378mg sod., 41g carb. (8g sugars, 6g fiber), 17g pro. **Diabetic exchanges:** 2½ starch, 2 lean meat, 1 vegetable, 1 fat.

GLAZED PORK ON SWEET POTATO BEDS

GLAZED PORK ON SWEET POTATO BEDS

When solving the "what's for dinner" puzzle, this maple-glazed pork tenderloin is often our top choice. Add sweet potatoes for a comfy side.
—Jessie Grearson, Falmouth, ME

Prep: 20 min. • **Cook:** 30 min.
Makes: 6 servings

- 1½ lbs. sweet potatoes, peeled and cubed
- 1 medium apple, peeled and cut into 8 pieces
- 2 Tbsp. butter
- 1 Tbsp. lemon juice
- 2 tsp. minced fresh gingerroot
- ½ tsp. salt
- ½ tsp. pepper

PORK

- 1 tsp. water
- ½ tsp. cornstarch
- 3 Tbsp. maple syrup
- 2 tsp. wasabi mustard
- 2 tsp. soy sauce
- ½ tsp. pepper
- 2 pork tenderloins (¾ lb. each), cut into 1-in. slices
- 1 Tbsp. olive oil
- 2 garlic cloves, minced

1. Place sweet potatoes and apple in a large saucepan with water to cover. Bring to a boil over high heat. Reduce heat to medium; cover and cook just until tender, 10-12 minutes. Drain. Mash the potatoes and apple. Stir in the next 5 ingredients; keep warm.
2. Stir water into the cornstarch until smooth; add syrup, mustard, soy sauce and pepper. Add pork; stir to coat.
3. In a large skillet, heat oil over medium heat. Brown pork. Add garlic; cook until meat is no longer pink, 3-5 minutes longer. Serve with sweet potatoes and pan juices.

3 oz. pork with ½ cup sweet potato mixture: 327 cal., 10g fat (4g sat. fat), 74mg chol., 473mg sod., 33g carb. (13g sugars, 4g fiber), 25g pro. **Diabetic exchanges:** 3 lean meat, 2 starch, 1 fat.

EASY CARIBBEAN CHICKEN

This is a very simple recipe that uses easy-to-find ingredients. Serve with some steamed vegetables for a complete meal. Use cubes of pork or even shrimp instead of the chicken.
—Courtney Stultz, Weir, KS

Takes: 20 min. • **Makes:** 4 servings

- 1 Tbsp. olive oil
- 1 lb. boneless skinless chicken breasts, cut into 1-in. pieces
- 2 tsp. garlic-herb seasoning blend
- 1 can (14½ oz.) fire-roasted diced tomatoes
- 1 can (8 oz.) unsweetened pineapple chunks
- ¼ cup barbecue sauce
  Hot cooked rice
  Fresh cilantro leaves, optional

In a large nonstick skillet, heat oil over medium-high heat. Add chicken and seasoning; saute until chicken is lightly browned and no longer pink, about 5 minutes. Add tomatoes, pineapple and barbecue sauce. Bring to a boil; cook and stir until flavors are blended and chicken is cooked through, 5-7 minutes. Serve with rice and, if desired, cilantro.

1 cup chicken mixture: 242 cal., 6g fat (1g sat. fat), 63mg chol., 605mg sod., 20g carb. (15g sugars, 1g fiber), 24g pro. **Diabetic exchanges:** 3 lean meat, 1 starch, ½ fat.

CURRIED SQUASH & SAUSAGE

(PICTURED ON P. 111)

This stovetop supper is easy to make, and it charms my whole family of curry lovers. My kids even like it cold and ask to have it packed that way for their lunch at school.
—Colette Lower, York, PA

Prep: 15 min. • **Cook:** 20 min.
Makes: 8 servings

- 1 lb. mild bulk Italian sausage
- 1 Tbsp. olive oil
- 1 medium onion, chopped
- 1 medium green pepper, chopped
- 1 large acorn squash or 6 cups butternut squash, seeded, peeled and cubed (½ in.)
- 1 large unpeeled apple, cubed (½ in.)
- 2 to 3 tsp. curry powder
- 1 tsp. salt
- 3 cups cooked small pasta shells
- ¼ cup water

1. In a stockpot, cook and crumble the sausage over medium heat until no longer pink, 5-6 minutes; remove.
2. In same pan, heat oil; cook and stir onion and pepper 3 minutes. Add squash; cook 5 minutes. Stir in the apple, curry powder and salt until the vegetables are crisp-tender, 3-4 minutes.
3. Return sausage to pan; add pasta and water. Heat through.

1⅓ cups: 385 cal., 18g fat (5g sat. fat), 38mg chol., 735mg sod., 44g carb. (7g sugars, 4g fiber), 14g pro.

EASY CARIBBEAN CHICKEN

BEEF FILETS WITH PORTOBELLO SAUCE
(PICTURED ON P. 111)

These tasty steaks are quick enough for everyday dinners, but they feel special, too. We enjoy the mushroom-topped filets with crusty French bread, mixed salad and a light lemon dessert.
—Christel Stein, Tampa, FL

Takes: 20 min. • **Makes:** 2 servings

- 2 beef tenderloin steaks (4 oz. each)
- 1¾ cups sliced baby portobello mushrooms (about 4 oz.)
- ½ cup dry red wine or reduced-sodium beef broth
- 1 tsp. all-purpose flour
- ½ cup reduced-sodium beef broth
- 1 tsp. ketchup
- 1 tsp. steak sauce
- 1 tsp. Worcestershire sauce
- ½ tsp. ground mustard
- ¼ tsp. pepper
- ⅛ tsp. salt
- 1 Tbsp. minced fresh chives, optional

1. Place a large skillet coated with cooking spray over medium-high heat; brown the steaks on both sides. Remove from pan.
2. Add the mushrooms and wine to pan; bring to a boil over medium heat, stirring to loosen browned bits from pan. Cook until liquid is reduced by half, 2-3 minutes. Mix flour and broth until smooth; stir into pan. Stir in all remaining ingredients except chives; bring to a boil.
3. Return steaks to pan; cook, uncovered, until meat reaches desired doneness (for medium-rare, a thermometer should read 135°; medium, 140°), 1-2 minutes per side. If desired, sprinkle with chives.
1 steak with ⅓ cup sauce: 247 cal., 7g fat (3g sat. fat), 51mg chol., 369mg sod., 7g carb. (3g sugars, 1g fiber), 27g pro. **Diabetic exchanges:** 3 lean meat, 1 vegetable.

ISRAELI COUSCOUS & CHICKEN SAUSAGE SKILLET

ISRAELI COUSCOUS & CHICKEN SAUSAGE SKILLET

Craving a plate full of comfort? My 30-minute recipe is hearty, satisfying and a little bit different. The family loves it.
—Angela Spengler, Niceville, FL

Takes: 30 min. • **Makes:** 4 servings

- 2 tsp. olive oil
- 1 pkg. (12 oz.) fully cooked spinach and feta chicken sausage links or flavor of your choice, sliced
- 1 small onion, finely chopped
- 1 celery rib, finely chopped
- 1 garlic clove, minced
- 1 cup reduced-sodium chicken broth
- 1 cup water
- ¼ tsp. crushed red pepper flakes
- 1¼ cups uncooked pearl (Israeli) couscous
- 2 Tbsp. minced fresh parsley
- ¼ cup crumbled feta cheese, optional

1. In a large nonstick skillet, heat oil over medium-high heat. Add sausage, onion and celery; cook and stir 6-8 minutes or until sausage is browned. Add garlic; cook 1 minute longer.
2. Stir in broth, water and pepper flakes; bring to a boil. Stir in couscous. Reduce heat; simmer, covered, 10-12 minutes or until liquid is absorbed. Remove from heat; let stand, covered, 5 minutes. Stir in the parsley. If desired, sprinkle with cheese.
1 cup: 343 cal., 10g fat (3g sat. fat), 65mg chol., 694mg sod., 41g carb. (1g sugars, 1g fiber), 22g pro. **Diabetic exchanges:** 3 starch, 3 lean meat, ½ fat.

BLACKENED CATFISH WITH MANGO AVOCADO SALSA

A delightful and tasty rub makes this quick recipe fantastic. While the fish is sitting to allow the flavors to blend, you can easily assemble the salsa. My family thinks this is marvelous.
—Laura Fisher, Westfield, MA

....

Prep: 20 min. + chilling • **Cook:** 10 min.
Makes: 4 servings (2 cups salsa)

- 2 tsp. dried oregano
- 2 tsp. ground cumin
- 2 tsp. paprika
- 2¼ tsp. pepper, divided
- ¾ tsp. salt, divided
- 4 catfish fillets (6 oz. each)
- 1 medium mango, peeled and cubed
- 1 medium ripe avocado, peeled and cubed
- ⅓ cup finely chopped red onion
- 2 Tbsp. minced fresh cilantro
- 2 Tbsp. lime juice
- 2 tsp. olive oil

1. Combine the oregano, cumin, paprika, 2 tsp. pepper and ½ tsp. salt; rub over the fillets. Refrigerate for at least 30 minutes.
2. Meanwhile, in a small bowl, combine the mango, avocado, red onion, cilantro, lime juice and remaining salt and pepper. Chill until serving.
3. In a large cast-iron skillet, cook fillets in oil over medium heat until fish flakes easily with a fork, 5-7 minutes on each side. Serve with salsa.

1 fillet with ½ cup salsa: 376 cal., 22g fat (4g sat. fat), 80mg chol., 541mg sod., 17g carb. (9g sugars, 6g fiber), 28g pro. **Diabetic exchanges:** 5 lean meat, 1 starch, ½ fat.

BLACKENED CATFISH WITH MANGO AVOCADO SALSA

BAVARIAN APPLE-SAUSAGE HASH

This awesome recipe reflects my German roots. In the cooler months, nothing is as comforting as a hearty hash. You can also serve this versatile dish as a holiday side, or as a brunch entree over cheddar grits or topped with a fried egg.
—Crystal Schlueter, Northglenn, CO

....

Takes: 30 min. • **Makes:** 4 servings

- 2 Tbsp. canola oil
- ½ cup chopped onion
- 4 fully cooked apple chicken sausages or flavor of your choice, sliced
- 1½ cups thinly sliced Brussels sprouts
- 1 large tart apple, peeled and chopped
- 1 tsp. caraway seeds
- ¼ tsp. salt
- ⅛ tsp. pepper
- 2 Tbsp. finely chopped walnuts
- 1 Tbsp. brown sugar
- 1 Tbsp. whole grain mustard
- 1 Tbsp. cider vinegar

1. In a large skillet, heat the oil over medium-high heat; saute onion until tender, 1-2 minutes. Add sausages, Brussels sprouts, apple and seasonings; saute until lightly browned, 6-8 minutes.
2. Stir in walnuts, brown sugar, mustard and vinegar; cook and stir 2 minutes.

1 cup: 310 cal., 17g fat (3g sat. fat), 60mg chol., 715mg sod., 25g carb. (19g sugars, 3g fiber), 16g pro.

CHUNKY COD STIR-FRY

Here's a flavorful new way to serve fish. Good-for-you cod is accented with crunchy vegetables, peanuts and a simple sauce.
—Dorothy Colette, Bourbonnais, IL

....

Takes: 30 min. • **Makes:** 4 servings

- 2 tsp. cornstarch
- ⅓ cup chicken broth
- 2 Tbsp. sherry or additional chicken broth
- 2 Tbsp. reduced-sodium soy sauce
- ⅛ tsp. crushed red pepepr flakes
- 1 garlic clove, minced
- 1 Tbsp. canola oil
- 1 pkg. (16 oz.) frozen stir-fry vegetable blend, thawed
- 1 small sweet red pepper, julienned
- 1 lb. cod, cut into 1-in. cubes
- ¼ cup chopped peanuts
- 3 cups hot cooked rice

1. In a bowl, combine first 5 ingredients; set aside. In a large nonstick skillet or wok, stir-fry garlic in oil for 30 seconds. Add the mixed vegetables and red pepper; stir-fry until crisp-tender, 4-5 minutes.

2. Remove and keep warm. Add half of the cod to skillet; gently stir-fry until fish flakes easily with a fork, 3-5 minutes. Remove and keep warm. Repeat with the remaining cod.

3. Stir broth mixture and add to the pan. Bring to a boil; cook and stir for 2 minutes or until thickened. Return vegetables and fish to the pan. Add the peanuts. Gently stir to coat. Cover and cook until heated through, about 1 minute. Serve over rice.

1 serving: 419 cal., 9g fat (1g sat. fat), 43mg chol., 507mg sod., 54g carb. (6g sugars, 4g fiber), 27g pro.

GARLIC-MUSHROOM TURKEY SLICES

GARLIC-MUSHROOM TURKEY SLICES

Even my daughter likes this turkey dish, and she's a picky eater! There's a minimum of fat, and it's delicious and inexpensive for weeknight dining.
—Rick Fleishman, Beverly Hills, CA

....

Takes: 30 min. • **Makes:** 4 servings

- ½ cup all-purpose flour
- ½ tsp. dried oregano
- ½ tsp. paprika
- ¾ tsp. salt, divided
- ¼ tsp. pepper, divided
- 1 Tbsp. olive oil
- 1 pkg. (17.6 oz.) turkey breast cutlets
- ½ lb. sliced fresh mushrooms
- ¾ cup reduced-sodium chicken broth
- ¼ cup dry white wine or additional broth
- 2 garlic cloves, minced

1. In a large shallow dish, mix the flour, oregano, paprika, ½ tsp. salt and ⅛ tsp. pepper. Dip cutlets in flour mixture to coat both sides; shake off excess.

2. In a large nonstick skillet, heat oil over medium heat. In batches, add turkey and cook 1-2 minutes on each side or until no longer pink; remove from pan.

3. Add remaining ingredients to skillet; stir in the remaining salt and pepper. Cook, uncovered, 4-6 minutes or until the mushrooms are tender, stirring occasionally. Return turkey to pan; heat through, turning to coat.

1 serving: 218 cal., 4g fat (1g sat. fat), 77mg chol., 440mg sod., 8g carb. (1g sugars, 1g fiber), 34g pro. **Diabetic exchanges:** 4 lean meat, ½ starch, ½ fat.

ITALIAN SAUSAGE VEGGIE SKILLET

We love Italian sausage sandwiches, but because the bread isn't diet-friendly for me, I created this recipe to satisfy my craving. If you like a little heat, use some hot peppers in addition to the sweet ones.
—Tina M. Howells, Salem, OH

Takes: 30 min. • **Makes:** 6 servings

- 4 cups uncooked whole wheat spiral pasta
- 1 lb. Italian turkey sausage, casings removed
- 1 medium onion, chopped
- 1 garlic clove, minced
- 2 medium zucchini, chopped
- 1 large sweet red pepper, chopped
- 1 large sweet yellow pepper, chopped
- 1 can (28 oz.) diced tomatoes, drained
- ¼ tsp. salt
- ¼ tsp. pepper

1. Cook pasta according to package directions; drain.
2. Meanwhile, in large skillet, cook the sausage and onion over medium-high heat 5-7 minutes or until sausage is no longer pink. Add garlic and cook 1 minute longer. Add the chopped zucchini and peppers; cook until crisp-tender, 3-5 minutes. Add tomatoes, salt and pepper. Cook and stir until the vegetables are tender and begin to release their juices, 5-7 minutes. Serve with whole wheat pasta.

1⅓ cups: 251 cal., 6g fat (1g sat. fat), 28mg chol., 417mg sod., 35g carb. (4g sugars, 6g fiber), 16g pro. **Diabetic exchanges:** 2 vegetable, 2 lean meat, 1½ starch.

SHRIMP WITH WARM GERMAN-STYLE COLESLAW
(PICTURED ON P. 111)

We love anything that's tangy or bacony. Fennel and tarragon make this dish especially savory. I use the medley from Minute Rice if I don't have time to make my own.
—Ann Sheehy, Lawrence, MA

Takes: 30 min. • **Makes:** 4 servings

- 6 bacon strips
- 2 Tbsp. canola oil, divided
- 3 cups finely shredded green cabbage
- ½ cup finely shredded carrot (1 medium carrot)
- 1 cup finely shredded red cabbage, optional
- ½ cup finely shredded fennel bulb, optional
- 6 green onions, finely chopped
- 3 Tbsp. minced fresh parsley
- 2 Tbsp. minced fresh tarragon or 2 tsp. dried tarragon
- ¼ tsp. salt
- ⅛ tsp. pepper
- ¼ cup red wine vinegar
- 1 lb. uncooked shrimp (26-30 per lb.), peeled and deveined
- 3 cups hot cooked rice or multigrain medley

1. In a large skillet, cook the bacon over medium heat until crisp. Remove to paper towels to drain. Pour off the drippings, discarding all but 2 Tbsp. Crumble bacon.
2. In same skillet, heat 1 Tbsp. drippings with 1 Tbsp. oil over medium heat. Add green cabbage and carrot and, if desired, red cabbage and fennel; cook and stir until vegetables are just tender, 1-2 minutes. Remove to a bowl. Stir in green onions, parsley, tarragon, salt and pepper; toss with vinegar. Keep warm.
3. Add remaining drippings and remaining oil to skillet. Add the shrimp; cook and stir over medium heat until shrimp turn pink, 2-3 minutes. Remove from heat.
4. To serve, spoon rice and coleslaw into soup bowls. Top with shrimp; sprinkle with crumbled bacon.

1 serving: 472 cal., 20g fat (5g sat. fat), 156mg chol., 546mg sod., 44g carb. (2g sugars, 3g fiber), 28g pro.

ITALIAN SAUSAGE VEGGIE SKILLET

PAN-SEARED SALMON WITH DILL SAUCE

PAN-SEARED SALMON WITH DILL SAUCE

This is one of my husband's favorite recipes. Salmon is a go-to for busy nights because it cooks so quickly and goes with so many different flavors. The creamy dill sauce tastes light and fresh, with a nice crunch from the cucumbers.

—Angela Spengler, Niceville, FL

Takes: 25 min. • **Makes:** 4 servings

- 1 Tbsp. canola oil
- 4 salmon fillets (6 oz. each)
- 1 tsp. Italian seasoning
- ¼ tsp. salt
- ½ cup reduced-fat plain yogurt
- ¼ cup reduced-fat mayonnaise
- ¼ cup finely chopped cucumber
- 1 tsp. snipped fresh dill

1. In a large skillet, heat oil over medium-high heat. Sprinkle the salmon with Italian seasoning and salt. Place in skillet, skin side down. Reduce heat to medium. Cook until fish just begins to flake easily with a fork, about 5 minutes on each side.

2. Meanwhile, in a small bowl, combine yogurt, mayonnaise, cucumber and dill. Serve with salmon.

1 salmon fillet with ¼ cup sauce: 366 cal., 25g fat (4g sat. fat), 92mg chol., 349mg sod., 4g carb. (3g sugars, 0 fiber), 31g pro. **Diabetic exchanges:** 4 lean meat, 2½ fat.

* **HEALTH TIP** * This nutritious salmon dish provides about 2 grams of omega-3 fatty acids. Salmon is one of the best sources for this healthy fat.

> **READER REVIEW**
>
> *"We enjoyed this dish along with a whole grain rice medley and fresh peas. Instead of using mayo and fresh dill, I used some dill pesto with the yogurt because I had some in the freezer. This saved on buying a bunch of fresh dill that I couldn't have finished up. We had some leftover fish, and it made a terrific salmon salad the next day! This recipe is definitely on the keeper list."*
>
> —ANNRMS, TASTEOFHOME.COM

TEX-MEX PORK CHOPS
(PICTURED ON P. 110)

I won a contest with these easy, flavorful chops. Salsa, cumin and chile peppers give this dish the kick it needs to be called Tex-Mex.

—Jo Ann Dalrymple, Claremore, OK

Takes: 20 min. • **Makes:** 6 servings

- Butter-flavored cooking spray
- 1 small onion, chopped
- 6 boneless pork loin chops (5 oz. each)
- 1 cup salsa
- 1 can (4 oz.) chopped green chiles
- ½ tsp. ground cumin
- ¼ tsp. pepper

1. In a large skillet coated with butter-flavored cooking spray, saute onion until tender. Add the pork chops; cook over medium heat until a thermometer reads 145°, 5-6 minutes on each side.

2. Combine the salsa, chiles, cumin and pepper; pour over pork. Bring to a boil. Reduce heat; cover and simmer until heated through.

1 serving: 223 cal., 8g fat (3g sat. fat), 68mg chol., 433mg sod., 9g carb. (3g sugars, 5g fiber), 32g pro. **Diabetic exchanges:** 4 lean meat, 1 vegetable.

WEEKNIGHT PASTA SQUIGGLES

This zesty pasta dish is ideal for busy weeknights. It's low on ingredients and easy to prep, and it tastes so comforting when the weather turns cool. A salad on the side makes it a meal.
—Stacey Brown, Spring, TX

Takes: 30 min. • **Makes:** 8 servings

- 1 pkg. (19½ oz.) Italian turkey sausage links, casings removed
- 1 can (28 oz.) whole plum tomatoes with basil
- 1 can (14½ oz.) no-salt-added whole tomatoes
- 4 cups uncooked spiral pasta (about 12 oz.)
- 1 can (14½ oz.) reduced-sodium chicken broth
- ¼ cup water
- ½ cup crumbled goat or feta cheese

1. In a Dutch oven, cook and crumble sausage over medium-high heat until no longer pink, 5-7 minutes. Meanwhile, coarsely chop tomatoes, reserving juices.
2. Add tomatoes and reserved juices to sausage; stir in pasta, broth and water. Bring to a boil. Reduce heat to medium; cook, uncovered, until pasta is al dente, 15-18 minutes, stirring occasionally. Top with cheese.

1½ cups: 278 cal., 7g fat (2g sat. fat), 34mg chol., 622mg sod., 38g carb. (5g sugars, 4g fiber), 16g pro. **Diabetic exchanges:** 2½ starch, 2 medium-fat meat.

TARRAGON CHICKEN WITH APPLES

When friends in Winnipeg served us this delicious chicken, I knew I had to have the recipe. It originally called for whipping cream, which is a little high in fat for me. I substituted 1% milk and found that it was just as tasty and not quite as rich.
—Karen Moffatt, Lake Cowichan, BC

Takes: 30 min. • **Makes:** 4 servings

- 4 boneless skinless chicken breast halves (4 oz. each)
- 2 Tbsp. butter, divided
- ¼ tsp. salt
- ⅛ tsp. pepper
- 2 medium tart apples, peeled and sliced
- ½ cup apple juice
- ½ cup 1% milk
- 1 tsp. cornstarch
- 1 Tbsp. water
- 1 Tbsp. minced fresh tarragon or 1 tsp. dried tarragon
  Hot cooked long grain and wild rice, optional

1. In a nonstick skillet, brown chicken in 1 Tbsp. butter for 3-4 minutes on each side. Sprinkle with salt and pepper; remove and keep warm. In the same skillet, cook apples in remaining butter for 6-8 minutes or until tender; remove and keep warm.
2. Add apple juice to pan; cook and stir over medium heat for 4 minutes or until juice is reduced by half. Add milk. Return chicken to pan; cook for 3 minutes or until chicken juices run clear.
3. Combine cornstarch and water until smooth; stir into pan juices. Bring to a boil; cook and stir for 2 minutes or until thickened. Add the apples and tarragon; heat through. Serve with rice if desired.

1 serving: 234 cal., 9g fat (5g sat. fat), 79mg chol., 263mg sod., 14g carb. (11g sugars, 1g fiber), 48g pro. **Diabetic exchanges:** 3 lean meat, 1½ fat, ½ fruit.

WEEKNIGHT PASTA SQUIGGLES

SOUTHWESTERN SPAGHETTI

Chili powder and cumin give a mild Mexican flavor to this colorful one-skillet supper. With chunks of fresh zucchini, it's a nice change of pace from typical spaghetti dishes.
—Beth Coffee, Hartford City, IN

Takes: 30 min. • **Makes:** 5 servings

- ¾ lb. lean ground beef (90% lean)
- 2¼ cups water
- 1 can (15 oz.) tomato sauce
- 2 tsp. chili powder
- ½ tsp. garlic powder
- ½ tsp. ground cumin
- ⅛ tsp. salt
- 1 pkg. (7 oz.) thin spaghetti, broken into thirds
- 1 lb. zucchini (about 4 small), cut into chunks
- ½ cup shredded cheddar cheese

1. In a large skillet, cook ground beef over medium heat until no longer pink; drain. Remove beef and set aside. In the same skillet, combine the water, tomato sauce, chili powder, garlic powder, cumin and salt; bring to a boil. Stir in spaghetti; return to a boil. Boil for 6 minutes.
2. Add the zucchini. Cook 4-5 minutes longer or until spaghetti and zucchini are tender, stirring several times. Stir in beef and heat through. Sprinkle with cheese.
1 cup: 340 cal., 11g fat (5g sat. fat), 54mg chol., 600mg sod., 38g carb. (5g sugars, 4g fiber), 24g pro. **Diabetic exchanges:** 2 starch, 2 lean meat, 2 vegetable, ½ fat.

READER REVIEW

"I'm so glad I tried this recipe; we really enjoyed it! I did saute the zucchini with some chopped onions until soft (we don't care for crisp-tender zucchini), and I doubled the seasonings. I also added oregano and some black olives. It was delicious. I will make this again!"
—SGRONHOLZ, TASTEOFHOME.COM

SUMMERTIME ORZO & CHICKEN

SUMMERTIME ORZO & CHICKEN

This easy-as-can-be main dish is likely to become a summer staple at your house. It's that good! If you prefer, grill the chicken breasts instead of cooking them in a skillet.
—Fran MacMillan, West Melbourne, FL

Takes: 30 min. • **Makes:** 4 servings

- ¾ cup uncooked orzo pasta
- 1 lb. boneless skinless chicken breasts, cut into 1-in. pieces
- 1 medium cucumber, chopped
- 1 small red onion, chopped
- ¼ cup minced fresh parsley
- 2 Tbsp. lemon juice
- 1 Tbsp. olive oil
- 1 tsp. salt
- ¼ tsp. pepper
- ¼ cup crumbled reduced-fat feta cheese

1. Cook orzo pasta according to package directions; drain.
2. Meanwhile, in a large skillet coated with cooking spray, cook and stir chicken over medium heat until no longer pink, 6-8 minutes. Transfer to a large bowl.
3. Add the cucumber, onion, parsley and pasta. In a small bowl, mix lemon juice, oil, salt and pepper; toss with chicken mixture. Serve immediately or refrigerate and serve cold. Top with cheese before serving.
1¼ cups: 320 cal., 7g fat (2g sat. fat), 65mg chol., 742mg sod., 32g carb. (3g sugars, 2g fiber), 30g pro. **Diabetic exchanges:** 3 lean meat, 2 starch, 1 fat.

* HEALTH TIP * Make this salad heart-healthier: A simple switch to whole wheat orzo pasta will add nearly 3 grams fiber per serving.

SPINACH & SHRIMP FRA DIAVOLO

This dish is spicy, garlicky, saucy, and loaded with delicious shrimp. Plus, with the addition of spinach you're also getting a serving of veggies. When you need a perfect low-fat weeknight meal that is quick to pull together, this is it. You can substitute arugula or kale for the spinach if you'd like.
—Julie Peterson, Crofton, MD

Prep: 20 min. • **Cook:** 30 min.
Makes: 4 servings

- 2 Tbsp. olive oil
- 1 medium onion, chopped
- 5 garlic cloves, minced
- ½ to 1 tsp. crushed red pepper flakes
- 1 cup dry white wine
- 1 can (14½ oz.) diced tomatoes, undrained
- 1 can (8 oz.) tomato sauce
- 3 Tbsp. minced fresh basil or 1 Tbsp. dried basil
- 1 tsp. dried oregano
- ¼ tsp. salt
- ¼ tsp. pepper
- 1 lb. uncooked shrimp (26-30 per lb.), peeled and deveined
- 3 cups finely chopped fresh spinach Grated Parmesan cheese, optional

1. In a large skillet, heat oil over medium-high heat. Add onion; cook and stir until tender, 8-10 minutes. Add the garlic and pepper flakes; cook 1 minute longer. Stir in wine. Bring to a boil; cook until liquid is reduced by half. Stir in tomatoes, tomato sauce, basil, oregano, salt and pepper. Cook and stir until the sauce is slightly thickened, about 10 minutes.
2. Add shrimp and spinach; cook and stir until the shrimp turn pink and spinach is wilted, 3-5 minutes. If desired, sprinkle with Parmesan cheese.

1½ cups: 235 cal., 9g fat (1g sat. fat), 138mg chol., 727mg sod., 14g carb. (6g sugars, 4g fiber), 22g pro. **Diabetic exchanges:** 3 lean meat, 2 vegetable, 1½ fat.

SNOW PEAS & BEEF STIR-FRY

Skip greasy takeout food and go for this healthy and fast dinner that's so much more enjoyable. To make it even easier, warm up ready-to-serve brown rice in the microwave and dinner is ready to go (with one less pan to wash).
—Donna Lindecamp, Morganton, NC

Takes: 30 min. • **Makes:** 6 servings

- ½ cup reduced-sodium soy sauce
- ½ cup sherry or water
- 2 Tbsp. cornstarch
- 2 tsp. sugar
- 2 Tbsp. canola oil, divided
- 2 garlic cloves, minced
- 1½ lbs. beef top sirloin steak, thinly sliced
- ½ lb. sliced fresh mushrooms
- 1 medium onion, cut into thin wedges
- ½ lb. fresh snow peas Hot cooked rice, optional

1. In a small bowl, whisk soy sauce, sherry, cornstarch and sugar. Transfer ¼ cup mixture to a large bowl; stir in 1 Tbsp. oil and garlic. Add the beef; toss to coat. Let stand 15 minutes.
2. Heat a large skillet over medium-high heat. Add half of the beef mixture; stir-fry 1-2 minutes or until no longer pink. Remove from pan; repeat with the remaining beef.
3. In same pan, heat remaining oil over medium-high heat until hot. Add the mushrooms and onion; cook and stir until mushrooms are tender. Add snow peas; cook 2-3 minutes longer or until crisp-tender.
4. Stir remaining soy sauce mixture and add to pan. Bring to a boil; cook and stir 1-2 minutes or until sauce is thickened. Return beef to pan; heat through. Serve with rice if desired.

1 cup: 265 cal., 9g fat (2g sat. fat), 46mg chol., 863mg sod., 12g carb. (5g sugars, 2g fiber), 28g pro. **Diabetic exchanges:** 3 lean meat, 2 vegetable, 1 fat.

SPINACH & SHRIMP FRA DIAVOLO

CHICKEN WITH CREAMY JALAPENO SAUCE

SPICY SAUSAGE & RICE SKILLET

The spicy sausage in this quick skillet dish gives it a kick, and the sliced apple is a pleasant, tart surprise.
—Jamie Jones, Madison, GA

Takes: 30 min. • **Makes:** 6 servings

- 1 pkg. (12 oz.) fully cooked spicy chicken sausage links, halved lengthwise and cut into ½-in. slices
- 1 Tbsp. olive oil
- 2 medium yellow summer squash, chopped
- 2 medium zucchini, chopped
- 1 large sweet red pepper, chopped
- 1 medium onion, chopped
- 1 medium tart apple, cut into ¼-in. slices
- 1 garlic clove, minced
- ½ tsp. salt
- 1 pkg. (8.8 oz.) ready-to-serve brown rice
- 1 can (15 oz.) black beans, rinsed and drained
- ¼ to ½ cup water

1. In a large nonstick skillet, cook the chicken sausage over medium-high heat, turning occasionally, until lightly browned. Remove from skillet.
2. In the same skillet, heat olive oil over medium-high heat. Saute squash, zucchini, pepper, onion, apple, garlic and salt until the vegetables are tender, 5-7 minutes. Add rice, beans, ¼ cup water and sausage; cook and stir until heated through, about 5 minutes, adding more water if needed.

1⅓ cups: 285 cal., 8g fat (2g sat. fat), 43mg chol., 668mg sod., 34g carb. (9g sugars, 6g fiber), 17g pro. **Diabetic exchanges:** 2 starch, 2 lean meat, 1 vegetable, ½ fat.

> **TEST KITCHEN TIP**
>
> If making rice from scratch, you'll need about 2 cups cooked rice. Skip the sausage and add more beans to make a meatless version.

CHICKEN WITH CREAMY JALAPENO SAUCE

My sister Amy came up with this recipe that makes standard chicken breasts a lot more exciting. My husband and I just love the wonderful sauce.
—Molly Cappone, Lewis Center, OH

Takes: 25 min.
Makes: 4 servings (2 cups sauce)

- 4 boneless skinless chicken breast halves (4 oz. each)
- ¼ tsp. salt
- 1 Tbsp. canola oil
- 2 medium onions, chopped
- ½ cup reduced-sodium chicken broth
- 2 jalapeno peppers, seeded and minced
- 2 tsp. ground cumin
- 3 oz. reduced-fat cream cheese, cubed
- ¼ cup reduced-fat sour cream
- 3 plum tomatoes, seeded and chopped
- 2 cups hot cooked rice

1. Sprinkle chicken with salt. In a large nonstick skillet over medium-high heat, brown chicken in oil on both sides.
2. Add the onions, broth, jalapenos and cumin. Bring to a boil. Reduce heat; cover and simmer until a thermometer reads 165°, 5-7 minutes. Remove chicken and keep warm.
3. Stir cream cheese and sour cream into onion mixture until blended. Stir in tomatoes; heat through. Serve with chicken and rice.

Note: Wear disposable gloves when cutting hot peppers; the oils can burn skin. Avoid touching your face.

1 serving: 376 cal., 13g fat (5g sat. fat), 83mg chol., 389mg sod., 34g carb. (8g sugars, 3g fiber), 30g pro. **Diabetic exchanges:** 3 lean meat, 2 vegetable, 2 fat, 1½ starch.

SPICY SAUSAGE & RICE SKILLET

SOFT FISH TACOS

My husband, Bill, and I were cooking together in the kitchen one day and we came up with these tasty fish tacos. The combination of tilapia, cabbage and a hint of cumin is fun. After one bite, everyone is hooked!

—Carrie Billups, Florence, OR

Takes: 25 min. • **Makes:** 5 servings

- 4 cups coleslaw mix
- ⅓ cup tartar sauce
- ½ tsp. salt
- ½ tsp. ground cumin
- ¼ tsp. pepper
- 1½ lbs. tilapia fillets
- 2 Tbsp. olive oil
- 1 Tbsp. lemon juice
- 10 corn tortillas (6 in.), warmed
    Optional: Shredded cheddar cheese, chopped tomato and sliced avocado

1. In a large bowl, toss the coleslaw mix, tartar sauce, salt, cumin and pepper; set aside. In a large nonstick skillet, cook tilapia in oil and lemon juice over medium heat for 4-5 minutes on each side or until fish flakes easily with a fork.
2. Place tilapia on tortillas; top with coleslaw mixture. Serve with shredded cheese, chopped tomato and sliced avocado if desired.

2 tacos: 309 cal., 11g fat (2g sat. fat), 66mg chol., 423mg sod., 26g carb. (4g sugars, 4g fiber), 29g pro. **Diabetic exchanges:** 4 lean meat, 2 starch, 2 fat.

VEGGIE-CASHEW STIR-FRY

VEGGIE-CASHEW STIR-FRY

Getting my meat-loving husband and two sons, ages 5 and 7, to eat more veggies had always been a struggle until I whipped up this stir-fry one night. I was shocked when they cleaned their plates and asked for seconds.

—Abbey Hoffman, Ashland, OH

Prep: 20 min. • **Cook:** 15 min.
Makes: 4 servings

- ¼ cup reduced-sodium soy sauce
- ¼ cup water
- 2 Tbsp. brown sugar
- 2 Tbsp. lemon juice
- 2 Tbsp. olive oil
- 1 garlic clove, minced
- 2 cups sliced fresh mushrooms
- ¼ lb. fresh baby carrots, coarsely chopped
- 1 small zucchini, cut into ¼-in. slices
- 1 small sweet red pepper, coarsely chopped
- 1 small green pepper, coarsely chopped
- 4 green onions, sliced
- 2 cups cooked brown rice
- 1 can (8 oz.) sliced water chestnuts, drained
- ½ cup honey-roasted cashews

1. In a small bowl, mix soy sauce, water, brown sugar and lemon juice until smooth; set aside.
2. In a large skillet, heat oil over medium-high heat. Stir-fry garlic for 1 minute. Add vegetables; cook until the vegetables are crisp-tender, 6-8 minutes.
3. Stir the soy sauce mixture and add to pan. Bring to a boil. Add brown rice and water chestnuts; heat through. Top with honey-roasted cashews.

1½ cups: 385 cal., 16g fat (3g sat. fat), 0 chol., 671mg sod., 56g carb. (15g sugars, 6g fiber), 9g pro.

FETTUCCINE WITH BLACK BEAN SAUCE

When my husband needed to go on a heart-smart diet, I had to come up with new ways to get more vegetables into our daily menus. This meatless spaghetti sauce is a winner; it's especially delicious with spinach fettuccine.
—Marianne Neuman, East Troy, WI

Takes: 30 min. • **Makes:** 5 servings

- 6 oz. uncooked fettuccine
- 1 small green pepper, chopped
- 1 small onion, chopped
- 1 Tbsp. olive oil
- 2 cups garden-style pasta sauce
- 1 can (15 oz.) black beans, rinsed and drained
- 2 Tbsp. minced fresh basil or 2 tsp. dried basil
- 1 tsp. dried oregano
- ½ tsp. fennel seed
- ¼ tsp. garlic salt
- 1 cup shredded part-skim mozzarella cheese
   Additional chopped fresh basil, optional

1. Cook fettuccine according to package directions. Meanwhile, in a large saucepan, saute green pepper and onion in oil until tender. Stir in the pasta sauce, black beans and seasonings.
2. Bring to a boil. Reduce heat; simmer, uncovered, for 5 minutes. Drain the fettuccine. Top with sauce and sprinkle with cheese. If desired, top with chopped fresh basil.

Note: This recipe was tested with Ragu Super Vegetable Primavera pasta sauce.

¾ cup sauce with ¾ cup pasta: 350 cal., 10g fat (3g sat. fat), 17mg chol., 761mg sod., 51g carb. (12g sugars, 8g fiber), 16g pro.

* HEALTH TIP * As long as you're eating a healthy dinner, switch up your noodle game, too. Try this recipe with whole wheat, buckwheat, quinoa, chickpea or multigrain pasta.

> **READER REVIEW**
>
> *"This was an awesome twist for our weekly meal rotation. My family loves pasta, and this black bean sauce tastes great! I could easily see putting some type of meat into this recipe, too!"*
> —CHANDRA_24, TASTEOFHOME.COM

FETTUCCINE WITH BLACK BEAN SAUCE

CREAMY PASTA WITH FLORETS

Cottage cheese is the surprising base for the wonderfully creamy sauce that coats the pasta and veggies in this side dish. My husband, who doesn't like to compromise good taste for low-fat foods, didn't even realize this recipe was lower in fat.
—Barbara Toher, Lexington, KY

Takes: 30 min. • **Makes:** 4 servings

- 1 cup 1% cottage cheese
- ½ cup 1% milk
- ¼ cup reduced-fat sour cream
- ¼ cup grated Parmesan cheese
- ½ tsp. salt
- ⅛ tsp. cayenne pepper
- 5 cups broccoli florets
- 4 cups cauliflowerets
- 4 oz. uncooked angel hair pasta
- 3 garlic cloves, minced
- 2 tsp. olive oil
- 2½ cups sliced fresh mushrooms

1. In a blender or food processor, combine the cottage cheese, milk, sour cream, Parmesan cheese, salt and cayenne; cover and process until smooth. Set aside.
2. In a saucepan, bring 1 in. of water to a boil; place broccoli and cauliflower in a steamer basket over water. Cover and steam for 3-4 minutes or until crisp-tender. Meanwhile, cook pasta according to package directions; drain.
3. In a large nonstick skillet, saute garlic in oil for 2 minutes. Add mushrooms; saute 5 minutes longer. Stir in the broccoli, cauliflower, pasta and cottage cheese mixture; heat through.

2 cups: 260 cal., 4g fat (2g sat. fat), 10mg chol., 699mg sod., 38g carb. (9g sugars, 6g fiber), 20g pro. **Diabetic exchanges:** 2½ starch, 1 medium-fat meat.

BEEF BARLEY SKILLET

BEEF BARLEY SKILLET

This versatile dish goes together fast since it's made with quick-cooking barley. You can make it with ground turkey or chicken, and any color bell pepper that you have on hand.
—Irene Tetreault, South Hadley, MA

Takes: 30 min. • **Makes:** 4 servings

- 1 lb. lean ground beef (90% lean)
- 1 small onion, chopped
- ¼ cup chopped celery
- ¼ cup chopped green pepper
- 1 can (14½ oz.) diced tomatoes, undrained
- 1½ cups water
- ¾ cup quick-cooking barley
- ½ cup chili sauce
- 1 tsp. Worcestershire sauce
- ½ tsp. dried marjoram
- ⅛ tsp. pepper
  Chopped parsley, optional

In a large skillet, cook beef, onion, celery and green pepper over medium-high heat until beef is no longer pink and vegetables are tender, breaking up the beef into crumbles, 5-7 minutes; drain. Stir in the remaining ingredients. Bring to a boil; reduce heat. Simmer, uncovered, until barley is tender, 5-10 minutes. If desired, top with chopped parsley.

1½ cups: 362 cal., 10g fat (4g sat. fat), 71mg chol., 707mg sod., 41g carb. (11g sugars, 8g fiber), 27g pro. **Diabetic exchanges:** 3 lean meat, 2 starch, 1 vegetable.

TEST KITCHEN TIP

You can also make this dish with ground turkey or chicken, or stir in leftover cooked meat toward the end of cooking. The texture is thick and hearty. If you want it more stew-like, stir in another can of diced tomatoes.

BRAISED PORK LOIN CHOPS

An easy herb rub gives sensational taste to these pork chops. The meat turns out tender and delicious.
—Marilyn Larsen, Port Orange, FL

Takes: 30 min. • **Makes:** 4 servings

- 1 garlic clove, minced
- 1 tsp. rubbed sage
- 1 tsp. dried rosemary, crushed
- ½ tsp. salt
- ⅛ tsp. pepper
- 4 boneless pork loin chops (½ in. thick and 4 oz. each)
- 1 Tbsp. butter
- 1 Tbsp. olive oil
- ¾ cup dry white wine or apple juice
- 1 Tbsp. minced fresh parsley

1. Mix first 5 ingredients; rub over both sides of pork chops. In a large nonstick skillet, heat butter and oil over medium-high heat; brown chops on both sides. Remove from pan.
2. In same pan, bring white wine to a boil, stirring to loosen browned bits from pan. Cook, uncovered, until liquid is reduced to ½ cup. Add chops; return to a boil. Reduce heat; simmer, covered, until pork is tender, 6-8 minutes. Sprinkle with parsley.

1 pork chop with 2 Tbsp. sauce: 218 cal., 13g fat (5g sat. fat), 62mg chol., 351mg sod., 3g carb. (2g sugars, 0 fiber), 22g pro. **Diabetic exchanges:** 3 lean meat, 1½ fat.

CHICKEN NUGGETS

I like to make these golden chicken nuggets because they're so quick and easy. My whole family loves them. You can also use the seasoning to cook chicken breast halves. Stack them on some rustic bread with mayo, lettuce and tomato for delicious sandwiches.
—Annette Ellyson, Carolina, WV

Takes: 30 min. • **Makes:** 8 servings

- 1 cup all-purpose flour
- 4 tsp. seasoned salt
- 1 tsp. poultry seasoning
- 1 tsp. ground mustard
- 1 tsp. paprika
- ½ tsp. pepper
- 2 lbs. boneless skinless chicken breasts
- ¼ cup canola oil

1. In a large shallow dish, combine the first 6 ingredients. Flatten chicken to ½-in. thickness, then cut into 1½-in. pieces. Add chicken, a few pieces at a time, to dish and turn to coat.
2. In a large skillet, cook chicken in oil in batches until no longer pink, 6-8 minutes.

3 oz. cooked chicken: 212 cal., 10g fat (2g sat. fat), 63mg chol., 435mg sod., 6g carb. (0 sugars, 0 fiber), 24g pro. **Diabetic exchanges:** 3 lean meat, 1½ fat, ½ starch.

BRAISED PORK LOIN CHOPS

DIJON-HONEY PORK CHOPS

Lemon pepper is my seasoning of choice for these pork chops. With the flavorful honey-orange Dijon sauce, there's no need to pass the salt.
—Shirley Goehring, Lodi, CA

Takes: 20 min. • **Makes:** 4 servings

- 4 boneless pork loin chops (5 oz. each)
- 1 tsp. salt-free lemon-pepper seasoning
- 2 tsp. canola oil
- ½ cup orange juice
- 1 Tbsp. Dijon mustard
- 1 Tbsp. honey

1. Sprinkle the pork chops with lemon pepper. In a large nonstick skillet, heat oil over medium heat. Brown pork chops on both sides.

2. In a small bowl, whisk orange juice, mustard and honey until blended; pour over chops. Bring to a boil. Reduce heat; simmer, covered, 5-8 minutes or until a thermometer inserted in pork reads 145°.

3. Remove chops from pan; keep warm. Bring sauce to a boil; cook until mixture is reduced to ¼ cup, stirring occasionally. Serve with chops.

1 pork chop with 1 Tbsp. sauce: 244 cal., 11g fat (3g sat. fat), 68mg chol., 134mg sod., 9g carb. (7g sugars, 0 fiber), 28g pro. **Diabetic exchanges:** 4 lean meat, ½ starch.

CHICKEN BULGUR SKILLET

CHICKEN BULGUR SKILLET

This recipe was passed on to me by a friend, and I've altered it slightly to suit our tastes. We like it with a fresh green salad.
—Leann Hillmer, Sylvan Grove, KS

Prep: 15 min. • **Cook:** 30 min.
Makes: 4 servings

- 1 lb. boneless skinless chicken breasts, cut into 1-in. cubes
- 2 tsp. olive oil
- 2 medium carrots, chopped
- ⅔ cup chopped onion
- 3 Tbsp. chopped walnuts
- ½ tsp. caraway seeds
- ¼ tsp. ground cumin
- 1½ cups bulgur
- 2 cups reduced-sodium chicken broth
- 2 Tbsp. raisins
- ¼ tsp. salt
- ⅛ tsp. ground cinnamon

1. In a large cast-iron or other heavy skillet, cook chicken in oil over medium-high heat until meat is no longer pink. Remove and keep warm. In the same skillet, cook and stir the carrots, onion, nuts, caraway seeds and cumin until onion starts to brown, 3-4 minutes.

2. Stir in bulgur. Gradually add broth; bring to a boil over medium heat. Reduce heat; add the raisins, salt, cinnamon and chicken. Cover and simmer until bulgur is tender, 12-15 minutes.

1½ cups: 412 cal., 8g fat (1g sat. fat), 66mg chol., 561mg sod., 51g carb. (8g sugars, 12g fiber), 36g pro.

GINGER VEGGIE BROWN RICE PASTA

Once I discovered brown rice pasta, I never looked back. Tossed with ginger, bright veggies and rotisserie chicken, this dish tastes like a deconstructed egg roll!
—Tiffany Ihle, Bronx, NY

Takes: 30 min. • **Makes:** 8 servings

- 2 cups uncooked brown rice elbow pasta
- 1 Tbsp. coconut oil
- ½ small red onion, sliced
- 2 tsp. ginger paste
- 2 tsp. garlic paste
- 1½ cups chopped fresh Brussels sprouts
- ½ cup chopped red cabbage
- ½ cup shredded carrots
- ½ medium sweet red pepper, chopped
- ½ tsp. salt
- ¼ tsp. ground ancho chili pepper
- ¼ tsp. coarsely ground pepper
- 1 shredded rotisserie chicken, skin removed
- 2 green onions, chopped

1. In a Dutch oven, cook pasta according to package directions.
2. Meanwhile, in a large skillet, heat the coconut oil over medium heat. Add red onion, ginger paste and garlic paste; saute 2 minutes. Stir in next 7 ingredients; cook until vegetables are crisp-tender, 4-6 minutes. Add chicken; heat through.
3. Drain pasta, reserving 1 cup pasta water. Return pasta to Dutch oven. Add vegetable mixture; toss to coat, adding enough reserved pasta water to moisten the pasta. Sprinkle with green onions before serving.

1 cup: 270 cal., 7g fat (3g sat. fat), 55mg chol., 257mg sod., 29g carb. (2g sugars, 2g fiber), 21g pro. **Diabetic exchanges:** 3 lean meat, 2 starch, 1 fat.

TEST KITCHEN TIP

If you have fresh garlic and ginger on hand, go ahead and mince 2 tsp. of each and add them to this dish instead of using the 2 tsp. each of ginger and garlic paste.

QUICK GINGER PORK

My husband and I are empty nesters. It was a challenge learning to cook for just two again, but recipes like this give us delicious scaled-down dinners.
—Esther Johnson Danielson, Lawton, PA

Takes: 20 min. • **Makes:** 2 servings

- ½ lb. pork tenderloin, cut into thin strips
- 1 Tbsp. canola oil
- 1 garlic clove, minced
- 2 Tbsp. reduced-sodium soy sauce
- ¼ tsp. sugar
- ⅛ to ¼ tsp. ground ginger
- ½ cup cold water
- 1½ tsp. cornstarch
  Hot cooked rice, optional
  Optional: Thinly sliced green onions and toasted sesame seeds

1. In a large skillet or wok, stir-fry pork in oil until no longer pink. Add garlic; cook 1 minute longer.
2. In a small bowl, combine the soy sauce, sugar and ginger; add to skillet. Combine water and cornstarch until smooth; add to skillet. Bring to a boil; cook and stir until thickened, about 2 minutes. If desired, serve with rice and top with green onions and sesame seeds.

1 serving: 216 cal., 11g fat (2g sat. fat), 64mg chol., 621mg sod., 4g carb. (1g sugars, 0 fiber), 24g pro. **Diabetic exchanges:** 3 lean meat, 1½ fat, ½ starch.
* HEALTH TIP * Cuts of pork with loin in the name are lean—pork tenderloin, pork loin roast and pork loin chops.

GINGER VEGGIE BROWN RICE PASTA

PORK TENDERLOIN WITH THREE-BERRY SALSA

PORK TENDERLOIN WITH THREE-BERRY SALSA

My husband came home from a work meeting that had served pork with a spicy blueberry salsa. He was amazed at how tasty it was, so I came up with my own rendition without seeing or tasting what he had. It took us several tries to perfect it, and this is the delicious result.
—Angie Phillips, Tarzana, CA

Prep: 30 min. + standing • **Cook:** 25 min.
Makes: 6 servings

- 1¼ cups fresh or frozen blackberries (about 6 oz.), thawed and drained
- 1¼ cups fresh or frozen raspberries (about 6 oz.), thawed and drained
- 1 cup fresh or frozen blueberries (about 6 oz.), thawed
- 1 medium sweet red pepper, finely chopped
- 1 jalapeno pepper, seeded and minced
- ½ medium red onion, finely chopped
- ¼ cup lime juice
- 3 Tbsp. minced fresh cilantro
- ¼ tsp. salt

PORK
- 2 pork tenderloins (¾ lb. each), cut into ¾-in. slices
- 1 tsp. salt
- ½ tsp. pepper
- 2 Tbsp. olive oil, divided
- ½ cup white wine or chicken stock
- 2 shallots, thinly sliced
- ½ cup chicken stock

1. Place the first 5 ingredients in a bowl; toss lightly to combine. Reserve 1 cup berry mixture for sauce. For salsa, gently stir onion, lime juice, cilantro and salt into remaining mixture; let stand 30 minutes.
2. Meanwhile, sprinkle pork with salt and pepper. In a large skillet, heat 1 Tbsp. oil over medium-high heat. Add half the pork and cook until a thermometer inserted in pork reads 145°, 2-4 minutes on each side. Remove from pan. Repeat with the remaining pork and oil.
3. Add wine, shallots and reserved berry mixture to the pan, stirring to loosen browned bits. Bring to a boil; cook until liquid is reduced to 1 Tbsp., 4-6 minutes. Stir in stock; cook until shallots are tender, about 5 minutes longer, stirring mixture occasionally. Return pork to pan; heat through. Serve with salsa.

ZIPPY TURKEY ZOODLES

3 oz. cooked pork with ⅔ cup salsa and 3 Tbsp. sauce: 239 cal., 9g fat (2g sat. fat), 64mg chol., 645mg sod., 15g carb. (7g sugars, 5g fiber), 25g pro. **Diabetic exchanges:** 3 lean meat, ½ starch, ½ fruit.

ZIPPY TURKEY ZOODLES

Eating healthy doesn't mean sacrificing flavor—and these spiced-up zoodles prove it. If you don't have a spiralizer, simply slice the zucchini julienne-style.
—Elizabeth Bramkamp, Gig Harbor, WA

Prep: 25 min. • **Cook:** 20 min.
Makes: 4 servings

- 4 tsp. olive oil, divided
- 1 lb. ground turkey
- 1 small onion, finely chopped
- 1 jalapeno pepper, seeded and chopped
- 2 garlic cloves, minced
- ¾ tsp. ground cumin
- ½ tsp. salt
- ¼ tsp. chili powder
- ¼ tsp. crushed red pepper flakes
- ¼ tsp. pepper
- 3 medium zucchini, spiralized
- 4 plum tomatoes, chopped
- 1 cup frozen corn, thawed
- 1 cup black beans, rinsed and drained
  Optional: Chopped fresh cilantro and shredded cheddar cheese

1. In a large nonstick skillet heat 2 tsp. olive oil over medium heat. Add turkey, onion, jalapeno and garlic and cook until turkey is no longer pink and vegetables are tender; breaking up turkey into crumbles, 8-10 minutes; drain. Stir in seasonings; remove and keep warm. Wipe out pan.
2. In the same pan, heat remaining olive oil and cook zucchini over medium heat until crisp-tender, 3-5 minutes. Stir in tomatoes, corn, beans and the reserved turkey mixture; heat through. Serve with cilantro and cheese, if desired.

1¾ cups: 332 cal., 14g fat (3g sat. fat), 75mg chol., 500mg sod., 26g carb. (7g sugars, 6g fiber), 29g pro. **Diabetic exchanges:** 3 medium-fat meat, 2 vegetable, 1 starch, 1 fat.

PORK PAPRIKA

I often scramble to put a meal on the table, but this comes together so quickly it's amazing. My family oohs and aahs the whole time they're eating it.
—Monette Johnson, San Antonio, TX

Takes: 30 min. • **Makes:** 4 servings

- 1 lb. pork tenderloin, cut into cubes
- 1 Tbsp. canola oil
- 1 large onion, chopped
- 1 medium green pepper, chopped
- 2 garlic cloves, minced
- 1 can (14½ oz.) diced tomatoes, undrained
- ½ cup white wine or chicken broth
- 4 tsp. paprika
- 1 tsp. sugar
- 1 tsp. grated lemon zest, optional
- ½ tsp. caraway seeds
- ½ tsp. dried marjoram
- ¼ tsp. salt
- ¼ tsp. pepper
  Hot cooked noodles, optional
- ¼ cup reduced-fat sour cream

In a large nonstick skillet, cook pork in oil until no longer pink; remove and keep warm. Add the onion, green pepper and garlic to pan; cook and stir until crisp-tender. Add the next 9 ingredients; bring to a boil. Reduce the heat; cover and simmer for 10-15 minutes or until slightly thickened. Stir in pork. Serve over noodles if desired. Dollop with sour cream.

1 cup: 258 cal., 9g fat (2g sat. fat), 65mg chol., 372mg sod., 15g carb. (8g sugars, 4g fiber), 26g pro. **Diabetic exchanges:** 3 lean meat, 2 vegetable, 1 fat.

SKILLET PLUM
CHICKEN TENDERS

SKILLET PLUM CHICKEN TENDERS

If you love plums, this recipe is for you! I combine the fruit with chicken tenders for a quick, easy and flavorful meal. Serve with brown rice or orzo pasta.
—Nancy Heishman, Las Vegas, NV

Prep: 20 min. • **Cook:** 15 min.
Makes: 4 servings

- ½ tsp. garlic salt
- ½ tsp. lemon-pepper seasoning
- 1½ lbs. chicken tenderloins
- 1 Tbsp. extra virgin olive oil
- 2 cups sliced fresh plums
- ½ cup diced red onion
- ⅓ cup apple jelly
- 1 Tbsp. grated fresh gingerroot
- 1 Tbsp. balsamic vinegar
- 2 tsp. reduced-sodium soy sauce
- 1 tsp. minced fresh thyme or ½ tsp. dried thyme
- 1 Tbsp. cornstarch
- 2 Tbsp. white wine
- 1 Tbsp. sesame seeds, toasted

1. Combine garlic salt and lemon pepper; sprinkle mixture over chicken. In a large nonstick skillet, heat oil over medium-high heat; brown chicken. Add plums and red onion; cook and stir 1-2 minutes.
2. Reduce heat. Stir in next 5 ingredients. Mix the cornstarch and white wine until smooth; gradually stir into pan. Cook, covered, until chicken juices run clear and the plums are tender, about 10 minutes. Just before serving, sprinkle with toasted sesame seeds.

1 serving: 343 cal., 6g fat (1g sat. fat), 83mg chol., 483mg sod., 33g carb. (26g sugars, 2g fiber), 41g pro.

QUICK MOROCCAN SHRIMP SKILLET

When my niece was attending West Point, she was sent to Morocco for five months. I threw her a going-away party with Moroccan decorations, costumes and cuisine, including this saucy shrimp dish. Whenever I make it now, I think of her and I smile.

—Barbara Lento, Houston, PA

Takes: 25 min. • **Makes:** 4 servings

- 1 Tbsp. canola oil
- 1 small onion, chopped
- ¼ cup pine nuts
- 1 lb. uncooked shrimp (16-20 per lb.), peeled and deveined
- 1 cup uncooked pearl (Israeli) couscous
- 2 Tbsp. lemon juice
- 3 tsp. Moroccan seasoning (ras el hanout)
- 1 tsp. garlic salt
- 2 cups hot water
  Minced fresh parsley, optional

1. In a large skillet, heat oil over medium-high heat; saute onion and pine nuts until onion is tender, 2-3 minutes. Stir in all remaining ingredients except parsley; bring just to a boil. Reduce heat; simmer, covered, 4-6 minutes or until the shrimp turn pink.

2. Remove from heat; let stand 5 minutes. If desired, top with parsley.

Note: This recipe was tested with McCormick Gourmet Moroccan Seasoning (ras el hanout).

1 cup: 335 cal., 11g fat (1g sat. fat), 138mg chol., 626mg sod., 34g carb. (1g sugars, 1g fiber), 24g pro.

* HEALTH TIP * Shrimp are naturally high in cholesterol, but not to worry. The greatest impact on blood cholesterol comes from saturated and trans fats, and shrimp has little saturated and no trans fat.

> **TEST KITCHEN TIP**
>
> Letting the mixture stand before serving helps the pasta absorb more liquid. It's still a saucy dish, so serve it in a shallow bowl.

MONGOLIAN BEEF

My family just loves this meal, including my husband—and he's truly a meat-and-potatoes guy. The dish uses inexpensive ingredients to offer big flavor in a small amount of time.

—Heather Blum, Coleman, WI

Takes: 25 min. • **Makes:** 4 servings

- 1 Tbsp. cornstarch
- ¾ cup reduced-sodium chicken broth
- 2 Tbsp. reduced-sodium soy sauce
- 1 Tbsp. hoisin sauce
- 2 tsp. sesame oil
- 1 lb. beef top sirloin steak, cut into thin strips
- 1 Tbsp. olive oil, divided
- 5 green onions, cut into 1-in. pieces
- 2 cups hot cooked rice

1. In a small bowl, combine cornstarch and broth until smooth. Stir in the soy sauce, hoisin sauce and sesame oil; set aside. In a large nonstick skillet or wok, stir-fry beef in 1½ tsp. hot olive oil until no longer pink. Remove and keep warm.

2. In the same skillet, stir-fry the onions in remaining olive oil 3-4 minutes or until crisp-tender. Stir cornstarch mixture and add to the pan. Bring to a boil; cook and stir until thickened, about 2 minutes. Add beef and heat through. Serve with rice.

1 serving: 328 cal., 11g fat (3g sat. fat), 46mg chol., 529mg sod., 28g carb. (2g sugars, 1g fiber), 28g pro. **Diabetic exchanges:** 3 lean meat, 2 starch, 1 fat.

QUICK MOROCCAN SHRIMP SKILLET

CHICKEN ORZO SKILLET

As a busy homemaker with a home-based business, I try to make quick dinners that are healthy for my husband and two young children. I combined two recipes to come up with this winning dish.
—Kathleen Farrell, Rochester, NY

Takes: 30 min. • **Makes:** 6 servings

- 1 cup uncooked orzo pasta
- 1 lb. boneless skinless chicken breasts, cubed
- 3 tsp. olive oil, divided
- 3 garlic cloves, minced
- 2 cans (14½ oz. each) stewed tomatoes, cut up
- 1 can (15 oz.) cannellini beans, rinsed and drained
- 1½ tsp. Italian seasoning
- ½ tsp. salt
- 1 pkg. (16 oz.) frozen broccoli florets, thawed

1. Cook orzo pasta according to package directions. Meanwhile, in a large nonstick skillet, cook the chicken in 2 tsp. oil for 6-7 minutes or until no longer pink. Remove and keep warm.

2. In the same skillet, cook garlic in remaining oil for 1 minute or until tender. Stir in stewed tomatoes, beans, Italian seasoning and salt. Bring to a boil. Stir in broccoli and chicken; heat through. Drain orzo; stir into chicken mixture.

1½ cups: 342 cal., 5g fat (1g sat. fat), 42mg chol., 589mg sod., 49g carb. (9g sugars, 7g fiber), 25g pro. **Diabetic exchanges:** 3 vegetable, 2 starch, 2 lean meat, ½ fat.

SAUCY MEDITERRANEAN CHICKEN WITH RICE
(PICTURED ON P. 110)

The hints of Mediterranean flavor in this chicken dish make it a family favorite.
—Tabitha Alloway, Edna, KS

Takes: 30 min. • **Makes:** 4 servings

- ¾ cup water
- 3 Tbsp. tomato paste
- 2 Tbsp. lemon juice
- ¾ tsp. salt
- 1 tsp. chili powder
- ½ tsp. garlic powder
- ½ tsp. ground ginger
- ¼ tsp. ground fennel seed
- ¼ tsp. ground turmeric
- 1 tsp. ground coriander, optional
- 3 Tbsp. olive oil
- 1 medium onion, chopped
- 1 lb. boneless skinless chicken breasts, cut into 1-in. cubes
- 3 cups hot cooked rice
  Minced fresh parsley, optional

1. In a small bowl, mix the water, tomato paste, lemon juice, salt, chili powder, garlic powder, ginger, fennel, turmeric and, if desired, coriander until smooth.

2. In a large skillet, heat oil over medium-high heat. Add onions; cook and stir until tender. Stir in chicken; brown 3-4 minutes. Pour water mixture into pan.

3. Bring to a boil. Reduce heat; simmer, uncovered, until chicken is no longer pink, 8-10 minutes. Serve with rice. If desired, top with parsley.

¾ cup chicken mixture with ¾ cup rice: 394 cal., 13g fat (2g sat. fat), 63mg chol., 527mg sod., 40g carb. (3g sugars, 2g fiber), 27g pro. **Diabetic exchanges:** 3 lean meat, 2½ starch, 2 fat.

TEST KITCHEN TIP

Long grain rice triples when cooked and instant rice doubles. So you'll need 1 cup uncooked long grain or 1½ cups uncooked instant to yield about 3 cups hot cooked rice.

WEEKNIGHT CHICKEN CHOP SUEY

If you'd like a little extra crunch with this colorful chop suey, serve it with chow mein noodles.
—George Utley, South Hill, VA

Takes: 30 min. • **Makes:** 6 servings

- 4 tsp. olive oil
- 1 lb. boneless skinless chicken breasts, cut into 1-in. cubes
- ½ tsp. dried tarragon
- ½ tsp. dried basil
- ½ tsp. dried marjoram
- ½ tsp. grated lemon zest
- 1½ cups chopped carrots
- 1 cup unsweetened pineapple tidbits, drained (reserve juice)
- 1 can (8 oz.) sliced water chestnuts, drained
- 1 medium tart apple, chopped
- ½ cup chopped onion
- 1 cup cold water, divided
- 3 Tbsp. unsweetened pineapple juice
- 3 Tbsp. reduced-sodium teriyaki sauce
- 2 Tbsp. cornstarch
- 3 cups hot cooked brown rice

1. In a large cast-iron or other heavy skillet, heat oil over medium heat. Add chicken, herbs and lemon zest; saute until lightly browned. Add next 5 ingredients. Stir in ¾ cup water, pineapple juice and teriyaki sauce; bring to a boil. Reduce the heat; simmer, covered, until the chicken is no longer pink and the carrots are tender, 10-15 minutes.
2. Combine cornstarch and remaining water. Gradually stir into the chicken mixture. Bring to a boil; cook and stir until thickened, about 2 minutes. Serve with brown rice.

1 cup chop suey with ½ cup rice: 330 cal., 6g fat (1g sat. fat), 42mg chol., 227mg sod., 50g carb. (14g sugars, 5g fiber), 20g pro.
Diabetic exchanges: 3 vegetable, 3 lean meat, 1 fruit, 1 fat.

TURKEY SAUSAGE & SPINACH ORECCHIETTE

It was fun to come up with a recipe on my own and have my picky husband love it! Little ear-shaped orecchiette pasta is delicious with spicy turkey sausage.
—Andrea Phillips, Lakeville, MN

Takes: 30 min. • **Makes:** 4 servings

- ½ lb. uncooked orecchiette or small tube pasta
- 3 hot Italian turkey sausage links, casings removed
- ¼ cup chopped onion
- 2 garlic cloves, minced
- ¼ tsp. crushed red pepper flakes
- 3 cups fresh spinach
- ½ cup shredded Asiago cheese
- ¼ cup grated Parmesan cheese
- ¼ cup rinsed and drained cannellini beans
- ¼ cup chopped roasted sweet red pepper
- ½ tsp. Italian seasoning
  Additional shredded Asiago cheese, optional

1. Cook orecchiette according to package directions.
2. In a large skillet, cook and stir the sausage, onion, garlic and pepper flakes over medium heat for 6-8 minutes or until sausage is no longer pink; drain. Add the spinach, Asiago, Parmesan, beans, red pepper and Italian seasoning; cook just until spinach is wilted, stirring occasionally.
3. Drain orecchiette; add to sausage mixture and toss to combine. Sprinkle with additional Asiago cheese if desired.

1¼ cups: 382 cal., 11g fat (4g sat. fat), 47mg chol., 593mg sod., 47g carb. (3g sugars, 3g fiber), 22g pro.

WEEKNIGHT CHICKEN CHOP SUEY

MUSHROOM & BROWN RICE HASH WITH POACHED EGGS

SPICY SALMON PATTIES

Made with canned salmon, these patties are good hot or cold. I usually serve them on buns with slices of ripe tomato, sweet red onion, and red and green bell pepper.
—Barbara Coston, Little Rock, AR

Takes: 30 min. • **Makes:** 4 servings

- 2 slices whole wheat bread
- 12 miniature pretzels
- 2 tsp. Italian seasoning
- 2 tsp. salt-free spicy seasoning blend
- ½ tsp. pepper
- 2 large eggs, lightly beaten
- 1 can (14¾ oz.) salmon, drained, bones and skin removed
- ½ cup finely chopped onion
- ⅓ cup finely chopped green pepper
- 1 Tbsp. finely chopped jalapeno pepper
- 2 garlic cloves, minced
- 2 Tbsp. olive oil

1. Place the first 5 ingredients in a blender or food processor; cover and process until mixture resembles fine crumbs.
2. In a bowl, combine the eggs, salmon, onion, green pepper, jalapeno, garlic and ½ cup crumb mixture. Shape into eight ½-in.-thick patties. Coat with remaining crumb mixture.
3. In a large nonstick skillet over medium heat, cook patties in oil until golden brown, 4-5 minutes on each side.
Note: Wear disposable gloves when cutting hot peppers; the oils can burn skin. Avoid touching your face.
2 patties: 339 cal., 18g fat (3g sat. fat), 176mg chol., 607mg sod., 13g carb. (2g sugars, 2g fiber), 30g pro. **Diabetic exchanges:** 4 lean meat, 2 fat, 1 starch.

MUSHROOM & BROWN RICE HASH WITH POACHED EGGS

I made my mother's famous roast beef hash healthier by using cremini mushrooms instead of beef, and brown rice instead of potatoes. It's ideal for a light main dish.
—Lily Julow, Lawrenceville, GA

Takes: 30 min. • **Makes:** 4 servings

- 2 Tbsp. olive oil
- 1 lb. sliced baby portobello mushrooms
- ½ cup chopped sweet onion
- 1 pkg. (8.8 oz.) ready-to-serve brown rice
- 1 large carrot, grated
- 2 green onions, thinly sliced
- ½ tsp. salt
- ¼ tsp. pepper
- ¼ tsp. caraway seeds
- 4 large eggs

1. In a large skillet, heat oil over medium-high heat; saute mushrooms until lightly browned, 5-7 minutes. Add sweet onion; cook 1 minute. Add rice and carrot; cook and stir until the vegetables are tender, 4-5 minutes. Stir in green onions, salt, pepper and caraway seeds; heat through.
2. Meanwhile, place 2-3 in. of water in a large saucepan or skillet with high sides. Bring to a boil; adjust heat to maintain a gentle simmer. Break cold eggs, one at a time, into a small bowl; holding bowl close to surface of water, slip egg into water.
3. Cook, uncovered, until whites are completely set and yolks begin to thicken but are not hard, 3-5 minutes. Using a slotted spoon, lift eggs out of water. Serve over rice mixture.
1 serving: 282 cal., 13g fat (3g sat. fat), 186mg chol., 393mg sod., 26g carb. (4g sugars, 3g fiber), 13g pro. **Diabetic exchanges:** 1½ starch, 1½ fat, 1 medium-fat meat.
* **HEALTH TIP** * This is a great weeknight dinner or brunch option for anyone following a gluten-free diet.

SPICY SALMON PATTIES

STIR-FRIED SCALLOPS

Scallops add interest to this mild tomato-based supper. Try serving the saucy mixture over rice or angel hair pasta, and garnish with cilantro if you'd like.
—Stephany Gocobachi, San Rafael, CA

Takes: 15 min. • **Makes:** 2 servings

- 1 small onion, chopped
- 3 garlic cloves, minced
- 1 Tbsp. olive oil
- ¾ lb. sea scallops, halved
- 2 medium plum tomatoes, chopped
- 2 Tbsp. lemon juice
- ⅛ tsp. pepper
  Hot cooked pasta or rice, optional

1. In a nonstick skillet or wok, stir-fry onion and garlic in hot oil until tender. Add scallops; stir-fry until scallops turn opaque. Add tomatoes; cook and stir until heated through, 1-2 minutes longer.
2. Stir in lemon juice and pepper. Serve over pasta or rice if desired.

1 cup: 213 cal., 8g fat (1g sat. fat), 41mg chol., 672mg sod., 14g carb. (4g sugars, 2g fiber), 22g pro. **Diabetic exchanges:** 3 lean meat, 2 vegetable, 1½ fat.

LEMON PORK
WITH MUSHROOMS

LEMON PORK WITH MUSHROOMS

This is my family's favorite go-to healthy dish—you wouldn't guess it's good for you. A little squeeze of lemon gives these crispy, seasoned chops a bright boost.
—Christine Datian, Las Vegas, NV

Takes: 30 min. • **Makes:** 4 servings

- 1 large egg, lightly beaten
- 1 cup seasoned bread crumbs
- 8 thin boneless pork loin chops (2 oz. each)
- ¼ tsp. salt
- ⅛ tsp. pepper
- 1 Tbsp. olive oil
- 1 Tbsp. butter
- ½ lb. sliced fresh mushrooms
- 2 garlic cloves, minced
- 2 tsp. grated lemon zest
- 1 Tbsp. lemon juice
  Lemon wedges, optional

1. Place egg and bread crumbs in separate shallow bowls. Sprinkle pork chops with salt and pepper; dip in egg, then coat with crumbs, pressing to adhere.

2. In a large skillet, heat oil over medium heat. In batches, cook pork until golden brown, 2-3 minutes per side. Remove from pan; keep warm.

3. Wipe pan clean. In skillet, heat butter over medium heat; saute mushrooms until tender, 2-3 minutes. Add garlic, lemon zest and juice; cook and stir 1 minute. Serve over pork. If desired, serve with lemon.

1 serving: 331 cal., 15g fat (5g sat. fat), 109mg chol., 601mg sod., 19g carb. (2g sugars, 1g fiber), 28g pro. **Diabetic exchanges:** 3 lean meat, 1½ fat, 1 starch.

> **TEST KITCHEN TIP**
>
> When adding a crumb coating, keep one hand for the wet ingredients (pork chops and eggs) and the other for the dry ingredients (crumb mixture) for less mess. A 1-pound pork tenderloin can be substituted for the pork chops. Cut the tenderloin into 8 slices, then pound to ¼-in. thickness.

QUICK ITALIAN VEGGIE SKILLET

When you don't know what to serve, Italian flavors are always a good starting point. We combine cannellini and garbanzo beans for this snappy rice dish.

—Sonya Labbe, West Hollywood, CA

Takes: 25 min. • **Makes:** 4 servings

- 1 can (15 oz.) no-salt-added garbanzo beans or chickpeas, rinsed and drained
- 1 can (15 oz.) no-salt-added cannellini beans, rinsed and drained
- 1 can (14½ oz.) no-salt-added stewed tomatoes, undrained
- 1 cup vegetable broth
- ¾ cup uncooked instant rice
- 1 tsp. Italian seasoning
- ¼ tsp. crushed red pepper flakes, optional
- 1 cup marinara sauce
- ¼ cup grated Parmesan cheese
  Minced fresh basil

In a skillet, combine first 6 ingredients and, if desired, pepper flakes; bring to a boil. Reduce heat; simmer, covered, until rice is tender, 7-9 minutes. Stir in marinara sauce; heat through, stirring occasionally. Top with cheese and basil.

1⅓ cups: 342 cal., 4g fat (1g sat. fat), 6mg chol., 660mg sod., 59g carb. (10g sugars, 11g fiber), 16g pro.

SUNSHINE CHICKEN
(PICTURED ON P. 110)

Since it is easily doubled and takes little time or effort to prepare, this recipe is great to serve for large groups. Even my husband, who usually doesn't enjoy cooking, likes to make this dish.

—Karen Gardiner, Eutaw, AL

Prep: 15 min. • **Cook:** 20 min.
Makes: 6 servings

- 2 to 3 tsp. curry powder
- 1¼ tsp. salt, divided
- ¼ tsp. pepper
- 6 boneless skinless chicken breast halves (5 oz. each)
- 1½ cups orange juice
- 1 cup uncooked long grain rice
- ¾ cup water
- 1 Tbsp. brown sugar
- 1 tsp. ground mustard
  Chopped fresh parsley

1. Combine curry powder, ½ tsp. salt and the pepper; rub over chicken. In a skillet, combine orange juice, rice, water, brown sugar, mustard and remaining salt. Add chicken pieces; bring to a boil. Reduce heat; cover and simmer until chicken juices run clear, 20-25 minutes.

2. Remove from the heat and let stand, covered, until all liquid has absorbed, about 5 minutes. Sprinkle with parsley.

1 serving: 317 cal., 4g fat (1g sat. fat), 78mg chol., 562mg sod., 36g carb. (8g sugars, 1g fiber), 32g pro. **Diabetic exchanges:** 4 lean meat, 2 starch.

QUICK ITALIAN VEGGIE SKILLET

CACCIATORE CHICKEN BREASTS

CACCIATORE CHICKEN BREASTS

This simple and fast recipe is my version of traditional chicken cacciatore. The tasty sauce and chicken can be served over rice or noodles. If you want to lower the sodium, use garlic powder instead of garlic salt.

—JoAnn McCauley, Dubuque, IA

Takes: 30 min. • **Makes:** 2 servings

- ½ medium onion, sliced and separated into rings
- ½ medium green pepper, sliced
- 1 Tbsp. olive oil
- 2 boneless skinless chicken breast halves (5 oz. each)
- ¾ cup canned stewed tomatoes
- 2 Tbsp. white wine or chicken broth
- ¼ tsp. garlic salt
- ¼ tsp. dried rosemary, crushed
- ⅛ tsp. pepper

1. In a large skillet, saute onion and green pepper in oil until crisp-tender. Remove and keep warm. Cook the chicken over medium-high heat until juices run clear, 4-5 minutes on each side. Remove and set aside.

2. Add the tomatoes, wine, garlic salt, rosemary and pepper to the skillet. Stir in onion mixture and heat through. Serve with chicken.

1 chicken breast half with ¾ cup sauce: 272 cal., 10g fat (2g sat. fat), 78mg chol., 462mg sod., 12g carb. (7g sugars, 2g fiber), 30g pro. **Diabetic exchanges:** 4 lean meat, 2 vegetable, 1½ fat.

PORK TENDERLOIN DIANE

We have pork at least once a week, and this is one dish we especially enjoy. The moist, tender pork medallions are served up in a savory sauce for a combination that's irresistible. This recipe is also nice for busy days because it's quick and easy to prepare.

—Janie Thorpe, Tullahoma, TN

Takes: 20 min. • **Makes:** 4 servings

- 1 pork tenderloin (about 1 lb.)
- 1 Tbsp. lemon-pepper seasoning
- 2 Tbsp. butter
- 2 Tbsp. lemon juice
- 1 tsp. Worcestershire sauce
- 1 tsp. Dijon mustard
- 1 Tbsp. minced fresh parsley

1. Cut tenderloin into 8 pieces; place each piece between 2 pieces of plastic wrap or waxed paper and flatten to ½-in. thickness. Sprinkle with lemon pepper.

2. Melt the butter in a large skillet over medium heat; cook pork for 3-4 minutes on each side or until no longer pink and juices run clear. Remove to a serving platter and keep warm.

3. To the pan juices, add lemon juice, Worcestershire sauce and mustard; heat through, stirring occasionally. Pour over the pork and sprinkle with parsley.

1 serving: 214 cal., 14g fat (0 sat. fat), 6mg chol., 491mg sod., 1g carb. (0 sugars, 0 fiber), 18g pro. **Diabetic exchanges:** 3 meat.

QUICK PEPPER STEAK

When I need a speedy skillet supper, this pepper steak comes to my rescue. The tender meat is slightly sweet, with a hint of brown sugar and molasses.
—Monica Williams, Burleson, TX

Takes: 25 min. • **Makes:** 6 servings

- 2 Tbsp. cornstarch
- 2 Tbsp. brown sugar
- 2 Tbsp. minced fresh gingerroot
- ¾ tsp. garlic powder
- 1 can (14½ oz.) beef broth
- 3 Tbsp. reduced-sodium soy sauce
- 1 Tbsp. molasses
- 1½ lbs. beef top sirloin steak, cut into ¼-in. strips
- 1 Tbsp. canola oil
- 2 large green peppers, cut into ½-in. strips
- 1½ cups sliced celery
- 3 green onions, chopped
- 4 tsp. lemon juice
  Hot cooked noodles, optional

1. In a bowl, combine the cornstarch, brown sugar, ginger and garlic powder. Stir in broth until smooth. Add soy sauce and molasses; set aside.
2. In a nonstick skillet or wok, stir-fry steak in oil for 4-5 minutes; remove and keep warm. Stir-fry peppers, celery and onions until crisp-tender, about 5 minutes. Stir broth mixture and add to the vegetables. Return meat to the pan. Bring to a boil; cook and stir until thickened, about 2 minutes. Stir in lemon juice. Serve over noodles if desired.

¾ cup: 233 cal., 7g fat (2g sat. fat), 46mg chol., 672mg sod., 14g carb. (9g sugars, 2g fiber), 26g pro. **Diabetic exchanges:** 3 lean meat, 1 vegetable, ½ starch, ½ fat.

CHICKEN PARMESAN WITH SPAGHETTI SQUASH

I grow spaghetti squash and herbs in my garden every year, so this recipe is the perfect way to use them up.
—Kristina Krummel, Elkins, AR

Takes: 30 min. • **Makes:** 4 servings

- 1 medium spaghetti squash
- 4 boneless skinless chicken breast halves (6 oz. each)
- 2 Tbsp. minced fresh parsley, plus more for topping
- 1 Tbsp. minced fresh oregano or ¾ tsp. dried oregano
- 1 Tbsp. minced fresh basil or ¾ tsp. dried basil
- 2 Tbsp. olive oil
- 1 jar (14 oz.) pasta sauce
- ½ cup shredded mozzarella cheese
- ¼ cup grated Parmesan cheese

1. Halve squash lengthwise; discard seeds. Place squash on a microwave-safe plate, cut side down; microwave on high until tender, about 15 minutes. Cool slightly.
2. Meanwhile, sprinkle the chicken with parsley, oregano and basil. In a large skillet, heat oil over medium heat. Add chicken; cook 7-9 minutes on each side or until a thermometer reads 165°. Stir in pasta sauce; sprinkle with cheeses. Cover and cook until cheese is melted, 3-5 minutes.
3. Separate strands of squash with a fork. Serve with chicken and sauce. If desired, top with chopped parsley.

1 chicken breast half with ¾ cup squash and ½ cup sauce: 501 cal., 19g fat (5g sat. fat), 109mg chol., 704mg sod., 43g carb. (8g sugars, 9g fiber), 43g pro.

* HEALTH TIP * Cup-for-cup, spaghetti squash is lower in carbs than white pasta, but it's also higher in fiber and vitamin C.

> **TEST KITCHEN TIP**
>
> Change up this recipe by using Alfredo sauce instead of a tomato-based sauce.

QUICK PEPPER STEAK

EASY CHANA MASALA

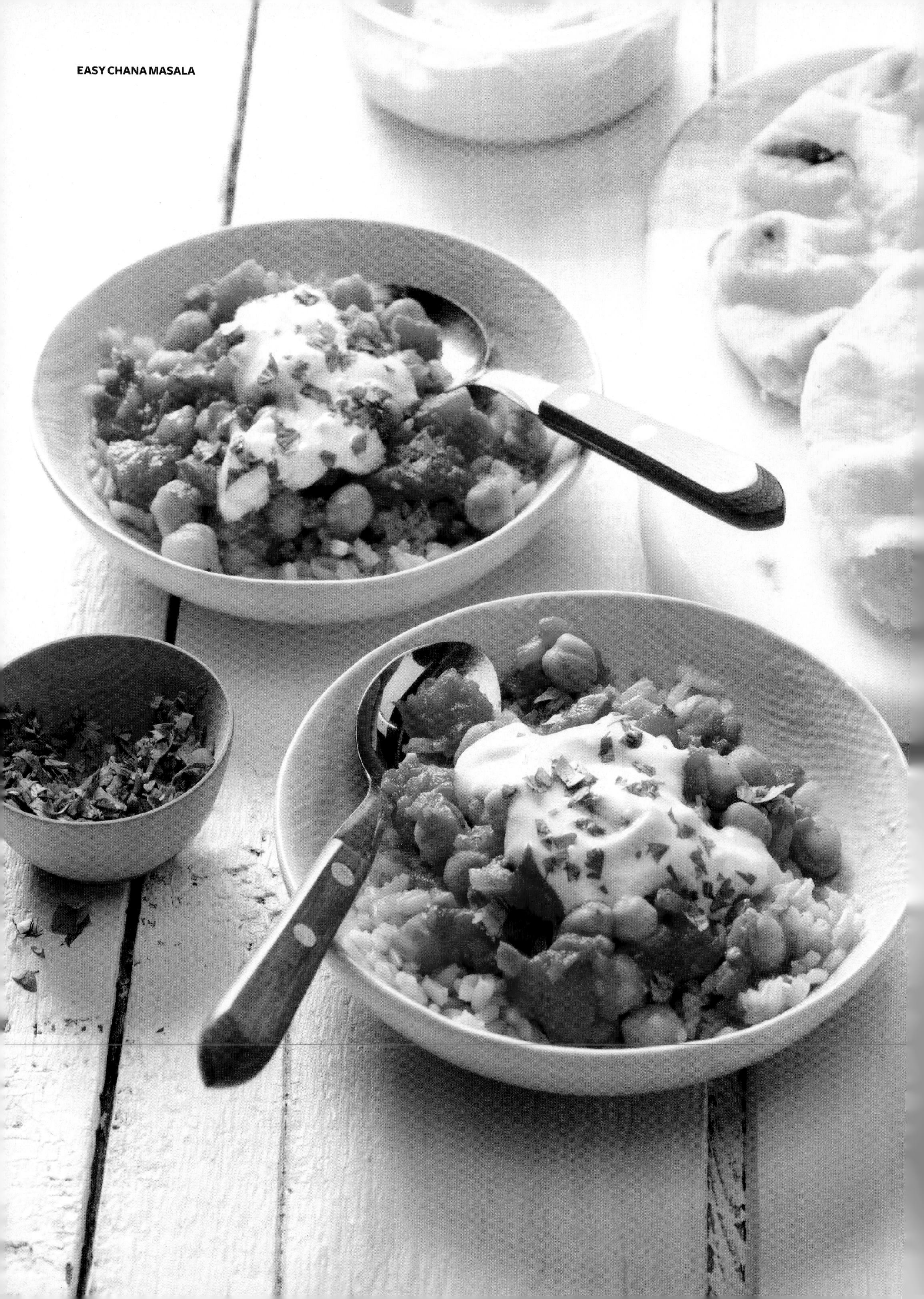

EASY CHANA MASALA

I love this quick and healthy Indian dish so much, I always make sure to have the ingredients stocked in my pantry. It makes weeknight dinners feel a little more special.
—Janeen Judah, Houston, TX

Takes: 30 min. • **Makes:** 4 servings

- 1   Tbsp. canola oil
- ½   cup finely chopped onion
- 1   Tbsp. minced fresh gingerroot
- 2   garlic cloves, minced
- 1   jalapeno pepper, seeded and finely chopped, optional
- ½   tsp. salt
- 1   tsp. garam masala
- ½   tsp. ground coriander
- ½   tsp. ground cumin
- 1   can (15 oz.) diced tomatoes, undrained
- 1   can (15 oz.) garbanzo beans or chickpeas, rinsed and drained
- 3   cups hot cooked brown rice
- ¼   cup plain yogurt
      Minced fresh cilantro

1. In a large skillet, heat oil over medium heat. Add the onion, ginger, garlic and, if desired, jalapeno; cook and stir until the onion is softened and lightly browned, 4-5 minutes. Add salt and spices; cook and stir 1 minute.

2. Stir in tomatoes and garbanzo beans; bring to a boil. Reduce the heat; simmer, covered, 12-15 minutes or until flavors are blended, stirring occasionally. Serve with rice. Top with yogurt and cilantro.

Freeze option: Freeze cooled garbanzo bean mixture in freezer containers. To use, partially thaw in the refrigerator overnight. Heat through in a saucepan, stirring occasionally and adding a little water if necessary.

¾ cup chickpea mixture with ¾ cup rice: 359 cal., 8g fat (1g sat. fat), 2mg chol., 616mg sod., 64g carb. (8g sugars, 9g fiber), 10g pro.

> **TEST KITCHEN TIP**
>
> This is a quick version of a popular Indian and Pakistani dish. Chana refers to the chickpeas.

HERB-GLAZED TURKEY SLICES

HERB-GLAZED TURKEY SLICES

In the mood for turkey, but don't want to prepare a whole bird? Here's the perfect solution! These savory slices with an easy-to-prepare herb glaze offer the goodness of turkey without the hassle.
—*Taste of Home* Test Kitchen

Takes: 20 min. • **Makes:** 4 servings

- 1   pkg. (17.6 oz.) turkey breast cutlets
- 1   Tbsp. canola oil
- ½   cup chicken broth
- ½   cup apple juice
- 1   Tbsp. honey
- 1   Tbsp. Dijon mustard
- ½   tsp. salt
- ¼   tsp. each dried basil, dried rosemary, crushed and garlic powder
- 1   Tbsp. cornstarch
- 1   Tbsp. water

1. In a large skillet, brown turkey slices on each side in oil. In a small bowl, combine the broth, apple juice, honey, mustard, salt, basil, rosemary and garlic powder; pour over turkey. Bring to a boil. Reduce heat; cover and simmer for 8 minutes or until the turkey is no longer pink.

2. Combine cornstarch and water until smooth; stir into skillet. Bring to a boil; cook and stir for 2 minutes or until thickened.

4 oz. cooked turkey: 213 cal., 4g fat (1g sat. fat), 78mg chol., 570mg sod., 11g carb. (8g sugars, 0 fiber), 31g pro. **Diabetic exchanges:** 4 lean meat, 1 fat, ½ starch.

OVEN
ENTREES

"When my aunt first told me about these shells, they sounded like a lot of work—but the recipe whips up in no time. Sometimes I add a little cooked bacon to the ricotta filling."
—Amelia Hopkin, Salt Lake City, UT

BLACK BEAN TORTILLA PIE

BLACK BEAN TORTILLA PIE

I found this southwestern entree a while ago but decreased the cheese and increased the herbs originally called for. It's one of my toddler's favorite meals. She always smiles when she sees it on the table.
—Wendy Kelly, Petersburg, NY

Prep: 50 min. • **Bake:** 15 min.
Makes: 6 servings

- 1 Tbsp. olive oil
- 1 medium green pepper, chopped
- 1 medium onion, chopped
- 1 tsp. ground cumin
- ¼ tsp. pepper
- 3 garlic cloves, minced
- 2 cans (15 oz. each) black beans, rinsed and drained
- 1 can (14½ oz.) vegetable broth
- 1 pkg. (10 oz.) frozen corn, thawed
- 4 green onions, sliced
- 4 flour tortillas (8 in.)
- 1 cup shredded reduced-fat cheddar cheese, divided

1. Preheat oven to 400°. In a large skillet, heat oil over medium-high heat. Add green pepper, onion, cumin and pepper; cook and stir until vegetables are tender. Add garlic; cook 1 minute longer.

2. Stir in beans and broth. Bring to a boil; cook until liquid is reduced to about ⅓ cup, stirring occasionally. Stir in corn and green onions; remove from heat.

3. Place 1 tortilla in a 9-in. springform pan coated with cooking spray. Layer with 1½ cups bean mixture and ¼ cup cheese. Repeat layers twice. Top with remaining tortilla. Place pan on a baking sheet.

4. Bake, uncovered, until heated through, 15-20 minutes. Sprinkle with remaining cheese. Loosen sides from pan with a knife; remove rim from the pan. Cut into 6 wedges.

1 slice: 353 cal., 9g fat (3g sat. fat), 14mg chol., 842mg sod., 53g carb. (6g sugars, 8g fiber), 17g pro.

STUFFED VEGETARIAN SHELLS
(PICTURED ON P. 147)

When my aunt first told me about these shells, they sounded like a lot of work— but the recipe whips up in no time. Sometimes I add a little cooked bacon to the ricotta filling.
—Amelia Hopkin, Salt Lake City, UT

Prep: 20 min. • **Bake:** 30 min.
Makes: 8 servings

- 24 uncooked jumbo pasta shells
- 1 carton (15 oz.) part-skim ricotta cheese
- 3 cups frozen chopped broccoli, thawed and drained
- 1 cup shredded part-skim mozzarella cheese
- 2 large egg whites
- 1 Tbsp. minced fresh basil or 1 tsp. dried basil
- ½ tsp. garlic salt
- ¼ tsp. pepper
- 1 jar (26 oz.) meatless spaghetti sauce
- 2 Tbsp. shredded Parmesan cheese

1. Cook pasta according to package directions. In a large bowl, combine the ricotta, broccoli, mozzarella, egg whites and seasonings. Drain pasta and rinse in cold water.

2. Spread half the spaghetti sauce into a 13x9-in. baking dish coated with cooking spray. Stuff pasta shells with the ricotta mixture; arrange over spaghetti sauce. Pour remaining sauce over pasta shells.

3. Cover and bake at 375° for 25 minutes. Uncover and sprinkle with the Parmesan cheese. Bake until heated through, about 5 minutes longer.

3 stuffed shells: 279 cal., 8g fat (5g sat. fat), 26mg chol., 725mg sod., 36g carb. (8g sugars, 4g fiber), 18g pro. **Diabetic exchanges:** 2½ starch, 2 lean meat.

HEARTY BAKED BEEF STEW

This is such an easy way to make a wonderful beef stew. You don't need to brown the meat first—just combine it with hearty chunks of carrots, potatoes and celery, then let it all cook together in a flavorful gravy. My daughter Karen came up with the recipe for her busy family.
—Doris Sleeth, Naples, FL

Prep: 15 min. • **Bake:** 1¾ hours
Makes: 8 servings

- 1 can (14½ oz.) diced tomatoes, undrained
- 1 cup water
- 3 Tbsp. quick-cooking tapioca
- 2 tsp. sugar
- 1½ tsp. salt
- ½ tsp. pepper
- 2 lbs. beef stew meat, cut into 1-in. cubes
- 4 medium carrots, cut into 1-in. chunks
- 3 medium potatoes, peeled and quartered
- 2 celery ribs, cut into ¾-in. chunks
- 1 medium onion, cut into chunks
- 1 slice bread, cubed

1. In a large bowl, combine the tomatoes, water, tapioca, sugar, salt and pepper. Stir in the remaining ingredients.

2. Pour into a greased 13x9-in. or 3-qt. baking dish. Cover and bake at 375° for 1¾-2 hours or until meat and vegetables are tender. Serve in bowls.

1 cup: 300 cal., 8g fat (3g sat. fat), 70mg chol., 628mg sod., 31g carb. (7g sugars, 4g fiber), 25g pro. **Diabetic exchanges:** 3 lean meat, 2 starch.

* HEALTH TIP * Beef that's sold for stew is typically from lean, tougher cuts, like round or chuck, that become tender and flavorful when braised.

WALNUT & OAT-CRUSTED SALMON

I think this recipe gives you the most Omega-3 fatty acid bang for your buck!
—Cristen Dutcher, Marietta, GA

Takes: 30 min. • **Makes:** 2 servings

- 2 salmon fillets (6 oz. each), skin removed
- ¼ tsp. salt
- ¼ tsp. pepper
- 3 Tbsp. quick-cooking oats, crushed
- 3 Tbsp. finely chopped walnuts
- 2 Tbsp. olive oil

Preheat oven to 400°. Place salmon on a baking sheet; sprinkle with salt and pepper. Combine the remaining ingredients; press onto salmon. Bake until fish just begins to flake easily with a fork, 12-15 minutes.

1 fillet: 484 cal., 37g fat (6g sat. fat), 85mg chol., 381mg sod., 7g carb. (0 sugars, 2g fiber), 32g pro. **Diabetic exchanges:** 5 lean meat, 3 fat, ½ starch.

> **TEST KITCHEN TIP**
>
> When you're shopping, buy wild-caught salmon if it's available. It has a significantly higher vitamin D content than farm-raised salmon.

HEARTY BAKED BEEF STEW

TUNA NOODLE CASSEROLE

Your family is sure to love the creamy texture and comforting taste of this traditional tuna casserole that goes together in a jiffy. A buttery topping adds a nice touch. I serve it with a green salad and warm rolls for a nutritious supper.
—Ruby Wells, Cynthiana, KY

Prep: 20 min. • **Bake:** 30 min.
Makes: 4 servings

- 1 can (10¾ oz.) reduced-fat reduced-sodium condensed cream of celery soup, undiluted
- ½ cup fat-free milk
- 2 cups yolk-free noodles, cooked
- 1 cup frozen peas, thawed
- 1 can (5 oz.) light water-packed tuna, drained and flaked
- 1 jar (2 oz.) diced pimientos, drained
- 2 Tbsp. dry bread crumbs
- 1 Tbsp. butter, melted

1. In a large bowl, combine soup and milk until smooth. Add the noodles, peas, tuna and pimientos; mix well.
2. Pour into a 1½-qt. baking dish coated with cooking spray. Bake, uncovered, at 400° for 25 minutes. Toss bread crumbs and butter; sprinkle over the top. Bake 5 minutes longer or until golden brown.
1 cup: 238 cal., 5g fat (2g sat. fat), 27mg chol., 475mg sod., 32g carb. (6g sugars, 4g fiber), 15g pro. **Diabetic exchanges:** 2 starch, 2 lean meat, ½ fat.

CORNMEAL OVEN-FRIED CHICKEN

CORNMEAL OVEN-FRIED CHICKEN

A crunchy coating of cornmeal and Parmesan really perks up fried chicken. It's a crisp, tasty, mess-free variation on regular fried chicken.
—Deborah Williams, Peoria, AZ

Prep: 20 min. • **Bake:** 40 min.
Makes: 6 servings

- ½ cup dry bread crumbs
- ½ cup cornmeal
- ⅓ cup grated Parmesan cheese
- ¼ cup minced fresh parsley or 4 tsp. dried parsley flakes
- ¾ tsp. garlic powder
- ½ tsp. salt
- ½ tsp. onion powder
- ½ tsp. dried thyme
- ½ tsp. pepper
- ½ cup buttermilk
- 1 broiler/fryer chicken (3 to 4 lbs.), cut up and skin removed
- 1 Tbsp. butter, melted

1. In a large shallow dish, combine the first 9 ingredients. Place the buttermilk in a shallow bowl. Dip chicken in buttermilk, then dip in bread crumb mixture, a few pieces at a time, and turn to coat.
2. Place in a 13x9-in. baking pan coated with cooking spray. Bake at 375° for 10 minutes; drizzle with butter. Bake until juices run clear, 30-40 minutes longer.
3 oz. cooked chicken: 244 cal., 9g fat (3g sat. fat), 82mg chol., 303mg sod., 11g carb. (1g sugars, 1g fiber), 27g pro. **Diabetic exchanges:** 3 lean meat, 1 starch, ½ fat.

TEST KITCHEN TIP

No buttermilk? Simply place 1½ tsp. white vinegar or lemon juice in a measuring cup and add enough milk to measure ½ cup. Stir, then let stand for 5 minutes.

COMPANY STUFFED PORK CHOPS

These pork chops bake to a perfect golden brown, and the stuffing is incredibly moist. It's one of my favorite dishes to serve to guests because I know they'll love it.

—Lorraine Darocha, Mountain City, TN

Prep: 40 min. • **Bake:** 30 min.
Makes: 6 servings

- 2 celery ribs, diced
- 1 small onion, chopped
- 1 tsp. olive oil
- 9 slices white bread, cubed
- ¼ cup minced fresh parsley
- ¼ tsp. salt
- ¼ tsp. rubbed sage
- ⅛ tsp. white pepper
- ⅛ tsp. dried marjoram
- ⅛ tsp. dried thyme
- ¾ cup reduced-sodium chicken broth

PORK CHOPS
- 6 pork rib chops (7 oz. each)
- 2 tsp. olive oil
- ¼ tsp. salt
- ¼ tsp. pepper

1. In a large skillet coated with cooking spray, saute celery and onion in 1 tsp. oil until tender; remove from the heat. In a large bowl, combine cubed bread and the seasonings. Add celery mixture and broth; toss to coat. Set aside.

2. Cut a pocket in each pork chop by making a horizontal slice almost to the bone. Recoat the same skillet with cooking spray. Cook chops in remaining 2 tsp. oil in batches over medium-high heat until browned, 1-2 minutes on each side. Fill chops with bread mixture; secure with toothpicks if necessary.

3. Transfer to a 13x9-in. baking dish coated with cooking spray. Sprinkle with salt and pepper. Cover and bake at 350° for 15 minutes. Uncover; bake until a thermometer inserted in center of stuffing reads 165° and thermometer inserted in pork reads at least 145°, 15-20 minutes longer. Discard toothpicks. Let pork stand for 5 minutes before serving.

1 serving: 314 cal., 12g fat (4g sat. fat), 64mg chol., 526mg sod., 20g carb. (3g sugars, 1g fiber), 29g pro. **Diabetic exchanges:** 4 lean meat, 1 starch.

GARLIC-HERB ROASTED CHICKEN

Since the garlic and herbs make this roasted chicken so flavorful, you can eliminate the salt from the recipe if you like.

—Cindy Steffen, Cedarburg, WI

Prep: 10 min. • **Bake:** 1½ hours + standing
Makes: 8 servings

- 1 roasting chicken (4 to 5 lbs.)
- 2 tsp. each minced fresh parsley, rosemary, sage and thyme
- ¾ tsp. salt
- ¼ tsp. pepper
- 20 garlic cloves, peeled and sliced
- 1 medium lemon, halved
- 1 large whole garlic bulb
- 1 sprig each fresh parsley, rosemary, sage and thyme

1. With fingers, carefully loosen skin around the chicken breast, leg and thigh. Combine minced parsley, rosemary, sage, thyme, salt and pepper; rub half under skin. Place sliced garlic cloves under skin. Squeeze half of the lemon into the cavity and place the squeezed half in the cavity.

2. Remove papery outer skin from whole garlic bulb (do not peel or separate cloves). Cut top off garlic bulb. Place garlic bulb and herb sprigs in the cavity. Skewer chicken openings; tie drumsticks together with kitchen string.

3. Place chicken breast side up on a rack in a roasting pan. Squeeze the remaining lemon half over chicken; rub remaining herb mixture over chicken.

4. Bake, uncovered, at 350° until a thermometer inserted in thickest part of a thigh reads 170°-175°, 1½-1¾ hours (cover loosely with foil if chicken browns too quickly). If desired, baste with the pan drippings.

5. Cover and let stand for 15 minutes. Remove and discard garlic, lemon and herbs from cavity before carving.

5 oz. cooked chicken: 163 cal., 6g fat (2g sat. fat), 67mg chol., 289mg sod., 3g carb. (0 sugars, 0 fiber), 23g pro. **Diabetic exchanges:** 3 lean meat.

COMPANY STUFFED PORK CHOPS

MINI TURKEY MEAT LOAVES

MINI TURKEY MEAT LOAVES

These turkey loaves are tender, hearty and loaded with flavor. I love this quick, easy dish!

—Janice Christofferson, Eagle River, WI

Prep: 25 min. • **Bake:** 25 min.
Makes: 6 servings

- 1 large egg, lightly beaten
- 1 large onion, finely chopped
- 1 small sweet red pepper, finely chopped
- ¾ cup shredded part-skim mozzarella cheese, divided
- ½ cup plus 6 Tbsp. spaghetti sauce, divided
- 3 Tbsp. grated Parmesan cheese, divided
- 3 Tbsp. quick-cooking oats
- 1 tsp. Italian seasoning
- ¼ tsp. salt
- ¼ tsp. pepper
- 1 lb. lean ground turkey

1. In a large bowl, combine the egg, onion, red pepper, ½ cup mozzarella cheese, ½ cup spaghetti sauce, 2 Tbsp. Parmesan cheese, oats and seasonings. Crumble turkey over mixture and mix well.
2. Coat 6 jumbo muffin cups with cooking spray; fill with turkey mixture. Bake at 350° for 20 minutes; drain.
3. Top each loaf with 1 Tbsp. spaghetti sauce, 2 tsp. mozzarella cheese and ½ tsp. Parmesan cheese. Bake 5-10 minutes longer or until a thermometer reads 165° and cheese is melted. Let stand for 5 minutes before removing from pan.
1 serving: 210 cal., 10g fat (4g sat. fat), 105mg chol., 447mg sod., 9g carb. (5g sugars, 2g fiber), 20g pro. **Diabetic exchanges:** 3 lean meat, ½ starch.

BUTTERNUT SQUASH MAC & CHEESE

BUTTERNUT SQUASH MAC & CHEESE

I created this dish after my father had triple bypass surgery. He loves comfort food, and I wanted him to be able to enjoy a rich and tasty dish like mac & cheese without all the fat and butter. It's also a smart way to sneak in some veggies for children.

—Megan Schwartz, New York, NY

Prep: 35 min. • **Bake:** 15 min.
Makes: 6 servings

- 8 oz. uncooked whole wheat elbow macaroni
- 1 medium butternut squash (about 3 lbs.), seeded and cubed
- ¼ cup plain Greek yogurt
- 1 cup fat-free milk
- 1 tsp. salt
- ¼ tsp. pepper
  Dash ground nutmeg
- 1½ cups (6 oz.) shredded sharp cheddar cheese
- ½ cup shredded Parmesan cheese
- ½ cup soft whole wheat bread crumbs

1. Preheat oven to 400°. Cook pasta according to package directions for al dente. Place squash in a large saucepan; add water to cover. Bring to a boil. Cook, covered, 8-10 minutes or until tender.
2. Meanwhile, place yogurt, milk, salt, pepper and nutmeg in a blender. Drain squash and transfer to blender; cover and process until pureed. Return mixture to saucepan; heat through. Stir in cheeses until melted.
3. Drain pasta; add to squash mixture. Toss to coat. Transfer to a greased 8-in. square baking dish. Sprinkle with the bread crumbs.
4. Bake, uncovered, until golden brown, 15-20 minutes.
1¼ cups: 422 cal., 13g fat (7g sat. fat), 36mg chol., 750mg sod., 60g carb. (10g sugars, 12g fiber), 20g pro.

BEEFY TOMATOES

My husband loves to garden, and I often fix this entree at the end of summer using the harvest from our backyard. The hollowed-out tomatoes are filled with a delicious beef and rice mixture.
—Liz Gallagher, Gilbertsville, PA

Prep: 20 min. • **Bake:** 20 min.
Makes: 6 servings

- 6 medium tomatoes
- 1 lb. lean ground beef (90% lean)
- 1 medium onion, chopped
- 2 tsp. dried basil
- 1 tsp. salt
- ¼ tsp. pepper
- ½ cup cooked rice
- ½ cup shredded reduced-fat cheddar cheese
- 1 large egg, lightly beaten

1. Cut a thin slice off the top of each tomato and discard; remove core. Carefully scoop out pulp, leaving a ½-in. shell. Reserve 1 cup pulp (discard remaining pulp or save for another use). Invert tomatoes onto paper towels to drain.
2. In a nonstick skillet, cook beef and onion over medium heat until meat is no longer pink; drain. Stir in the basil, salt, pepper and reserved tomato pulp; bring to a boil. Reduce the heat; simmer, uncovered, for 10-12 minutes or until the liquid has evaporated. Stir in the rice, cheese and egg; heat through. Spoon into tomato shells.
3. Place in a shallow 2-qt. baking dish coated with cooking spray. Bake, uncovered, at 350° for 20-25 minutes or until heated through.

1 stuffed tomato: 208 cal., 9g fat (4g sat. fat), 85mg chol., 516mg sod., 11g carb. (4g sugars, 2g fiber), 20g pro. **Diabetic exchanges:** 3 lean meat, 1 vegetable, ½ fat.

APRICOT CRAB STUFFED ACORN SQUASH

APRICOT CRAB STUFFED ACORN SQUASH

This light squash recipe is quick, simple and bursting with rich flavors. It looks so elegant when served on a lovely platter.
—Judy Armstrong, Prairieville, LA

Prep: 20 min. • **Bake:** 35 min.
Makes: 8 servings

- 2 large acorn squash, quartered and seeds removed
- ½ cup apricot nectar, divided
- 1 tsp. salt, divided
- 1 tsp. white pepper, divided
- 1 tsp. butter
- 1 tsp. olive oil
- 4 green onions, thinly sliced, plus additional for garnish
- ⅓ cup dried apricots, chopped
- 1 garlic clove, minced
- ½ cup half-and-half cream
- 4 cans (6 oz. each) lump crabmeat, drained

1. Preheat oven to 375°. Place squash in a greased 13x9-in. baking pan; add ¼ cup apricot nectar. Sprinkle with ½ tsp. each salt and white pepper. Bake, covered, until fork-tender, 35-40 minutes.
2. Meanwhile, in a large skillet, heat butter and oil over medium-high heat. Add green onions; cook and stir 3-5 minutes or until tender. Add apricots and garlic; cook for 1 minute longer. Stir in half-and-half and the remaining apricot nectar, salt and white pepper. Bring to a boil; reduce heat. Simmer for 5 minutes. Gently stir in crab; heat through.
3. Arrange squash on a serving dish; spoon crab mixture over top. Sprinkle with additional green onions.

1 serving: 217 cal., 3g fat (2g sat. fat), 91mg chol., 794mg sod., 31g carb. (11g sugars, 4g fiber), 18g pro. **Diabetic exchanges:** 2 starch, 2 lean meat, ½ fat.

HONEY-ORANGE GLAZED PORK LOIN

After finding this idea in a magazine, I changed it up to make it my own. I like to keep a pork loin in the freezer so we can have this special dish anytime.
—Marlys Peterson, Centerville, SD

Prep: 10 min. • **Bake:** 1¼ hours + standing
Makes: 12 servings

- 1 cup orange juice
- ½ cup cider vinegar
- ½ cup packed brown sugar
- ¼ cup honey
- 2 Tbsp. chili powder
- 1 Tbsp. ground coriander
- 1 Tbsp. ground cumin
- 1½ tsp. ground cinnamon
- 1 boneless pork loin roast (4 lbs.)
- 1 tsp. salt
- ¼ tsp. pepper

1. In a small saucepan, combine the first 8 ingredients. Bring to a boil. Reduce heat; simmer, uncovered, for 45 minutes or until glaze is reduced to 1 cup.
2. Meanwhile, sprinkle pork with salt and pepper. Place on a rack in a shallow roasting pan lined with heavy-duty foil. Roast at 350° for 1¼-1¾ hours or until a thermometer reads 145°, brushing with glaze 2-3 times after first hour of roasting. Let stand for 10-15 minutes before slicing.

4 oz. cooked pork: 263 cal., 7g fat (3g sat. fat), 75mg chol., 258mg sod., 19g carb. (17g sugars, 1g fiber), 30g pro. **Diabetic exchanges:** 4 lean meat, 1 starch.

CRUMB-TOPPED SOLE

Looking for a low-carb supper that's ready in a pinch? This buttery sole is topped with a rich sauce and covered with toasty bread crumbs.
—*Taste of Home* Test Kitchen

Takes: 15 min. • **Makes:** 4 servings

- 3 Tbsp. reduced-fat mayonnaise
- 3 Tbsp. grated Parmesan cheese, divided
- 2 tsp. mustard seed
- ¼ tsp. pepper
- 4 sole fillets (6 oz. each)
- 1 cup soft bread crumbs
- 1 green onion, finely chopped
- ½ tsp. ground mustard
- 2 tsp. butter, melted
  Thinly sliced green onions, optional

1. Combine the mayonnaise, 2 Tbsp. cheese, mustard seed and pepper; spread over tops of fillets. Place on a broiler pan coated with cooking spray. Broil 4 in. from the heat until fish flakes easily with a fork, 3-5 minutes.
2. Meanwhile, in a small bowl, combine the bread crumbs, onion, ground mustard and remaining cheese; stir in butter. Spoon over fillets; spritz topping with cooking spray. Broil until golden brown, 1-2 minutes longer. Sprinkle with green onions if desired.

1 fillet: 267 cal., 10g fat (3g sat. fat), 94mg chol., 378mg sod., 8g carb. (1g sugars, 1g fiber), 35g pro. **Diabetic exchanges:** 5 lean meat, 1 fat, ½ starch.

HONEY-ORANGE GLAZED PORK LOIN

LEMON-PARSLEY TILAPIA

I like to include seafood in our weekly dinner rotation but don't want to bother with anything complicated. My family adores this dish, and it's a breeze to prepare. Cod and snapper work well here, too—simply adjust the cooking time if needed.
—Trisha Kruse, Eagle, ID

Takes: 20 min. • **Makes:** 4 servings

- 4 tilapia fillets (about 4 oz. each)
- 2 Tbsp. lemon juice
- 1 Tbsp. butter, melted
- 2 Tbsp. minced fresh parsley
- 2 garlic cloves, minced
- 2 tsp. grated lemon zest
- ½ tsp. salt
- ¼ tsp. pepper

1. Preheat oven to 375°. Place tilapia in a parchment-lined 15x10x1-in. pan. Drizzle with lemon juice, then melted butter.
2. Bake until fish just begins to flake easily with a fork, 11-13 minutes. Meanwhile, mix remaining ingredients. Remove fish from oven; sprinkle with parsley mixture.

1 fillet: 124 cal., 4g fat (2g sat. fat), 63mg chol., 359mg sod., 1g carb. (0 sugars, 0 fiber), 21g pro. **Diabetic exchanges:** 3 lean meat, 1 fat.

SNEAKY TURKEY MEATBALLS

SNEAKY TURKEY MEATBALLS

Like most kids, mine refuse to eat certain veggies. In order to get healthy foods into their diets, I have to be sneaky sometimes. The recipe's veggies give the meatballs a pleasing texture while providing valuable nutrients—and I'm happy to say that my kids love 'em.
—Courtney Stultz, Weir, KS

Prep: 15 min. • **Bake:** 20 min.
Makes: 6 servings

- ¼ head cauliflower, broken into florets
- ½ cup finely shredded cabbage
- 1 Tbsp. potato starch or cornstarch
- 1 Tbsp. balsamic vinegar
- 1 tsp. sea salt
- 1 tsp. dried basil
- ½ tsp. pepper
- 1 lb. ground turkey
  Optional: Barbecue sauce and fresh basil leaves

1. Preheat oven to 400°. Place cauliflower in a food processor; pulse until finely chopped. Transfer to a large bowl. Add the cabbage, potato starch, vinegar, salt, basil and pepper.
2. Add turkey; mix lightly but thoroughly. With ice cream scoop or with wet hands, shape into 1½-in. balls. Place meatballs on a greased rack in a 15x10x1-in. baking pan. Bake 20-24 minutes or until cooked through. If desired, toss with barbecue sauce and top with basil.

2 meatballs: 125 cal., 6g fat (1g sat. fat), 50mg chol., 370mg sod., 4g carb. (1g sugars, 1g fiber), 15g pro. **Diabetic exchanges:** 2 medium-fat meat.

BAKED BARBECUE PORK CHOPS

My mom used to prepare this recipe for dinner when I was growing up. Our whole family loved it. Now I enjoy preparing this same dish for my husband and our four children. They seem to enjoy it as much as I did when I was a kid.
—Bonnie Schiltz, Oakley, KS

Prep: 20 min. • **Bake:** 15 min.
Makes: 4 servings

 4   boneless pork loin chops (4 oz. each)
 ½   tsp. salt, divided
 ¼   tsp. pepper
 2   tsp. canola oil
 ⅓   cup water
 ¼   cup ketchup
 2   Tbsp. cider vinegar
 ¼   tsp. celery seed
 ⅛   tsp. ground nutmeg
 1   bay leaf

1. Sprinkle pork chops with ¼ tsp. salt and the pepper. In a large cast-iron or other ovenproof skillet, cook chops in oil until browned, 3-4 minutes on each side.
2. In a small bowl, combine the water, ketchup, vinegar, celery seed, nutmeg, bay leaf and remaining salt; pour over pork. Bring to a boil.
3. Cover and bake at 350° until a thermometer reads 145°, 15-20 minutes. Discard bay leaf.

1 pork chop: 190 cal., 9g fat (3g sat. fat), 55mg chol., 505mg sod., 5g carb. (2g sugars, 0 fiber), 22g pro. **Diabetic exchanges:** 3 lean meat, ½ fat.

SPANISH CHICKEN & RICE

Using leftover chicken, this meaty dish is a snap to put on the table.
—Patricia Rutherford, Winchester, IL

Takes: 30 min. • **Makes:** 2 servings

 ⅔   cup finely chopped onion
 ¼   cup sliced fresh mushrooms
 1¼   cups cubed cooked chicken breast
 2   plum tomatoes, peeled and chopped
 ½   cup cooked long grain rice
 ½   cup reduced-sodium tomato juice
 ½   cup reduced-sodium chicken broth
 ⅓   cup frozen peas
 1   Tbsp. chopped pimientos
 ⅛   tsp. dried tarragon
 ⅛   tsp. dried savory
     Pinch pepper

In a skillet coated with cooking spray, saute onion and mushrooms for 4 minutes or until tender. Place in an ungreased 1-qt. baking dish. Stir in the remaining ingredients. Cover and bake at 375° for 15-20 minutes or until liquid is absorbed.

1½ cups: 254 cal., 3g fat (1g sat. fat), 67mg chol., 264mg sod., 25g carb. (8g sugars, 4g fiber), 30g pro. **Diabetic exchanges:** 3 lean meat, 1 starch, 1 vegetable.

BAKED BARBECUE PORK CHOPS

MEXICAN-STYLE
CHICKEN MANICOTTI

ALMOND-TOPPED FISH

A co-worker gave me this recipe some time ago, but I didn't try it until recently. What a mistake it was to wait! It's easier than dipping, coating and frying—and the flavor is outstanding. Once you've tried this tender fish, you'll never go back to fried.
—Heidi Kirsch, Waterloo, IA

Takes: 30 min. • **Makes:** 4 servings

1 Tbsp. butter
1 small onion, thinly sliced
4 cod or haddock fillets (6 oz. each)
1 tsp. seasoned salt
½ tsp. dill weed
¼ tsp. pepper
¼ cup grated Parmesan cheese
¼ cup reduced-fat mayonnaise
1 Tbsp. minced fresh parsley
1 Tbsp. lemon juice
2 Tbsp. sliced almonds, toasted

1. Place butter in a 13x9-in. baking dish; place in a 400° oven until melted. Spread butter over bottom of dish; cover with the onion slices.
2. Arrange fish over onion; sprinkle with salt, dill and pepper. Combine the Parmesan cheese, mayonnaise, parsley and lemon juice; spread over fish.
3. Bake, uncovered, at 400° until fish flakes easily with a fork, 18-20 minutes. Sprinkle with almonds.

1 fillet: 220 cal., 9g fat (2g sat. fat), 74mg chol., 658mg sod., 5g carb. (2g sugars, 1g fiber), 29g pro. **Diabetic exchanges:** 4 lean meat, 2 fat.

MEXICAN-STYLE CHICKEN MANICOTTI

Combining an Italian pasta dish with Mexican ingredients results in something extra tasty. This recipe is well liked even in Cajun Country.
—Larry Phillips, Shreveport, LA

Prep: 25 min. • **Bake:** 25 min.
Makes: 2 servings

4 uncooked manicotti shells
1 cup cubed cooked chicken breast
1 cup salsa, divided
½ cup reduced-fat ricotta cheese
2 Tbsp. sliced ripe olives
4 tsp. minced fresh parsley
1 Tbsp. diced pimientos
1 green onion, thinly sliced
1 small garlic clove, minced
¼ to ½ tsp. hot pepper sauce
⅓ cup shredded Monterey Jack cheese

1. Cook manicotti according to package directions. In a small bowl, combine the chicken, ¼ cup salsa, ricotta cheese, olives, parsley, pimientos, green onion, garlic and pepper sauce. Drain manicotti; fill with chicken mixture.
2. Spread ¼ cup salsa in an 8-in. square baking dish coated with cooking spray. Top with manicotti shells and remaining salsa.
3. Cover and bake at 400° for 20 minutes. Uncover; sprinkle with Monterey Jack cheese and bake until the cheese is melted and the filling is heated through, 5-10 minutes longer.

2 shells: 352 cal., 10g fat (4g sat. fat), 71mg chol., 708mg sod., 34g carb. (6g sugars, 2g fiber), 30g pro. **Diabetic exchanges:** 4 lean meat, 2 starch.

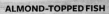
ALMOND-TOPPED FISH

ARTICHOKE CHICKEN

ARTICHOKE CHICKEN

Rosemary, mushrooms and artichokes combine to give chicken a wonderful, savory flavor. I've served this dish for a large group by doubling the recipe. It's always a big hit with everyone—especially my family!
—Ruth Stenson, Santa Ana, CA

Prep: 15 min. • **Bake:** 40 min.
Makes: 8 servings

- 8 boneless skinless chicken breast halves (4 oz. each)
- 2 Tbsp. butter
- 2 jars (6 oz. each) marinated quartered artichoke hearts, drained
- 1 jar (4½ oz.) whole mushrooms, drained
- ½ cup chopped onion
- ⅓ cup all-purpose flour
- 1½ tsp. dried rosemary, crushed
- ¾ tsp. salt
- ¼ tsp. pepper
- 2 cups chicken broth or 1 cup broth and 1 cup dry white wine
  Hot cooked noodles
  Minced fresh parsley

1. In a large skillet, brown chicken in butter. Remove chicken to an ungreased 13x9-in. baking dish. Arrange artichokes and mushrooms on top of the chicken; set aside.
2. Saute onion in pan juices until crisp-tender. Combine the flour, rosemary, salt and pepper. Stir into pan until blended. Add chicken broth. Bring to a boil; cook and stir until thickened and bubbly, about 2 minutes. Spoon over chicken.
3. Bake, uncovered, at 350° until a thermometer inserted in the chicken reads 165°, about 40 minutes. Serve with noodles and sprinkle with parsley.
Freeze option: Cool unbaked casserole; cover and freeze. To use, partially thaw in refrigerator overnight. Remove from refrigerator 30 minutes before baking. Preheat oven to 350°. Bake casserole as directed, increasing time as necessary to heat through and for a thermometer inserted in the chicken to read 165°.
1 serving: 232 cal., 9g fat (3g sat. fat), 81mg chol., 752mg sod., 7g carb. (1g sugars, 1g fiber), 28g pro. **Diabetic exchanges:** 4 lean meat, 1½ fat, ½ starch.

HADDOCK WITH LIME-CILANTRO BUTTER
(PICTURED ON P. 147)

In Louisiana, the good times roll when we broil fish and serve it with lots of lime juice, cilantro and butter.
—Darlene Morris, Franklinton, LA

Takes: 15 min. • **Makes:** 4 servings

- 4 haddock fillets (6 oz. each)
- ½ tsp. salt
- ¼ tsp. pepper
- 3 Tbsp. butter, melted
- 2 Tbsp. minced fresh cilantro
- 1 Tbsp. lime juice
- 1 tsp. grated lime zest

1. Preheat broiler. Sprinkle fillets with salt and pepper. Place on a greased broiler pan. Broil 4-5 in. from heat until fish flakes easily with a fork, 5-6 minutes.
2. In a small bowl, mix the remaining ingredients. Serve over fish.
1 fillet with 1 Tbsp. butter mixture: 227 cal., 10g fat (6g sat. fat), 121mg chol., 479mg sod., 1g carb. (0 sugars, 0 fiber), 32g pro. **Diabetic exchanges:** 4 lean meat, 2 fat.

ROASTED VEGETABLE PASTA PRIMAVERA

Roasting makes these end-of-summer veggies irresistible. Toss them with balsamic and pasta for a dinner that's light yet satisfying.

—Carly Curtin, Ellicott City, MD

Prep: 15 min. • **Bake:** 20 min.
Makes: 4 servings

- 4 medium carrots, sliced
- 2 medium zucchini, coarsely chopped (about 3 cups)
- 1⅔ cups cherry tomatoes
- ¼ cup olive oil
- 3 Tbsp. balsamic vinegar
- 1 Tbsp. minced fresh thyme or 1 tsp. dried thyme
- 2 tsp. minced fresh rosemary or ½ tsp. dried rosemary, crushed
- 1 tsp. salt
- ½ tsp. garlic powder
- 8 oz. uncooked rigatoni or whole wheat rigatoni
- ¼ cup shredded Parmesan cheese

1. Preheat the oven to 400°. Combine carrots, zucchini and tomatoes in a greased 15x10x1-in. baking pan. Whisk together the next 6 ingredients; reserve half. Drizzle remaining balsamic mixture over vegetables; toss to coat. Bake until carrots are crisp-tender, 20-25 minutes.
2. Meanwhile, cook rigatoni according to package directions; drain. Toss rigatoni with roasted vegetables, pan juices and reserved balsamic mixture. Sprinkle with cheese.
1½ cups: 410 cal., 17g fat (3g sat. fat), 4mg chol., 731mg sod., 56g carb. (12g sugars, 5g fiber), 12g pro.

TEST KITCHEN TIP

If your garden is overflowing with large tomatoes, use 2, cut into chunks, in place of the cherry tomatoes. And don't be afraid to sprinkle on additional fresh herbs just before serving. You'll be amazed at how they can perk up a dish.

CONTEST-WINNING GREEK PASTA BAKE

(PICTURED ON P. 147)

I've taken this hot dish to potlucks and it's received rave reviews. There's never a morsel left. Best of all, it's a simple, healthy and hearty supper made with ingredients that are easy to find.

—Anne Taglienti, Kennett Square, PA

Prep: 20 min. • **Bake:** 25 min.
Makes: 8 servings

- 3⅓ cups uncooked whole grain spiral or penne pasta
- 4 cups cubed cooked chicken breast
- 1 can (29 oz.) tomato sauce
- 1 can (14½ oz.) no-salt-added diced tomatoes, drained
- 1 pkg. (10 oz.) frozen chopped spinach, thawed and squeezed dry
- 2 cans (2¼ oz. each) sliced ripe olives, drained
- ¼ cup chopped red onion
- 2 Tbsp. chopped green pepper
- 1 tsp. dried basil
- 1 tsp. dried oregano
- 1 cup shredded part-skim mozzarella cheese
- ½ cup crumbled feta cheese
  Chopped fresh oregano or basil, optional

1. Cook pasta according to package directions; drain. In a large bowl, combine pasta, chicken, tomato sauce, tomatoes, spinach, olives, onion, green pepper, basil and oregano.
2. Transfer to a 13x9-in. baking dish coated with cooking spray. Sprinkle with cheeses. Bake, uncovered, at 400° for 25-30 minutes or until heated through and cheese is melted. If desired, sprinkle with oregano or basil.
Freeze option: Cool unbaked casserole; cover and freeze. To use, partially thaw in refrigerator overnight. Remove from refrigerator 30 minutes before baking. Preheat oven to 400°. Bake casserole as directed, increasing time as necessary to heat through and for a thermometer inserted in center to read 165°.
1½ cups: 398 cal., 10g fat (3g sat. fat), 67mg chol., 832mg sod., 47g carb. (5g sugars, 9g fiber), 34g pro.

ROASTED VEGETABLE PASTA PRIMAVERA

HORSERADISH-ENCRUSTED BEEF TENDERLOIN

HORSERADISH-ENCRUSTED BEEF TENDERLOIN

Wow friends and family with this tender beef in a golden horseradish crust. Roasted garlic boosts the robust flavor even more.
—Laura Bagozzi, Dublin, OH

Prep: 35 min. + cooling
Bake: 45 min. + standing
Makes: 8 servings

- 1 whole garlic bulb
- 1 tsp. olive oil
- ⅓ cup prepared horseradish
- ¼ tsp. salt
- ¼ tsp. dried basil
- ¼ tsp. dried thyme
- ¼ tsp. pepper
- ⅓ cup soft bread crumbs
- 1 beef tenderloin roast (3 lbs.)

1. Remove papery outer skin from garlic (do not peel or separate cloves). Cut top off garlic bulb; brush with oil. Wrap in heavy-duty foil. Bake at 425° until softened, 30-35 minutes. Cool for 10-15 minutes.

2. Squeeze softened garlic into a small bowl; stir in the horseradish, salt, basil, thyme and pepper. Add bread crumbs; toss to coat. Spread over top of tenderloin. Place on a rack in a large shallow roasting pan.

3. Bake at 400° until meat reaches desired doneness (for medium-rare, a thermometer should read 135°; medium, 140°; medium-well, 145°), 45-55 minutes. Let stand for 10 minutes before slicing.

5 oz. cooked beef: 268 cal., 11g fat (4g sat. fat), 75mg chol., 119mg sod., 4g carb. (1g sugars, 1g fiber), 37g pro. **Diabetic exchanges:** 5 lean meat.

CHICKEN VEGGIE PACKETS

CHICKEN VEGGIE PACKETS

People think I went to a lot of trouble when I serve these packets. Individual aluminum foil pouches hold the juices in during baking to keep the herbed chicken moist and tender. The foil saves time and makes cleanup a breeze.
—Edna Shaffer, Beulah, MI

Takes: 30 min. • **Makes:** 4 servings

- 4 boneless skinless chicken breast halves (4 oz. each)
- ½ lb. sliced fresh mushrooms
- 1½ cups fresh baby carrots
- 1 cup pearl onions
- ½ cup julienned sweet red pepper
- ¼ tsp. pepper
- 3 tsp. minced fresh thyme
- ½ tsp. salt, optional
  Lemon wedges, optional

1. Flatten chicken breasts to ½-in. thickness; place each on a piece of heavy-duty foil (about 12 in. square). Layer the mushrooms, carrots, onions and red pepper over chicken; sprinkle with pepper, thyme and salt if desired.

2. Fold foil around chicken and vegetables and seal tightly. Place on a baking sheet. Bake at 375° for 30 minutes or until chicken juices run clear. If desired, serve with lemon wedges.

1 serving: 175 cal., 3g fat (1g sat. fat), 63mg chol., 100mg sod., 11g carb. (6g sugars, 2g fiber), 25g pro. **Diabetic exchanges:** 3 lean meat, 2 vegetable.

CHILI MAC CASSEROLE

TURKEY ALFREDO PIZZA

A longtime family favorite, this thin-crust pizza is packed with flavor and nutrition—and it's an excellent way to use up leftover turkey during the holidays.
—Edie DeSpain, Logan, UT

Takes: 25 min. • **Makes:** 6 servings

- 1 prebaked 12-in. thin pizza crust
- 1 garlic clove, peeled and halved
- ¾ cup reduced-fat Alfredo sauce, divided
- 1 pkg. (10 oz.) frozen chopped spinach, thawed and squeezed dry
- 2 tsp. lemon juice
- ¼ tsp. salt
- ⅛ tsp. pepper
- 2 cups shredded cooked turkey breast
- ¾ cup shredded Parmesan cheese
- ½ tsp. crushed red pepper flakes

1. Place the crust on a baking sheet; rub with cut sides of garlic. Discard garlic. Spread ½ cup Alfredo sauce over crust.
2. In a small bowl, combine the spinach, lemon juice, salt and pepper; spoon evenly over sauce. Top with turkey; drizzle with remaining Alfredo sauce. Sprinkle with Parmesan cheese and pepper flakes.
3. Bake at 425° until heated through and cheese is melted, 11-13 minutes.

1 piece: 300 cal., 9g fat (4g sat. fat), 60mg chol., 823mg sod., 27g carb. (2g sugars, 2g fiber), 25g pro. **Diabetic exchanges:** 3 lean meat, 2 starch, ½ fat.

CHILI MAC CASSEROLE

This nicely spiced entree uses several of my family's favorite ingredients, including macaroni, kidney beans, tomatoes and cheese. Just add a green salad for a complete meal.
—Marlene Wilson, Rolla, ND

Prep: 15 min. • **Bake:** 30 min.
Makes: 10 servings

- 1 cup uncooked elbow macaroni
- 2 lbs. lean ground beef (90% lean)
- 1 medium onion, chopped
- 2 garlic cloves, minced
- 1 can (28 oz.) diced tomatoes, undrained
- 1 can (16 oz.) kidney beans, rinsed and drained
- 1 can (6 oz.) tomato paste
- 1 can (4 oz.) chopped green chiles
- 1¼ tsp. salt
- 1 tsp. chili powder
- ½ tsp. ground cumin
- ½ tsp. pepper
- 2 cups shredded reduced-fat Mexican cheese blend
  Thinly sliced green onions, optional

1. Cook macaroni according to package directions. Meanwhile, in a large nonstick skillet, cook the beef, onion and garlic over medium heat until meat is no longer pink; drain. Stir in the tomatoes, beans, tomato paste, chiles and seasonings. Drain macaroni; add to beef mixture.
2. Transfer to a 13x9-in. baking dish coated with cooking spray. Cover and bake at 375° until bubbly, 25-30 minutes. Uncover; sprinkle with cheese. Bake until cheese is melted, 5-8 minutes longer. If desired, top with sliced green onions.

1 cup: 313 cal., 13g fat (6g sat. fat), 69mg chol., 758mg sod., 22g carb. (6g sugars, 5g fiber), 30g pro. **Diabetic exchanges:** 3 lean meat, 1½ starch, 1 fat.

TURKEY ALFREDO PIZZA

CHICKEN VEGGIE FAJITAS
(PICTURED ON P. 146)

Our family loves the spicy flavor of these fajitas. I also appreciate the fact that they're fast to fix.
—Eleanor Martens, Rosenort, MB

Takes: 20 min. • **Makes:** 4 servings

- 3 Tbsp. lemon juice
- 1 Tbsp. soy sauce
- 1 Tbsp. Worcestershire sauce
- 2 tsp. canola oil
- 1 garlic clove, minced
- ½ tsp. ground cumin
- ½ tsp. dried oregano
- ¾ lb. boneless skinless chicken breasts, cut into ½-in. strips
- 1 small onion, sliced and separated into rings
- ½ each medium green, sweet red and yellow pepper, julienned
- 4 flour tortillas (6 in.), warmed
  Shredded cheddar cheese, optional

1. In a small bowl, combine the first 7 ingredients. Place chicken strips and vegetables in a single layer in a greased 15x10x1-in. baking pan; drizzle with ¼ cup lemon juice mixture. Broil 4-6 in. from the heat for 4 minutes.
2. Turn chicken and vegetables; drizzle with remaining lemon juice mixture. Broil 4 minutes longer or until chicken juices run clear. Serve on tortillas, with cheese if desired.

1 fajita: 231 cal., 7g fat (1g sat. fat), 47mg chol., 460mg sod., 20g carb. (3g sugars, 1g fiber), 21g pro. **Diabetic exchanges:** 2½ lean meat, 1 starch, 1 vegetable.

APPLE-ONION PORK TENDERLOIN

APPLE-ONION PORK TENDERLOIN

This slightly sweet and tender pork roast is quick enough to make for a weeknight, but I often serve it on special occasions. It tastes amazing served with mashed potatoes or over egg noodles.
—Trisha Kruse, Eagle, ID

Takes: 30 min. • **Makes:** 4 servings

- 2 Tbsp. canola oil, divided
- 1 pork tenderloin (1 lb.), cut in half
- 3 Tbsp. honey mustard
- 2 medium apples, thinly sliced
- 1 large onion, halved and thinly sliced
- ½ cup white wine or apple cider
- ⅛ tsp. salt
- ⅛ tsp. pepper

1. Preheat oven to 425°. In an ovenproof skillet, heat 1 Tbsp. oil over medium-high heat. Brown tenderloin halves on all sides; remove pan from heat. Spread the pork with mustard; roast in oven until a thermometer reads 145°, 15-20 minutes.
2. Meanwhile, in another skillet, heat the remaining oil over medium heat; saute apples and onion 7 minutes. Stir in wine; bring to a boil. Reduce heat; simmer, uncovered, until apples and onion are tender, 5-8 minutes. Stir in salt and pepper.
3. Remove pork from oven; let stand 5 minutes before slicing. Serve with the apple mixture.

3 oz. cooked pork with ½ cup apple mixture: 294 cal., 12g fat (2g sat. fat), 64mg chol., 218mg sod., 20g carb. (13g sugars, 3g fiber), 24g pro. **Diabetic exchanges:** 3 lean meat, 1½ fat, ½ starch, ½ fruit.

BAKED CHICKEN WITH BACON-TOMATO RELISH

We eat a lot of chicken for dinner, so I'm always trying to do something a little different with it. My children love the crispiness of this chicken, and my husband and I love the flavorful relish—you can never go wrong with bacon!
—Elisabeth Larsen, Pleasant Grove, UT

Takes: 30 min. • **Makes:** 4 servings

- 1 cup panko (Japanese) bread crumbs
- 2 Tbsp. plus 1 tsp. minced fresh thyme, divided
- ½ tsp. salt, divided
- ½ tsp. pepper, divided
- ⅓ cup all-purpose flour
- 1 large egg, beaten
- 1 lb. chicken tenderloins
- 4 bacon strips, cut into ½-in. pieces
- 1½ cups grape tomatoes, halved
- 1 Tbsp. red wine vinegar
- 1 Tbsp. brown sugar

1. Preheat oven to 425°. In a shallow bowl, mix bread crumbs, 2 Tbsp. thyme, and ¼ tsp. each salt and pepper. Place flour and egg in separate shallow bowls. Dip chicken in flour; shake off excess. Dip in egg, then in crumb mixture, patting to help coating adhere. Place chicken on a greased rack in a 15x10x1-in. baking pan. Bake until a thermometer reads 165°, about 15 minutes.

2. Meanwhile, in a large skillet, cook bacon over medium heat until crisp, stirring occasionally, about 5 minutes. Remove with a slotted spoon; drain on paper towels. Reserve 2 Tbsp. drippings in pan; discard remaining drippings.

3. Add tomatoes, vinegar, sugar and remaining salt and pepper to drippings; cook and stir until tomatoes are tender, 2-3 minutes. Stir in bacon and remaining thyme. Serve with chicken.

2 chicken tenders with ¼ cup relish:
326 cal., 13g fat (4g sat. fat), 95mg chol., 602mg sod., 19g carb. (6g sugars, 2g fiber), 34g pro. **Diabetic exchanges:** 4 lean meat, 2 fat, 1 starch.

BAKED CHICKEN WITH BACON-TOMATO RELISH

MEDITERRANEAN CHICKEN

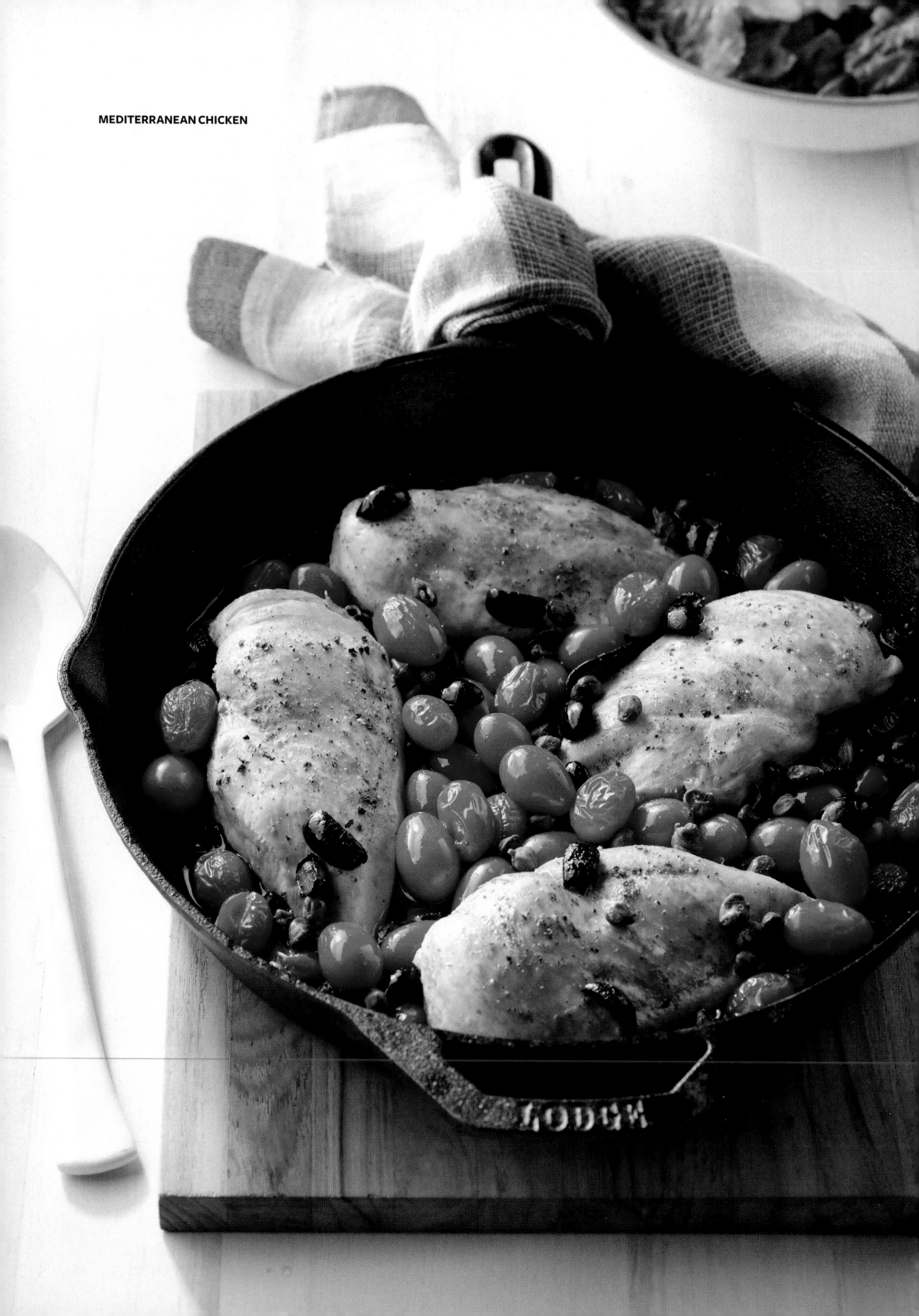

MEDITERRANEAN CHICKEN

Chicken goes Mediterranean in this skillet creation, a warm welcome to the table.
—Mary Relyea, Canastota, NY

Takes: 25 min. • **Makes:** 4 servings

- 4 boneless skinless chicken breast halves (6 oz. each)
- ¼ tsp. salt
- ¼ tsp. pepper
- 3 Tbsp. olive oil
- 1 pint grape tomatoes
- 16 pitted Greek or ripe olives, sliced
- 3 Tbsp. capers, drained

1. Sprinkle chicken with salt and pepper. In a large ovenproof skillet, cook chicken in oil over medium heat until golden brown, 2-3 minutes on each side. Add tomatoes, olives and capers.
2. Bake, uncovered, at 475° until a thermometer reads 170°, 10-14 minutes.

1 serving: 336 cal., 18g fat (3g sat. fat), 94mg chol., 631mg sod., 6g carb. (3g sugars, 2g fiber), 36g pro. **Diabetic exchanges:** 5 lean meat, 3 fat, 1 vegetable.

PORTOBELLO POLENTA STACKS

PORTOBELLO POLENTA STACKS

My friends and I have recently started growing portobello mushrooms from kits we found at a farmers market. We love to try new recipes like this one with our harvest.
—Breanne Heath, Chicago, IL

Takes: 30 min. • **Makes:** 4 servings

- 1 Tbsp. olive oil
- 3 garlic cloves, minced
- 2 Tbsp. balsamic vinegar
- 4 large portobello mushrooms (about 5 in.), stems removed
- ¼ tsp. salt
- ¼ tsp. pepper
- 1 tube (18 oz.) polenta, cut into 12 slices
- 4 slices tomato
- ½ cup grated Parmesan cheese
- 2 Tbsp. minced fresh basil

1. Preheat oven to 400°. In a small saucepan, heat oil over medium heat. Add garlic; cook and stir until tender, 1-2 minutes (do not allow to brown). Stir in vinegar; remove from heat.
2. Place mushrooms in a 13x9-in. baking dish, gill side up. Brush with the vinegar mixture; sprinkle with salt and pepper. Top with polenta and tomato slices; sprinkle with cheese.
3. Bake, uncovered, until mushrooms are tender, 20-25 minutes. Sprinkle with basil.

1 serving: 219 cal., 6g fat (2g sat. fat), 9mg chol., 764mg sod., 32g carb. (7g sugars, 3g fiber), 7g pro. **Diabetic exchanges:** 1½ starch, 1 lean meat, 1 vegetable, 1 fat.

TUSCAN FISH PACKETS
(PICTURED ON P. 146)

My husband does a lot of fishing, so I'm always looking for different ways to serve his catches. A professional chef was kind enough to share this recipe with me, and I played around with some different veggie combinations until I found the one my family liked best.
—Kathy Morrow, Hubbard, OH

Takes: 30 min. • **Makes:** 4 servings

- 1 can (15 oz.) great northern beans, rinsed and drained
- 4 plum tomatoes, chopped
- 1 small zucchini, chopped
- 1 medium onion, chopped
- 1 garlic clove, minced
- ¼ cup white wine
- ¾ tsp. salt, divided
- ¼ tsp. pepper, divided
- 4 tilapia fillets (6 oz. each)
- 1 medium lemon, cut into 8 thin slices

1. Preheat oven to 400°. In a bowl, combine beans, tomatoes, zucchini, onion, garlic, wine, ½ tsp. salt and ⅛ tsp. pepper.

2. Rinse fish and pat dry. Place each fillet on an 18x12-in. piece of heavy-duty foil; season with remaining salt and pepper. Spoon bean mixture over fish; top with lemon slices. Fold foil around fish and crimp edges to seal. Transfer packets to a baking sheet.

3. Bake until fish just begins to flake easily with a fork and vegetables are tender, 15-20 minutes. Be careful of escaping steam when opening packet.

1 serving: 270 cal., 2g fat (1g sat. fat), 83mg chol., 658mg sod., 23g carb. (4g sugars, 7g fiber), 38g pro. **Diabetic exchanges:** 5 lean meat, 1 starch, 1 vegetable.

TEST KITCHEN TIP

If you hate to open a bottle of wine just for ¼ cup, look for wine in single-portion plastic bottles. The small bottles are convenient for using in recipes.

MAPLE-GLAZED PORK TENDERLOIN

MAPLE-GLAZED PORK TENDERLOIN

My husband and I think this roasted pork tenderloin tastes like a fancy restaurant dish, but it couldn't be simpler to make at home. The maple-mustard glaze makes it extra special.
—Colleen Mercier, Salmon Arm, BC

Takes: 30 min. • **Makes:** 4 servings

- ¾ tsp. salt
- ¾ tsp. rubbed sage
- ½ tsp. pepper
- 2 pork tenderloins (¾ lb. each)
- 1 tsp. butter
- ¼ cup maple syrup
- 3 Tbsp. cider vinegar
- 1¾ tsp. Dijon mustard

1. Preheat oven to 425°. Mix seasonings; sprinkle over pork. In a large nonstick skillet, heat butter over medium heat; brown tenderloins on all sides. Transfer to a foil-lined 15x10x1-in. pan. Roast for 10 minutes.

2. Meanwhile, for glaze, in same skillet, mix syrup, vinegar and mustard; bring to a boil, stirring to loosen browned bits from pan. Cook and stir until slightly thickened, 1-2 minutes; remove from heat.

3. Brush 1 Tbsp. glaze over pork; continue roasting until a thermometer inserted in pork reads 145°, 7-10 minutes, brushing halfway through with remaining glaze. Let stand 5 minutes before slicing.

5 oz. cooked pork: 264 cal., 7g fat (3g sat. fat), 98mg chol., 573mg sod., 14g carb. (12g sugars, 0 fiber), 34g pro. **Diabetic exchanges:** 5 lean meat, 1 starch.

CRANBERRY CHIPOTLE CHICKEN ENCHILADAS

Cranberry sauce delivers a healthy dose of vitamins to this dish. A little bit sweet, a little bit smoky, these enchiladas are a delightful way to use leftover chicken or turkey.
—Julie Peterson, Crofton, MD

Prep: 30 min. • **Bake:** 30 min.
Makes: 8 servings

- 2½ cups shredded cooked chicken or turkey
- 1 can (15 oz.) black beans, rinsed and drained
- 1 cup (4 oz.) shredded reduced-fat Colby-Monterey Jack cheese, divided
- 1 can (14 oz.) whole-berry cranberry sauce, divided
- ½ cup reduced-fat sour cream
- 1½ cups salsa, divided
- 4 green onions, sliced
- ¼ cup minced fresh cilantro
- 1 to 2 Tbsp. finely chopped chipotle peppers in adobo sauce
- 1 tsp. ground cumin
- 1 tsp. chili powder
- ½ tsp. pepper
- 8 whole wheat tortilla or flour tortillas (8 in.), warmed

1. Preheat the oven to 350°. Combine chicken, beans, ¾ cup shredded cheese, ⅔ cup cranberry sauce, sour cream, ½ cup salsa, green onions, cilantro, chipotle peppers, cumin, chili powder and pepper. Place ¾ cup turkey mixture off center on each tortilla. Roll up and place in a greased 13x9-in. baking dish, seam side down.

2. Combine the remaining salsa and cranberry sauce; pour over enchiladas. Cover and bake 25 minutes. Uncover and sprinkle with remaining cheese. Bake until cheese is melted, 5-10 minutes longer.

To make ahead: Cover and refrigerate unbaked enchiladas overnight. Remove from refrigerator 30 minutes before baking. Preheat oven to 350°. Cover dish with foil; bake as directed, increasing covered time to 35-40 minutes or until heated through and a thermometer inserted in center reads 165°. Uncover; sprinkle with remaining cheese. Bake until cheese is melted, 5-10 minutes longer.

1 enchilada: 368 cal., 6g fat (3g sat. fat), 53mg chol., 623mg sod., 54g carb. (15g sugars, 6g fiber), 24g pro.

CRANBERRY
CHIPOTLE CHICKEN
ENCHILADAS

DEVILED CHICKEN THIGHS

MAKEOVER SHRIMP RICE CASSEROLE

The cooks at Taste of Home *made a lightened-up version of my shrimp casserole, and I love it. The makeover has only half the calories and sodium of my original recipe, and less fat, too.*
—Marie Roberts, Lake Charles, LA

Prep: 40 min. • **Bake:** 30 min.
Makes: 6 servings

- 1 lb. uncooked medium shrimp, peeled and deveined
- 2 Tbsp. butter, divided
- 12 oz. fresh mushrooms, sliced
- 1 large green pepper, chopped
- 1 medium onion, chopped
- 3 Tbsp. all-purpose flour
- ¾ tsp. salt
- ⅛ tsp. cayenne pepper
- 1⅓ cups fat-free milk
- 3 cups cooked brown rice
- 1 cup shredded reduced-fat cheddar cheese, divided

1. In a large nonstick skillet, saute shrimp in 1 Tbsp. butter for 2-3 minutes or until shrimp turn pink. Remove and set aside. In the same skillet, saute the mushrooms, green pepper and onion in the remaining butter until tender.
2. Stir in the flour, salt and cayenne. Gradually add milk until blended. Bring to a boil; cook and stir for 2 minutes or until thickened. Add rice, ½ cup cheese and the shrimp; stir until combined.
3. Pour into a 1½-qt. baking dish coated with cooking spray. Cover and bake at 325° for 30-35 minutes or until heated through. Sprinkle with remaining cheese; cover and let stand for 5 minutes or until cheese is melted.
1 cup: 318 cal., 10g fat (6g sat. fat), 137mg chol., 621mg sod., 35g carb. (7g sugars, 4g fiber), 24g pro. **Diabetic exchanges:** 3 lean meat, 2 starch, 1 vegetable, 1 fat.

DEVILED CHICKEN THIGHS

I make this dish when I invite my neighbor over for supper. It makes just enough for the two of us. The chicken stays tender and moist, and the cashews add a perfect bit of crunch. Serve it alongside roasted vegetables or rice for a complete meal.
—Bernice Morris, Marshfield, MO

Takes: 30 min. • **Makes:** 2 servings

- 1 tsp. butter, softened
- 1 tsp. cider vinegar
- 1 tsp. prepared mustard
- 1 tsp. paprika
  Dash pepper
- 2 boneless skinless chicken thighs (about ½ lb.)
- 3 Tbsp. soft bread crumbs
- 2 Tbsp. chopped cashews

1. In a large bowl, combine the butter, vinegar, mustard, paprika and pepper. Spread over chicken thighs. Place in a greased 11x7-in. baking dish. Sprinkle with bread crumbs.
2. Bake at 400° for 15 minutes. Sprinkle with the cashews. Bake until chicken juices run clear and topping is golden brown, 7-12 minutes longer.
1 chicken thigh: 246 cal., 14g fat (4g sat. fat), 81mg chol., 189mg sod., 6g carb. (1g sugars, 1g fiber), 23g pro. **Diabetic exchanges:** 3 lean meat, 1 fat, ½ starch.

MAKEOVER SHRIMP
RICE CASSEROLE

**DIJON-RUBBED
PORK WITH
RHUBARB SAUCE**

DIJON-RUBBED PORK
WITH RHUBARB SAUCE

*A tender pork loin roast served with a
rhubarb-orange sauce is simply delicious!
Here's an excellent choice for company—
it makes for a memorable meal.*
—Marilyn Rodriguez, Sparks, NV

Prep: 15 min. • **Bake:** 1 hour + standing
Makes: 12 servings (1½ cups sauce)

- 1   boneless pork loin roast (3 lbs.)
- ¼   cup Dijon mustard
- 6   garlic cloves, minced
- 1   Tbsp. minced fresh rosemary or
     1 tsp. dried rosemary, crushed
- ¾   tsp. salt
- ½   tsp. pepper

SAUCE
- 3   cups sliced fresh or frozen rhubarb
- ⅓   cup orange juice
- ⅓   cup sugar
- 1   Tbsp. cider vinegar

1. Score the surface of the pork, making
diamond shapes ¼ in. deep. In a small
bowl, combine the mustard, garlic,
rosemary, salt and pepper; rub over pork.

2. Coat a roasting pan and rack with
cooking spray; place pork on rack in pan.
Bake, uncovered, at 350° for 1 hour or
until a thermometer reads 145°. Let stand
for 10 minutes before slicing.

3. In a small saucepan, bring the sauce
ingredients to a boil. Reduce heat; cover
and simmer for 8-12 minutes or until
rhubarb is tender. Serve warm with pork.
Note: If using frozen rhubarb, measure
rhubarb while still frozen, then thaw
completely. Drain in a colander, but
do not press liquid out.

3 oz. cooked pork: 181 cal., 6g fat (2g sat.
fat), 56mg chol., 308mg sod., 9g carb.
(7g sugars, 1g fiber), 23g pro. **Diabetic
exchanges:** 3 lean meat, ½ starch.

BROILED SCALLOPS

*These quick scallops are perfect for two.
They look as if they were prepared in a
fancy restaurant.*
—Susan Coryell, Huddleston, VA

Takes: 25 min. • **Makes:** 2 servings

- 2   green onions, sliced
- 1   garlic clove, minced
- 2   tsp. olive oil
- 12 oz. sea scallops
- 2   tsp. minced fresh parsley
- 1   tsp. finely chopped fresh basil
- ¼   cup vermouth or chicken broth
- ⅛   tsp. salt
- ⅛   tsp. white pepper
- ⅓   cup soft bread crumbs
- 2   tsp. butter

1. In a nonstick skillet, saute onions and
garlic in oil until tender. Add the scallops,
parsley and basil; cook and stir over
medium heat until scallops are firm and
opaque. Add the vermouth or broth,
salt and pepper; cook, uncovered, over
medium-low heat for 1 minute.

2. Divide the mixture evenly between
2 ovenproof 1½-cup dishes. Sprinkle
with bread crumbs; dot with butter.
Broil 4-6 in. from heat until scallops
are firm and opaque and bread crumbs
are golden brown.

5 oz.: 296 cal., 10g fat (3g sat. fat), 66mg chol.,
506mg sod., 13g carb. (4g sugars, 1g fiber), 30g
pro. **Diabetic exchanges:** 4 very lean meat,
2 fat, 1 starch.

GARLICKY CHICKEN DINNER

Roasted chicken brings the flavor, which is enhanced by herbs, lemon and hearty vegetables in this simple sheet-pan dinner.
—Shannon Norris, Cudahy, WI

Prep: 25 min. • **Bake:** 45 min.
Makes: 8 servings

- 1¼ lbs. small red potatoes, quartered
- 4 medium carrots, cut into ½-in. slices
- 1 medium red onion, cut into thin wedges
- 1 Tbsp. olive oil
- 6 garlic cloves, minced
- 2 tsp. minced fresh thyme, divided
- 1½ tsp. salt, divided
- 1 tsp. pepper, divided
- 1 tsp. paprika
- 4 chicken drumsticks
- 4 bone-in chicken thighs
- 1 small lemon, sliced
- 1 pkg. (5 oz.) fresh spinach

1. Preheat the oven to 425°. In a large bowl, combine potatoes, carrots, onion, oil, garlic, 1 tsp. thyme, ¾ tsp. salt and ½ tsp. pepper; toss to coat. Transfer to a 15x10x1-in. baking pan coated with cooking spray.
2. In a small bowl, mix paprika and the remaining thyme, salt and pepper. Sprinkle chicken with paprika mixture; arrange over vegetables. Top with lemon slices. Roast until a thermometer inserted in chicken reads 170°-175° and vegetables are just tender, 35-40 minutes.
3. Remove chicken to a serving platter; keep warm. Top vegetables with spinach. Roast until vegetables are tender and spinach is wilted, 8-10 minutes longer. Stir the vegetables to combine; serve with chicken.

1 piece chicken with 1 cup vegetables: 264 cal., 12g fat (3g sat. fat), 64mg chol., 548mg sod., 18g carb. (3g sugars, 3g fiber), 21g pro. **Diabetic exchanges:** 3 medium-fat meat, 1 starch, 1 vegetable, ½ fat.

GARLICKY CHICKEN DINNER

TOMATO-BASIL BAKED FISH

This recipe works successfully with many kinds of fish, while the rest of the ingredients are things you're likely to have on hand. Baked fish is so simple and so good for you. I make this often!
—Annie Hicks, Zephyrhills, FL

Takes: 15 min. • **Makes:** 2 servings

- 1 Tbsp. lemon juice
- 1 tsp. olive oil
- 8 oz. red snapper, cod or haddock fillets
- ¼ tsp. dried basil
- ⅛ tsp. salt
- ⅛ tsp. pepper
- 2 plum tomatoes, thinly sliced
- 2 tsp. grated Parmesan cheese

1. In a shallow bowl, combine the lemon juice and oil. Add fish fillets; turn to coat. Place in a greased 9-in. pie plate. Sprinkle with half of the basil, salt and pepper. Arrange tomatoes over top; sprinkle with cheese and remaining seasonings.
2. Cover; bake at 400° for 10-12 minutes or until the fish flakes easily with a fork.

1 serving: 121 cal., 4g fat (1g sat. fat), 24mg chol., 256mg sod., 4g carb. (2g sugars, 1g fiber), 18g pro. **Diabetic exchanges:** 3 lean meat, 1 vegetable, ½ fat.

**SALMON WITH
ROOT VEGETABLES**

SPINACH & FETA
STUFFED CHICKEN

*My chicken bundles are simple, clean and
comforting. Serve them with wild rice and
green beans for one of our favorite meals.*
—Jim Knepper, Mount Holly Springs, PA

Takes: 30 min. • **Makes:** 2 servings

    8 oz. fresh spinach (about 10 cups)
 1½ tsp. cider vinegar
   ½ tsp. sugar
   ⅛ tsp. pepper
    2 boneless skinless chicken thighs
   ½ tsp. chicken seasoning
    3 Tbsp. crumbled feta cheese
    1 tsp. olive oil
   ¾ cup reduced-sodium chicken broth
    1 tsp. butter

1. Preheat oven to 375°. In a large skillet,
cook and stir spinach over medium-high
heat until wilted. Stir in vinegar, sugar
and pepper; cool slightly.
2. Pound chicken thighs with a meat
mallet to flatten slightly; sprinkle with
chicken seasoning. Top chicken with
spinach mixture and cheese. Roll up
chicken from a long side; tie securely
with kitchen string.
3. In an ovenproof skillet, heat oil over
medium-high heat; add chicken and brown
on all sides. Transfer to oven; roast until
a thermometer inserted in chicken reads
170°, 13-15 minutes.
4. Remove chicken from pan; keep warm.
On stovetop, add broth and butter to
skillet; bring to a boil, stirring to loosen
browned bits from pan. Cook until
slightly thickened, 3-5 minutes. Serve
with chicken.

Note: This recipe was tested with
McCormick's Montreal Chicken
Seasoning. Look for it in the spice aisle.

1 chicken roll-up with 2 Tbsp. sauce:
253 cal., 14g fat (5g sat. fat), 86mg chol.,
601mg sod., 5g carb. (2g sugars, 2g fiber),
26g pro. **Diabetic exchanges:** 3 lean meat,
2 vegetable, 1½ fat.

SALMON WITH
ROOT VEGETABLES

*This cozy hash is loaded with protein and
healthy fats that keep you going on busy
days. We've been known to devour it at
breakfast, lunch and dinner!*
—Courtney Stultz, Weir, KS

Takes: 25 min. • **Makes:** 6 servings

    2 Tbsp. olive oil
    2 medium sweet potatoes, peeled
       and cut into ¼-in. cubes
    2 medium red potatoes, cut into
       ¼-in. cubes
    2 medium turnips, peeled and diced
    2 medium carrots, peeled and diced
    1 tsp. sea salt, divided
    1 tsp. chili powder
   ¾ tsp. pepper, divided
   ½ tsp. ground cinnamon
   ½ tsp. ground cumin
    6 salmon fillets (6 oz. each)

1. Preheat oven to 400°. In a large skillet,
heat oil over medium heat. Add potatoes,
turnips and carrots. Combine ½ tsp. salt,
chili powder, ½ tsp. pepper, cinnamon and
cumin; sprinkle over vegetables. Cook,
stirring frequently, until vegetables are
tender, 15-20 minutes.
2. Meanwhile, place salmon, skin side
down, in a foil-lined 15x10x1-in. baking
pan. Sprinkle with remaining salt and
pepper. Bake 10 minutes. Preheat broiler;
broil until fish just begins to flake easily,
2-5 minutes. Serve fish with vegetables.

1 serving: 417 cal., 21g fat (4g sat. fat), 85mg
chol., 464mg sod., 26g carb. (9g sugars, 4g
fiber), 31g pro. **Diabetic exchanges:** 4 lean
meat, 2 starch, 1 fat.

> **TEST KITCHEN TIP**
>
> Nestle a poached egg in the
> vegetables, and you'll get
> a 6g boost of protein.

**SPINACH & FETA
STUFFED CHICKEN**

GRILLED
SPECIALTIES

"Kids like assembling these kabobs almost as much as they like devouring them. The whole family is sure to enjoy this sensational twist on a taco-night favorite."
—Dixie Terry, Goreville, IL

Grilled Angel Food Cake with Fruit Salsa (p. 193) **Cajun Grilled Shrimp** (p. 192) **Juicy Turkey Burgers** (p. 191)
Herbed Pork Chops (p. 190) **Tacos on a Stick** (p. 184) **Grilled Three-Potato Salad** (p.181)

GRILLED PATTYPANS

A few minutes and a handful of sauce ingredients are all you'll need for this scrumptious side dish. Hoisin sauce and rice vinegar give pattypans Asian flair.
—*Taste of Home* Test Kitchen

Takes: 15 min. • **Makes:** 6 servings

- 6 cups pattypan squash (about 1½ lbs.)
- ¼ cup apricot spreadable fruit
- 2 tsp. hoisin sauce
- 1 tsp. rice vinegar
- ½ tsp. sesame oil
- ¼ tsp. salt
- ⅛ tsp. ground ginger

1. Place squash in a grill wok or basket coated with cooking spray. Grill, covered, over medium heat until tender, 4 minutes on each side.
2. Meanwhile, in a small bowl, combine the remaining ingredients. Transfer squash to a serving bowl; add the sauce and toss gently to coat.
Note: If you do not have a grill wok or basket, use a disposable foil pan. Poke holes in the bottom of the pan with a meat fork to allow liquid to drain.
¾ cup: 54 cal., 0 fat (0 sat. fat), 0 chol., 127mg sod., 12g carb. (8g sugars, 1g fiber), 1g pro.
Diabetic exchanges: 1 vegetable, ½ starch.

CORN & SQUASH QUESADILLAS

CORN & SQUASH QUESADILLAS

Grilled vegetables give these quesadillas their distinctive richness, while cumin and jalapeno peppers add a little zip.
—Mildred Sherrer, Fort Worth, TX

Prep: 40 min. • **Cook:** 10 min.
Makes: 6 servings

- 2 medium ears sweet corn, husks removed
- 2 medium yellow summer squash, halved lengthwise
- ½ small sweet onion, cut into ¼-in. slices
- 1 to 2 jalapeno peppers
- 1 Tbsp. minced fresh basil
- 1½ tsp. minced fresh oregano
- 1 garlic clove, minced
- ¼ tsp. salt
- ¼ tsp. ground cumin
- 6 flour tortillas (8 in.), warmed
- 1 cup shredded Monterey Jack cheese
- 1 Tbsp. canola oil

1. Grill corn, covered, over medium heat for 10 minutes; turn. Place the squash, onion and jalapenos on grill; cover and cook for 5-6 minutes on each side. When vegetables are cool enough to handle, remove corn from the cobs, chop the squash and onion, and seed and chop jalapenos. Place in a large bowl.
2. Stir in the basil, oregano, garlic, salt and cumin. Place ½ cup filling on one side of each tortilla; sprinkle with cheese. Fold tortillas over filling. On a griddle or large skillet, cook quesadillas in oil over medium heat for 1-2 minutes on each side or until heated through. Cut into wedges.
Note: Wear disposable gloves when cutting hot peppers; the oils can burn skin. Avoid touching your face.
1 quesadilla: 301 cal., 12g fat (5g sat. fat), 17mg chol., 454mg sod., 38g carb. (5g sugars, 3g fiber), 11g pro. **Diabetic exchanges:** 2 starch, 1 medium-fat meat, 1 vegetable, ½ fat.

SUMMER TURKEY KABOBS

These kabobs let you enjoy Thanksgiving flavors any time of the year! We like grilling and serving them outdoors in summer.

—Angela Mathews, Fayetteville, NY

Takes: 30 min. • **Makes:** 6 kabobs

- 2 small yellow summer squash
- 2 small zucchini
- 1 can (about 15 oz.) whole potatoes, drained
- 2 Tbsp. olive oil
- 1 pkg. (20 oz.) turkey breast tenderloins
- ½ tsp. pepper
- ¼ tsp. salt
- 1 pkg. (5 oz.) torn mixed salad greens
- 1 cup salad croutons
- ½ cup red wine vinaigrette

1. Trim ends of the yellow squash and zucchini; cut crosswise into 1-in. slices. Place slices in a large bowl; add potatoes. Pour oil over mixture, tossing to coat.

2. Cut turkey into 24 cubes; add to the vegetables. Sprinkle with pepper and salt; toss again.

3. On 6 metal or soaked wooden skewers, alternately thread turkey cubes, squash, zucchini and potatoes. Grill, covered, over medium heat, turning occasionally, until turkey is no longer pink and vegetables are crisp-tender, 12-15 minutes. Serve kabobs on greens with croutons. Drizzle with red wine vinaigrette.

1 kabob: 274 cal., 13g fat (1g sat. fat), 38mg chol., 720mg sod., 15g carb. (3g sugars, 2g fiber), 26g pro. **Diabetic exchanges:** 2 lean meat, 1 vegetable, 1 fat, ½ starch.

GRILLED THREE-POTATO SALAD
(PICTURED ON P. 179)

Everyone in our extended family loves to cook, so I put together all of our favorite recipes in a cookbook to be handed down from generation to generation. This recipe comes from the cookbook. It's a delicious twist on traditional potato salad.

—Suzette Jury, Keene, CA

Prep: 25 min. + cooling • **Grill:** 10 min.
Makes: 6 servings

- ¾ lb. Yukon Gold potatoes
- ¾ lb. red potatoes
- 1 medium sweet potato, peeled
- ½ cup thinly sliced green onions
- ¼ cup canola oil
- 2 to 3 Tbsp. white wine vinegar
- 1 Tbsp. Dijon mustard
- 1 tsp. salt
- ½ tsp. celery seed
- ¼ tsp. pepper

1. Place the potatoes and sweet potato in a Dutch oven; cover with water. Bring to a boil. Reduce heat; cover and simmer for 15-20 minutes or until tender. Drain and cool. Cut into 1-in. chunks.

2. Place the potatoes in a grill wok or basket. Grill, uncovered, over medium heat for 8-12 minutes or until browned and tender, stirring frequently. Transfer to a large salad bowl; add onions.

3. Whisk the oil, vinegar, mustard, salt, celery seed and pepper. Drizzle over potato mixture and toss to coat. Serve warm or at room temperature.

Note: If you do not have a grill wok or basket, use a disposable foil pan. Poke holes in the bottom of the pan with a meat fork to allow liquid to drain.

¾ cup: 191 cal., 10g fat (1g sat. fat), 0 chol., 466mg sod., 24g carb. (3g sugars, 3g fiber), 3g pro. **Diabetic exchanges:** 2 fat, 1½ starch.

SUMMER TURKEY KABOBS

GRILLED CABBAGE

I don't really like cabbage, but when I fixed this recipe, I couldn't believe how good it was. We threw some burgers on the grill and our dinner was complete. I never thought I'd skip dessert because I was full from eating too much cabbage—but I did.
—Elizabeth Wheeler, Thornville, OH

Takes: 30 min. • **Makes:** 8 servings

- 1 medium head cabbage (about 1½ lbs.)
- ⅓ cup butter, softened
- ¼ cup chopped onion
- ½ tsp. garlic salt
- ¼ tsp. pepper

1. Cut cabbage into 8 wedges; place on a double thickness of heavy-duty foil (about 24x12 in.). Spread cut sides with butter. Sprinkle cabbage with onion, garlic salt and pepper.
2. Fold foil around cabbage and seal tightly. Grill, covered, over medium heat for 20 minutes or until tender. Open foil carefully to allow steam to escape.

1 wedge: 98 cal., 8g fat (5g sat. fat), 20mg chol., 188mg sod., 7g carb. (4g sugars, 3g fiber), 2g pro. **Diabetic exchanges:** 1½ fat, 1 vegetable.

TACOS ON A STICK

TACOS ON A STICK

Kids like assembling these kabobs almost as much as they like devouring them. The whole family is sure to enjoy this sensational twist on a taco-night favorite.
—Dixie Terry, Goreville, IL

Prep: 15 min. + marinating • **Grill:** 15 min.
Makes: 6 servings

- 1 envelope taco seasoning
- 1 cup tomato juice
- 2 Tbsp. canola oil
- 2 lbs. beef top sirloin steak, cut into 1-in. cubes
- 1 medium green pepper, cut into chunks
- 1 medium sweet red pepper, cut into chunks
- 1 large onion, cut into wedges
- 16 cherry tomatoes
  Salsa con queso or sour cream, optional

1. In a large shallow dish, combine the taco seasoning, tomato juice and oil; mix well. Remove ½ cup for basting; refrigerate. Add beef and turn to coat. Cover; refrigerate for at least 5 hours.
2. Drain and discard marinade from beef. On metal or soaked wooden skewers, alternately thread beef, peppers, onion and tomatoes. Grill, uncovered, over medium heat for 3 minutes on each side. Baste with reserved marinade. Continue turning and basting for 8-10 minutes or until meat reaches desired doneness. If desired, serve with salsa con queso or sour cream.

1 serving: 277 cal., 10g fat (3g sat. fat), 61mg chol., 665mg sod., 12g carb. (4g sugars, 2g fiber), 34g pro. **Diabetic exchanges:** 4 lean meat, 2 vegetable, 1 fat.

BALSAMIC GRILLED VEGETABLE & BARLEY SALAD

This side dish is both unique and delicious. The barley is a tasty alternative to rice, and the balsamic glaze complements the grilled vegetables perfectly. Make it even better when you use veggies straight out of the garden.
—Carly Curtin, Ellicott City, MD

Prep: 25 min. + marinating • **Grill:** 10 min.
Makes: 9 servings

- 2 Tbsp. olive oil
- ¼ tsp. salt
- 1¼ cups balsamic vinegar, divided
- 3 medium yellow summer squash, quartered and cut into 1-in. slices
- 3 medium zucchini, quartered and cut into 1-in. slices
- 2 cups grape tomatoes, halved
- 1 Tbsp. brown sugar
- 1 Tbsp. honey
- 2 fresh thyme sprigs
- 1 fresh rosemary sprig
- ½ tsp. garlic powder
- 1¾ cups reduced-sodium chicken broth
- 1 cup quick-cooking barley
- 2 Tbsp. minced fresh basil or 2 tsp. dried basil

1. In a large shallow bowl, combine the oil, salt and ¼ cup of vinegar. Add the yellow squash, zucchini and tomatoes; turn to coat. Cover; refrigerate for up to 4 hours.

2. In a small saucepan, combine the brown sugar, honey, thyme, rosemary, garlic powder and remaining vinegar. Bring to a boil; cook until liquid is reduced by half. Discard thyme and rosemary; set glaze aside.

3. In a large saucepan, bring broth to a boil. Stir in barley. Reduce heat; cover and simmer for 10-12 minutes or until barley is tender.

4. Meanwhile, drain the vegetables and discard marinade. Place vegetables in a grill wok or basket. Grill, uncovered, over medium heat for 8-12 minutes or until tender, stirring frequently and brushing occasionally with glaze.

5. Remove barley from the heat; let stand for 5 minutes. Transfer to a large serving bowl. Add vegetables and basil; toss to coat. Serve warm with a slotted spoon.

Note: If you do not have a grill wok or basket, use a disposable foil pan. Poke holes in the bottom of the pan with a meat fork to allow liquid to drain.

¾ cup: 145 cal., 2g fat (0 sat. fat), 0 chol., 154mg sod., 29g carb. (12g sugars, 5g fiber), 5g pro. **Diabetic exchanges:** 1½ starch, 1 vegetable.

BALSAMIC GRILLED VEGETABLE & BARLEY SALAD

GRILLED VEGGIE WRAPS

The key to this recipe's success is the three-cheese spread. My father is a meat-and-potatoes man, but he really liked these wraps.
—Britani Sepanski, Indianapolis, IN

Prep: 15 min. + marinating • **Grill:** 15 min.
Makes: 4 servings

- 2 Tbsp. balsamic vinegar
- 1½ tsp. minced fresh basil
- 1½ tsp. olive oil
- 1½ tsp. molasses
- ¾ tsp. minced fresh thyme
- ⅛ tsp. salt
- ⅛ tsp. pepper
- 1 medium zucchini, cut lengthwise into ¼-in. slices
- 1 medium sweet red pepper, cut into 1-in. pieces
- 1 medium red onion, cut into ½-in. slices
- 4 oz. whole fresh mushrooms, cut into ½-in. pieces
- 4 oz. fresh sugar snap peas
- ½ cup crumbled feta cheese
- 3 Tbsp. reduced-fat cream cheese
- 2 Tbsp. grated Parmesan cheese
- 1 Tbsp. reduced-fat mayonnaise
- 4 flour tortillas (8 in.)
- 4 romaine leaves

1. In a large shallow dish, combine the first 7 ingredients; add vegetables and turn to coat. Cover; refrigerate for 2 hours, turning once.
2. Drain and reserve marinade, setting aside 1 tsp. for tortillas. Transfer the vegetables to a grill wok or basket. Grill, uncovered, over medium-high heat for 5 minutes. Turn or stir vegetables; baste with remaining marinade. Grill 5-8 minutes longer or until tender, stirring frequently.
3. In a small bowl, combine cheeses and mayonnaise; set aside. Brush one side of each tortilla with reserved marinade. Place tortillas, marinade side down, on grill for 1-3 minutes or until lightly toasted.
4. Spread 3 tablespoons of the cheese mixture over ungrilled side of each tortilla. Top with romaine leaf and 1 cup of grilled vegetables; roll up.
1 serving: 332 cal., 14g fat (6g sat. fat), 26mg chol., 632mg sod., 39g carb. (9g sugars, 4g fiber), 13g pro. **Diabetic exchanges:** 2 starch, 2 vegetable, 2 fat.

GRILLED BUTTERMILK CHICKEN

GRILLED BUTTERMILK CHICKEN

I created this recipe years ago after one of our farmers market customers, a chef, shared the idea of marinating chicken in buttermilk. The chicken is easy to prepare and always turns out moist and delicious. I bruise the thyme sprigs by twisting them before adding to the buttermilk mixture; this tends to release the oils in the leaves and flavor the chicken better.
—Sue Gronholz, Beaver Dam, WI

Prep: 10 min. + marinating • **Grill:** 10 min.
Makes: 12 servings

- 1½ cups buttermilk
- 4 fresh thyme sprigs
- 4 garlic cloves, halved
- ½ tsp. salt
- 12 boneless skinless chicken breast halves (about 4½ lbs.)

1. Place the buttermilk, thyme, garlic and salt in a large bowl or shallow dish. Add chicken and turn to coat. Refrigerate 8 hours or overnight, turning occasionally.
2. Drain chicken, discarding marinade. Grill, covered, over medium heat until a thermometer reads 165°, 5-7 minutes per side.
1 chicken breast half: 189 cal., 4g fat (1g sat. fat), 95mg chol., 168mg sod., 1g carb. (1g sugars, 0 fiber), 35g pro.
Diabetic exchanges: 5 lean meat.

SPICY GRILLED BROCCOLI

My kids eat this spiced broccoli without cheese; it's that good. It transports easily to the beach, park or tailgate party, and it also works on an indoor grill.
—Kathy Lewis-Martinez, Spring Valley, CA

Prep: 20 min. standing • **Grill:** 10 min.
Makes: 6 servings

2 bunches broccoli

MARINADE
- ½ cup olive oil
- ¼ cup cider vinegar
- 1 tsp. onion powder
- 1 tsp. garlic powder
- 1 tsp. smoked paprika
- ½ tsp. salt
- ½ tsp. crushed red pepper flakes
- ¼ tsp. pepper

1. Cut each broccoli bunch into 6 pieces. In a 6-qt. stockpot, place a steamer basket over 1 in. of water. Place the broccoli in basket. Bring water to a boil. Reduce heat to maintain a simmer; steam, covered, 4-6 minutes or until crisp-tender.
2. In a large bowl, whisk the marinade ingredients until blended. Add broccoli; gently toss to coat. Let stand, covered, 15 minutes.
3. Drain broccoli, reserving marinade. Grill broccoli, covered, over medium heat or broil 4 in. from heat 6-8 minutes or until broccoli is tender, turning once. If desired, serve with reserved marinade.
2 pieces: 122 cal., 6g fat (1g sat. fat), 0 chol., 135mg sod., 15g carb. (4g sugars, 6g fiber), 6g pro. **Diabetic exchanges:** 2 vegetable, 1 fat.

ZIPPY SHRIMP SKEWERS

These flavorful skewers deliver a mouthwatering kick with minimal effort. Fix them for your next party and watch them disappear.
—Jalayne Luckett, Marion, IL

Prep: 10 min. + marinating • **Grill:** 5 min.
Makes: 6 servings

- 2 Tbsp. brown sugar
- 2 tsp. cider vinegar
- 1½ tsp. canola oil
- 1 tsp. chili powder
- ½ tsp. salt
- ½ tsp. paprika
- ¼ tsp. hot pepper sauce
- ¾ lb. uncooked medium shrimp, peeled and deveined

1. In a large shallow dish, combine the first 7 ingredients; add shrimp. Turn to coat; cover and refrigerate for 2-4 hours.
2. Drain and discard marinade. Thread shrimp onto 6 metal or soaked wooden skewers. Grill, uncovered, on a lightly oiled rack over medium heat or broil 4 in. from the heat until the shrimp turn pink, about 2-3 minutes on each side.
1 skewer: 57 cal., 1g fat (0 sat. fat), 84mg chol., 199mg sod., 2g carb. (2g sugars, 0 fiber), 9g pro. **Diabetic exchanges:** 1 lean meat.

SPICY GRILLED BROCCOLI

SWEET & SMOKY SALSA

covered with water. Bring to a boil; process 15 minutes. Remove jars and cool.
Note: Wear disposable gloves when cutting hot peppers; the oils can burn skin. Avoid touching your face. If you do not have a grilling grid, use a disposable foil pan. Poke holes in the bottom of the pan with a meat fork to allow liquid to drain.

¼ cup: 49 cal., 0 fat (0 sat. fat), 0 chol., 180mg sod., 11g carb. (9g sugars, 1g fiber), 1g pro. **Diabetic exchanges:** ½ starch.

BACON-CORN STUFFED PEPPERS

These grilled pepper halves filled with corn, salsa, green onions, mozzarella cheese and bacon are sure to liven up your next cookout. With a wonderful flavor they give a fancy twist to the old standby corn on the cob.
—Mitzi Sentiff, Annapolis, MD

Prep: 20 min. • **Grill:** 25 min.
Makes: 4 servings

- 2 cups frozen corn, thawed
- ⅓ cup salsa
- 6 green onions, chopped
- 1 medium green pepper, halved and seeded
- 1 medium sweet red pepper, halved and seeded
- ¼ cup shredded part-skim mozzarella cheese
- 2 bacon strips, cooked and crumbled
  Additional salsa, optional

1. In a large bowl, combine the corn, salsa and onions. Spoon into pepper halves. Place each stuffed pepper half on a piece of heavy-duty foil (about 18x12 in.). Fold foil around peppers and seal tightly.
2. Grill, covered, over medium heat until peppers are crisp-tender, 25-30 minutes. Carefully open packets to allow steam to escape. Sprinkle with cheese and bacon. Return to the grill until cheese is melted, 3-5 minutes. If desired serve peppers with additional salsa.

1 stuffed pepper half: 130 cal., 4g fat (1g sat. fat), 9mg chol., 207mg sod., 21g carb. (5g sugars, 3g fiber), 6g pro. **Diabetic exchanges:** 1 starch, 1 vegetable, ½ fat.

SWEET & SMOKY SALSA

I love the roasted flavor that comes from grilling, so I decided to make a salsa from grilled vegetables. I think this recipe would also taste great using only plum tomatoes instead of a tomatillo blend. If you don't have wood chips for smoking on the grill, you might add a little liquid smoke to the salsa as it cooks.
—Shelly Bevington, Hermiston, OR

Prep: 1 hour • **Process:** 15 min.
Makes: 4 pints

- 1 cup soaked mesquite wood chips
- 2 medium onions
- 12 garlic cloves, peeled
- 3 tsp. barbecue seasoning, divided
- 2 lbs. tomatillos, husks removed (about 12)
- 2 lbs. plum tomatoes (about 8)
- 6 jalapeno peppers
- 1½ cups cider vinegar
- 1¼ cups packed brown sugar
- 1½ tsp. salt
- ½ tsp. pepper
- ⅓ cup minced fresh cilantro

1. Add wood chips to grill according to manufacturer's directions.
2. Cut onions into quarters; place in a small bowl. Add the garlic and 1½ tsp. barbecue seasoning; toss to coat. Arrange on a grilling grid; place on greased grill rack. Grill onions, covered, over medium heat 10-15 minutes or until tender, turning occasionally.
3. Meanwhile, cut tomatillos, tomatoes and jalapenos in half; place in a large bowl. Add remaining barbecue seasoning; toss to coat. Grill in batches, covered, over medium heat 4-6 minutes or until tender, turning occasionally.
4. When cool enough to handle, chop vegetables. Transfer to a Dutch oven; stir in vinegar, brown sugar, salt and pepper. Bring to a boil. Reduce the heat; simmer, uncovered, 15-20 minutes or until slightly thickened. Immediately stir in cilantro.
5. Carefully ladle hot mixture into 4 hot 1-pint jars, leaving ½-in. of headspace. Remove air bubbles and adjust headspace, if necessary, by adding hot mixture. Wipe rims. Center lids on jars; screw on bands until fingertip tight.
6. Place jars into canner with simmering water, ensuring that they are completely

WHITE BALSAMIC BLUEBERRY, CORN, & FETA SALAD

WHITE BALSAMIC BLUEBERRY, CORN, & FETA SALAD

I'm not typically a huge fan of summer corn, but when it comes to this sweet, salty, refreshing salad, I can't put my fork down.

Try different types of white balsamic vinegar. A favorite of mine is one with a pomegranate quince flavor.
—Colleen Delawder, Herndon, VA

Prep: 30 min. + soaking • **Grill:** 20 min.
Makes: 10 servings

- 8 medium ears sweet corn
- 3 Tbsp. olive oil
- 3 Tbsp. white balsamic vinegar
- 1 Tbsp. minced fresh chives, plus more for garnish
- ¾ tsp. kosher salt
- ¼ tsp. pepper
- 1 cup fresh blueberries
- ½ cup crumbled feta cheese

1. Carefully peel back corn husks to within 1 in. of bottoms; remove silk. Rewrap corn in husks; secure with kitchen string. Place in a stockpot; cover with cold water. Soak 20 minutes; drain.
2. Grill corn, covered, over medium heat about 20 minutes or until tender, turning often. Cut string and peel back husks. Cool slightly. Cut corn from cobs; transfer to a large bowl.
3. In a small bowl, whisk the oil, vinegar, chives, salt and pepper. Pour over corn; toss to coat. Gently fold in blueberries and feta. Garnish with additional chives as desired.

¾ cup: 133 cal., 6g fat (1g sat. fat), 3mg chol., 210mg sod., 19g carb. (8g sugars, 2g fiber), 4g pro. **Diabetic exchanges:** 1 starch, 1 fat.

TEST KITCHEN TIP

If you don't have white balsamic vinegar, you can use traditional balsamic vinegar instead, but the corn and feta will take on some of that darker color.

HERBED PORK CHOPS
(PICTURED ON P. 178)

Herbs are a fast and flavorful way to dress up pork chops. I prepare these year-round as a way to capture the taste of summer.
—Dianne Esposite, New Middletown, OH

Takes: 20 min. • **Makes:** 4 servings

- 4 boneless pork loin chops (4 oz. each)
- 2 tsp. lemon juice
- 2 Tbsp. chopped fresh parsley
- ½ tsp. dried rosemary, crushed
- ½ tsp. dried thyme, crushed
- ¼ tsp. pepper

1. Sprinkle pork chops with lemon juice. Combine the parsley, rosemary, thyme and pepper; rub over chops.
2. Grill, covered, over medium heat for 4-5 minutes on each side or until a thermometer reads 145°. Let stand for 5 minutes before serving.

1 pork chop: 154 cal., 6g fat (2g sat. fat), 55mg chol., 33mg sod., 1g carb. (0 sugars, 0 fiber), 22g pro. **Diabetic exchanges:** 3 lean meat.

GRILLED STEAK PINWHEELS

I've been serving this dish to family and friends for 20 years and seldom have any leftovers. We try to keep the house cool, so we grill out often. I get most of the herbs in this recipe from my son's garden.
—Rhonda Knight, Scottsdale, AZ

Prep: 25 min. •**Grill:** 10 min.
Makes: 8 servings

- 2 beef flank steaks (1 lb. each), trimmed
- ½ lb. bacon strips, cooked and crumbled
- 1 cup finely chopped fresh mushrooms
- 1 cup finely chopped green onions
- ¼ cup finely chopped fresh basil or 4 tsp. dried basil
- 2 Tbsp. minced chives

1. Flatten steaks to ¼-in. thickness. In a large bowl, combine the bacon, mushrooms, onions, basil and chives; spread evenly over steaks.
2. Roll meat up and secure with skewers or toothpicks. Cut each roll into ½-¾-in. slices and secure with a toothpick.
3. Grill pinwheels over medium-hot heat for 4-6 minutes on each side until meat reaches desired doneness (for medium-rare, a thermometer should read 135°; medium, 140°; medium-well, 145°). Remove toothpicks.
2 pinwheels: 224 cal., 12g fat (5g sat. fat), 64mg chol., 250mg sod., 1g carb. (0 sugars, 0 fiber), 26g pro. **Diabetic exchanges:** 3 medium-fat meat.

JUICY TURKEY BURGERS
(PICTURED ON P. 179)

My husband enjoys these grilled turkey burgers with their herb flavor and garden-fresh garnish. They make an ideal summer sandwich.
—Trina Hopsecger, Elkhart, IN

Takes: 25 min. • **Makes:** 6 servings

- 1 medium apple, peeled and finely shredded
- ½ cup cooked brown rice
- 2 Tbsp. grated onion
- 2 garlic cloves, minced
- 1½ tsp. rubbed sage
- 1 tsp. salt
- ½ tsp. pepper
- ½ tsp. dried thyme
- ¼ tsp. ground allspice
- ¼ tsp. cayenne pepper
- 1 lb. lean ground turkey
- 2 Tbsp. minced fresh parsley
- 6 whole wheat hamburger buns, split
- 6 lettuce leaves
- 6 tomato slices

1. In a large bowl, combine the first 10 ingredients. Crumble turkey over the mixture and mix well. Shape into six ½-in.-thick patties.
2. Lightly grease grill rack. Prepare grill for indirect heat.
3. Grill burgers, covered, over indirect medium heat or broil 4 in. from the heat for 6-7 minutes on each side or until a thermometer reads 165° and juices run clear. Sprinkle with parsley. Serve on buns with lettuce and tomato.
1 serving: 265 cal., 9g fat (2g sat. fat), 60mg chol., 663mg sod., 28g carb. (0 sugars, 3g fiber), 18g pro. **Diabetic exchanges:** 2 starch, 2 lean meat.

GRILLED STEAK PINWHEELS

CAJUN GRILLED SHRIMP
(PICTURED ON P. 178)

I love to try new recipes for my husband and me, and also when we entertain—which is often. I collect recipes and cookbooks from all over the world, and I actually use them daily. When I find a winning recipe like this party-worthy shrimp, I put a copy of it in a clear plastic sleeve and file it one of my many three-ring recipe binders.
—Sharon Delaney-Chronis,
South Milwaukee, WI

Takes: 30 min. • **Makes:** 6 servings

- 3 green onions, finely chopped
- 2 Tbsp. lemon juice
- 1 Tbsp. olive oil
- 3 garlic cloves, minced
- 2 tsp. paprika
- 1 tsp. salt
- ¼ tsp. pepper
- ¼ tsp. cayenne pepper
- 2 lbs. uncooked medium shrimp, peeled and deveined with tails on
- 4 medium lemons, each cut into 8 wedges

1. In a large shallow dish, combine the first 8 ingredients. Add shrimp and turn to coat. Cover; refrigerate for 15 minutes.
2. Drain shrimp, discarding marinade. On 12 metal or soaked wooden skewers, thread the shrimp and the lemon wedges.
3. Grill, covered, over medium heat or broil 4 in. from the heat until shrimp turn pink, turning once, 6-8 minutes.
2 skewers: 168 cal., 5g fat (1g sat. fat), 184mg chol., 575mg sod., 7g carb. (1g sugars, 2g fiber), 25g pro. **Diabetic exchanges:** 3 lean meat, ½ fruit, ½ fat.

GRILLED SUMMER VEGETABLE & COUSCOUS SALAD

This healthy salad features the eggplant, peppers and herbs we manage to grow in pots and a raised bed at our small condo. Feel free to add a little crumbled goat cheese or tangy feta.
—Patricia Levenson, Santa Ana, CA

Prep: 35 min. • **Grill:** 10 min.
Makes: 10 servings

- ½ cup olive oil
- ⅓ cup balsamic vinegar

GRILLED SUMMER VEGETABLE & COUSCOUS SALAD

- 4 tsp. capers, drained
- 4 tsp. lemon juice
- 2 garlic cloves, minced
- ¾ tsp. Dijon mustard
- 1¼ tsp. minced fresh rosemary or ½ tsp. dried rosemary, crushed
- 1¼ tsp. minced fresh thyme or ½ tsp. dried thyme
- ⅛ tsp. salt
- ⅛ tsp. pepper

SALAD

- 1 pkg. (10 oz.) uncooked couscous
- 2 medium zucchini or yellow summer squash, halved lengthwise
- 2 medium sweet yellow or red peppers, quartered
- 1 Japanese eggplant, halved lengthwise
- 2 Tbsp. olive oil
- ¼ tsp. salt
- ¼ tsp. pepper
- 1 cup grape tomatoes, halved
- ½ cup Greek olives, pitted and sliced
- 1 Tbsp. minced fresh parsley or 1 tsp. dried parsley flakes
- 1 Tbsp. minced fresh basil or 1 tsp. dried basil

1. In a small bowl, whisk the first 10 ingredients. Refrigerate until serving.
2. Cook couscous according to package directions. Meanwhile, brush the zucchini, yellow peppers and eggplant with oil; sprinkle with salt and pepper. Grill, covered, over medium heat until crisp-tender, 10-12 minutes, turning once.
3. Chop grilled vegetables; place in a large bowl. Add the tomatoes, olives, parsley, basil and couscous. Pour dressing over salad and toss to coat. Serve salad warm or chilled.
¾ cup: 272 cal., 16g fat (2g sat. fat), 0 chol., 244mg sod., 29g carb. (5g sugars, 3g fiber), 5g pro. **Diabetic exchanges:** 2 fat, 1½ starch, 1 vegetable.

TEST KITCHEN TIP

Since this can be served warm or chilled, it's a great make-and-take for potlucks and picnics.

GRILLED GUACAMOLE

If you're a guacamole lover, try this version where grilling gives it a smoky flavor. The veggies tend to darken a bit when heated, so stir the guacamole gently to prevent further discoloration.
—Lindsay Sprunk, Brooklyn, NY

Prep: 10 min. • **Grill:** 10 min. + cooling
Makes: 12 servings

- 1 medium red onion, cut into ½-in. slices
- 2 plum tomatoes, halved and seeded
- 1 jalapeno pepper, halved and seeded
- 2 Tbsp. canola oil, divided
- 3 medium ripe avocados, halved and pitted
- ¼ cup fresh cilantro leaves, chopped
- 2 Tbsp. lime juice
- 2 tsp. ground cumin
- ¾ tsp. salt
  Tortilla chips

1. In a large bowl, combine the onion, tomatoes, pepper and 1 Tbsp. oil; gently toss to coat. Grill, covered, over medium-high heat or broil 4 in. from heat for 6-8 minutes or until tender and charred, turning occasionally. Brush avocados with remaining oil. Grill or broil avocados, cut side down, 4-6 minutes or until charred. Cool vegetables completely.
2. Chop onion, tomatoes and pepper; set aside. Peel avocados; transfer to a large bowl and mash with a fork. Stir in grilled vegetables, cilantro, lime juice, cumin and salt. Serve immediately with chips.
Note: Wear disposable gloves when cutting hot peppers; the oils can burn skin. Avoid touching your face.
¼ cup: 85 cal., 8g fat (1g sat. fat), 0 chol., 152mg sod., 5g carb. (1g sugars, 3g fiber), 1g pro. **Diabetic exchanges:** 1½ fat.

GRILLED GUACAMOLE

GRILLED ANGEL FOOD CAKE WITH FRUIT SALSA

When I need dessert fast, I go with angel food cake. Mix fruit salsa ahead of time, and pop the cake on the grill.
—Glorimar Jimenez, Indianapolis, IN

Takes: 15 min. • **Makes:** 6 servings

- ½ cup each fresh raspberries, blueberries and chopped strawberries
- 1 medium kiwifruit, peeled and chopped
- 2 Tbsp. sugar
- 1 Tbsp. lime juice
- 1 loaf-shaped angel food cake (10½ oz.), split horizontally
  Whipped topping, optional

1. In a small bowl, combine berries, kiwi, sugar and lime juice.
2. Grill cake, cut side down, over medium heat or broil 4 in. from heat 1-3 minutes or until lightly browned. Cut into slices. Serve with the fruit salsa and, if desired, whipped topping.
1 slice with ¼ cup salsa: 169 cal., 1g fat (0 sat. fat), 0 chol., 372mg sod., 39g carb. (30g sugars, 2g fiber), 3g pro.

TRIPLE TOMATO FLATBREAD

TRIPLE TOMATO FLATBREAD

Tomatoes are the reason I have a vegetable garden, and I developed this recipe as a way to show off my garden's plum, sun-dried and cherry tomatoes. It's easy and is sure to impress.

—Rachel Kimbrow, Portland, OR

Takes: 20 min. • **Makes:** 8 pieces

- 1 tube (13.8 oz.) refrigerated pizza crust
  Cooking spray
- 3 plum tomatoes, finely chopped (about 2 cups)
- ½ cup soft sun-dried tomato halves (not packed in oil), julienned
- 2 Tbsp. olive oil
- 1 Tbsp. dried basil
- ¼ tsp. salt
- ¼ tsp. pepper
- 1 cup shredded Asiago cheese
- 2 cups yellow and/or red cherry tomatoes, halved

1. Unroll and press dough into a 15x10-in. rectangle. Transfer dough to an 18x12-in. piece of heavy-duty foil coated with cooking spray; spritz dough with cooking spray. In a large bowl, toss plum tomatoes and sun-dried tomatoes with the oil and the seasonings.

2. Carefully invert dough onto grill rack; remove foil. Grill, covered, over medium heat 2-3 minutes or until bottom is golden brown. Turn; grill 1-2 minutes longer or until second side begins to brown.

3. Remove from grill. Spoon plum tomato mixture over crust; top with cheese and cherry tomatoes. Return flatbread to grill. Grill, covered, 2-4 minutes or until crust is golden brown and cheese is melted.

To bake flatbread: Preheat oven to 425°. Unroll and press the dough onto the bottom of a 15x10x1-in. baking pan coated with cooking spray. Bake for about 6-8 minutes or until lightly browned. Assemble the flatbread as directed. Bake 8-10 minutes longer or until the crust is golden and cheese is melted.

1 piece: 235 cal., 9g fat (3g sat. fat), 12mg chol., 476mg sod., 29g carb. (7g sugars, 3g fiber), 8g pro. **Diabetic exchanges:** 1½ starch, 1½ fat, 1 vegetable.

GRILLED STEAK & MUSHROOM SALAD

GRILLED STEAK & MUSHROOM SALAD

My husband loves this salad, especially during summertime. He says he feels as if he's eating a healthy salad and getting his steak, too! I always serve it with some great homemade bread.

—Julie Cashion, Sanford, FL

Takes: 30 min. • **Makes:** 6 servings

- 6 Tbsp. olive oil, divided
- 2 Tbsp. Dijon mustard, divided
- ½ tsp. salt
- ¼ tsp. pepper
- 1 beef top sirloin steak (1½ lbs.)
- 1 lb. sliced fresh mushrooms
- ¼ cup red wine vinegar
- 1 medium bunch romaine, torn

1. Whisk 1 Tbsp. oil, 1 Tbsp. mustard, salt and pepper; set aside.

2. Grill steak, covered, over medium-hot heat for 4 minutes. Turn; spread with mustard mixture. Grill 4 minutes longer or until meat reaches desired doneness (for medium-rare, a thermometer should read 135°; medium, 140°; medium-well, 145°).

3. Meanwhile, in a large skillet, cook the mushrooms in 1 Tbsp. oil until tender. Stir in the vinegar and the remaining oil and mustard.

4. Thinly slice steak across the grain; add to mushroom mixture. Serve immediately over romaine.

1 serving: 299 cal., 20g fat (4g sat. fat), 63mg chol., 378mg sod., 6g carb. (1g sugars, 2g fiber), 25g pro.

**GRILLED GARDEN
VEGGIE PIZZA**

GRILLED GARDEN
VEGGIE PIZZA

Pile on the veggies—this crisp, grilled crust can take it! This colorful, healthy pizza looks as fresh as it tastes.

—Diane Halferty, Corpus Christi, TX

Takes: 30 min. • **Makes:** 6 servings

- 1 **medium red onion, cut crosswise into ½-in. slices**
- 1 **large sweet red pepper, halved, stemmed and seeded**
- 1 **small zucchini, cut lengthwise into ½-in. slices**
- 1 **yellow summer squash, cut lengthwise into ½-in. slices**

- 2 **Tbsp. olive oil**
- ½ **tsp. salt**
- ¼ **tsp. pepper**
- 1 **prebaked 12-in. thin whole wheat pizza crust**
- 3 **Tbsp. jarred roasted minced garlic**
- 2 **cups shredded part-skim mozzarella cheese, divided**
- ⅓ **cup torn fresh basil**

1. Brush vegetables with oil; sprinkle with salt and pepper. Grill, covered, over medium heat until tender, 4-5 minutes per side for onion and pepper, 3-4 minutes per side for zucchini and squash.

2. Separate onion into rings; cut pepper into strips. Spread pizza crust with garlic; sprinkle with 1 cup cheese. Top with grilled vegetables, then remaining cheese.

3. Grill pizza, covered, over medium heat until bottom is golden brown and cheese is melted, 5-7 minutes. Top with basil.

1 slice: 324 cal., 15g fat (6g sat. fat), 24mg chol., 704mg sod., 30g carb. (5g sugars, 5g fiber), 16g pro. **Diabetic exchanges:** 2 starch, 2 medium-fat meat, 1 fat.

CHICKEN WITH PEACH-AVOCADO SALSA

This super fresh dinner is pure summer—juicy peaches, creamy avocado, grilled chicken and a kick of hot sauce and lime. To get it on the table even quicker, make the salsa ahead of time.
—Shannon Norris, Cudahy, WI

Takes: 30 min. • **Makes:** 4 servings

- 1 medium peach, peeled and chopped
- 1 medium ripe avocado, peeled and cubed
- ½ cup chopped sweet red pepper
- 3 Tbsp. finely chopped red onion
- 1 Tbsp. minced fresh basil
- 1 Tbsp. lime juice
- 1 tsp. hot pepper sauce
- ½ tsp. grated lime zest
- ¾ tsp. salt, divided
- ½ tsp. pepper, divided
- 4 boneless skinless chicken breast halves (6 oz. each)

1. For salsa, in a small bowl, combine peaches, avocado, red pepper, onion, basil, lime juice, hot sauce, lime peel, ¼ tsp. salt and ¼ tsp. pepper.
2. Sprinkle chicken with remaining salt and pepper. On a lightly greased grill rack, grill chicken, covered, over medium heat 5 minutes. Turn; grill until a thermometer reads 165°, about 7-9 minutes longer. Serve with salsa.

1 chicken breast half with ½ cup salsa: 265 cal., 9g fat (2g sat. fat), 94mg chol., 536mg sod., 9g carb. (4g sugars, 3g fiber), 36g pro.
Diabetic exchanges: 5 lean meat, 1 fat, ½ starch.

CHICKEN WITH PEACH-AVOCADO SALSA

EASY GRILLED SQUASH

This is one of my favorite ways to use butternut squash, which I love not just for its flavor but also because it's full of vitamin A. I usually make this when I am grilling steak or chicken.
—Esther Horst, Monterey, TN

Takes: 20 min. • **Makes:** 4 servings

- 3 Tbsp. olive oil
- 2 garlic cloves, minced
- ¼ tsp. salt
- ¼ tsp. pepper
- 1 small butternut squash, peeled and cut lengthwise into ½-in. slices

1. In a small bowl, combine the oil, garlic, salt and pepper. Brush over squash slices.
2. Grill squash, covered, over medium heat or broil 4 in. from the heat for 4-5 minutes on each side or until tender.

2 slices: 178 cal., 10g fat (1g sat. fat), 0 chol., 156mg sod., 23g carb. (5g sugars, 7g fiber), 2g pro. **Diabetic exchanges:** 1½ starch, 1½ fat.

DAN'S PEPPERY LONDON BROIL

I was bored making the usual London broil, so I got a little creative and sparked up the flavor.

—Dan Wright, San Jose, CA

Prep: 5 min. + marinating • **Grill:** 10 min.
Makes: 2 servings

- 1 beef flank steak (about ¾ lb.)
- 1 garlic clove, minced
- ½ tsp. seasoned salt
- ⅛ tsp. crushed red pepper flakes
- ¼ cup Worcestershire sauce

1. With a meat fork, poke holes in both sides of meat. Make a paste with garlic, seasoned salt and red pepper flakes; rub over both sides of meat. Place the steak in a large shallow dish. Add Worcestershire sauce; turn meat. Cover and refrigerate for at least 4 hours, turning once.

2. Drain and discard the marinade. Grill, uncovered, over hot heat or broil 4 in. from the heat for 4-5 minutes on each side or until meat reaches desired doneness (for medium-rare a thermometer should read 135°; medium, 140°; medium-well, 145°). To serve, thinly slice meat across the grain.

5 oz. cooked beef: 270 cal., 12g fat (5g sat. fat), 81mg chol., 578mg sod., 5g carb. (2g sugars, 0 fiber), 33g pro. **Diabetic exchanges:** 5 lean meat.

TOMATO, AVOCADO & GRILLED CORN SALAD

TOMATO, AVOCADO & GRILLED CORN SALAD

With ripe tomatoes, fresh basil and grilled corn off the cob, this sunny salad tastes just like summertime.

—Angela Spengler, Niceville, FL

Prep: 20 min. • **Grill:** 10 min. + cooling
Makes: 8 servings

- 1 medium ear sweet corn, husks removed
- 3 large red tomatoes, sliced
- 3 large yellow tomatoes, sliced
- ¾ tsp. kosher salt, divided
- ½ tsp. pepper, divided
- 2 medium ripe avocados, peeled and sliced
- ¼ cup olive oil
- 2 Tbsp. red wine vinegar
- 1 Tbsp. minced fresh basil, plus more for garnish
- ⅓ cup crumbled feta cheese

1. Grill corn, covered, over medium heat 10-12 minutes or until lightly browned and tender, turning occasionally. Cool slightly. Cut corn from cob.

2. Arrange tomato on large serving platter. Sprinkle with ½ tsp. salt and ¼ tsp. pepper. Top with avocado slices. Whisk together the oil, vinegar, basil and the remaining salt and pepper; drizzle half over the tomatoes and avocado. Top with grilled corn and feta; drizzle remaining dressing over top. Garnish with additional chopped basil.

1 serving: 164 cal., 13g fat (2g sat. fat), 3mg chol., 237mg sod., 11g carb. (4g sugars, 4g fiber), 3g pro. **Diabetic exchanges:** 2 fat, 1 vegetable, ½ starch.

TEST KITCHEN TIP

This dish is so spectacular with fresh heirloom tomatoes. In fact, you don't need that much salt to bring out the flavors. For a quick, healthy dinner, top the salad with grilled chicken.

GINGER-GLAZED GRILLED SALMON

Our family loves salmon prepared this way, and it's a real treat to make on a warm summer evening. You can bake the fillets in the oven at 450° for 18 minutes, basting occasionally.
—Wanda Toews, Cromer, MB

....

Takes: 15 min. • **Makes:** 4 servings

- 2 Tbsp. reduced-sodium soy sauce
- 2 Tbsp. maple syrup
- 2 tsp. minced fresh gingerroot
- 2 garlic cloves, minced
- 4 salmon fillets (6 oz. each)

1. For glaze, mix first 4 ingredients.

2. Place salmon on an oiled grill rack over medium heat, skin side up. Grill, covered, until fish just begins to flake easily with a fork, 4-5 minutes per side; brush top with half of the glaze after turning. Brush with remaining glaze before serving.

1 fillet: 299 cal., 16g fat (3g sat. fat), 85mg chol., 374mg sod., 8g carb. (6g sugars, 0 fiber), 29g pro. **Diabetic exchanges:** 4 lean meat, ½ starch.

APPLE SKEWERS

We enjoy these flavorful grilled apples with a lightly spiced coating all year. Best of all, they're a cinch to grill, and cleanup's a breeze.
—Doris Sowers, Hutchinson, KS

....

Takes: 30 min. • **Makes:** 4 servings

- 4 medium apples, peeled and quartered
- 4 tsp. sugar
- 1¼ tsp. ground cinnamon

1. Thread apples on 4 metal or soaked wooden skewers. Lightly spray with cooking spray. Combine the sugar and cinnamon; sprinkle over apples.

2. Lightly oil the grill rack. Grill apples, covered, over medium heat until golden, for 6-8 minutes. Turn; cook 8-10 minutes longer or until golden and tender. Serve apples warm.

1 serving: 80 cal., 0 fat (0 sat. fat), 0 chol., 0 sod., 21g carb. (18g sugars, 2g fiber), 0 pro. **Diabetic exchanges:** 1 fruit.

GINGER-GLAZED GRILLED SALMON

SLOW-COOKED SUPPERS

"This dish always seems to develop a devoted following. Prepared sauce makes it easy to bring the rich flavors of Indian cuisine to your family. Feel free to use more or less tikka masala sauce according to your personal taste."
—Erica Polly, Sun Prairie, WI

**SLOW-COOKED
MEXICAN MEAT LOAF**

SLOW-COOKED MEXICAN MEAT LOAF

Chopped onion and garlic plus spicy seasonings add outstanding flavor to this meat loaf.
—*Taste of Home* Test Kitchen

Prep: 25 min. • **Cook:** 4 hours
Makes: 8 servings

- 6 Tbsp. ketchup, divided
- 2 Tbsp. Worcestershire sauce
- 12 saltines, crushed
- 1 medium onion, finely chopped
- 6 garlic cloves, minced
- 1 tsp. paprika
- ½ tsp. salt
- ½ tsp. pepper
- ⅛ tsp. cayenne pepper
- 2 lbs. lean ground beef (90% lean)

1. Cut three 20x3-in. strips of heavy-duty foil; crisscross so they resemble spokes of a wheel. Place strips on the bottom and up the sides of a 3-qt. slow cooker. Coat strips with cooking spray.

2. In a large bowl, combine 2 Tbsp. ketchup, Worcestershire sauce, saltines, onion, garlic, paprika, salt, pepper and cayenne. Crumble beef over mixture and mix well.

3. Shape mixture into a round loaf. Place in the center of the strips. Cover and cook on low until no pink remains and a thermometer reads 160°, 4-5 hours.

4. Using foil strips as handles, remove the meat loaf to a platter. Spread remaining ketchup over top.

1 slice: 222 cal., 10g fat (4g sat. fat), 71mg chol., 447mg sod., 10g carb. (5g sugars, 1g fiber), 23g pro. **Diabetic exchanges:** 3 lean meat, ½ starch.

BBQ PORK & PEPPERS

(PICTURED ON P. 201)

This was the first recipe I ever made in a slow cooker, and it was the first recipe my husband taught me! We like this with white rice and a salad.
—Rachael Hughes, Southampton, PA

Prep: 10 min. • **Cook:** 8 hours
Makes: 4 servings

- 4 bone-in pork loin chops (7 oz. each)
- 1 large onion, chopped
- 1 large sweet red pepper, chopped
- 1 large green pepper, chopped
- 1 cup barbecue sauce
  Chopped fresh parsley, optional

Place chops in a 4-qt. slow cooker coated with cooking spray. Top with onion, peppers and barbecue sauce. Cover and cook on low 8-10 hours or until pork is tender. If desired, top with chopped fresh parsley.

1 chop with ¾ cup vegetable mixture: 291 cal., 10g fat (3g sat. fat), 86mg chol., 638mg sod., 17g carb. (12g sugars, 3g fiber), 33g pro. **Diabetic exchanges:** 4 lean meat, 1 vegetable, ½ starch.

CREOLE CHICKEN THIGHS

Cajun seasoning adds loads of flavor and spice to this easy meal. The slow cooker does the work so you don't have to!
—Matthew Laman, Hummelstown, PA

Prep: 25 min. • **Cook:** 4 hours
Makes: 8 servings

- 1 can (16 oz.) red beans, rinsed and drained
- 1½ cups uncooked converted rice (not instant)
- 2 medium tomatoes, chopped
- 1 medium green pepper, chopped
- 2 Tbsp. minced fresh parsley
- 3¼ cups reduced-sodium chicken broth
- 1½ tsp. plus 2 Tbsp. Cajun seasoning, divided
- 8 bone-in chicken thighs (about 3 lbs.), skin removed
- 1 Tbsp. canola oil

1. In a 6-qt. slow cooker, combine the first 6 ingredients and 1½ tsp. Cajun seasoning.
2. Sprinkle chicken with remaining Cajun seasoning. In a large skillet, heat oil over medium heat; brown chicken, about 5 minutes per side. Place in slow cooker.
3. Cook, covered, on low until a thermometer inserted in chicken reads at least 170°-175°, 4-5 hours (rice will be saucy).
Note: This recipe was tested with Uncle Ben's original converted rice.
1 serving: 394 cal., 12g fat (3g sat. fat), 87mg chol., 802mg sod., 38g carb. (2g sugars, 3g fiber), 31g pro.

SLOW-COOKED COFFEE BEEF ROAST
(PICTURED ON P. 200)

Coffee is the key to this flavorful beef roast that simmers in the slow cooker until it's fall-apart tender. Try it once, and I'm sure you'll cook it again.
—Charles Trahan, San Dimas, CA

Prep: 15 min. • **Cook:** 8 hours
Makes: 6 servings

- 1 beef sirloin tip roast (2½ lbs.), cut in half
- 2 tsp. canola oil
- 1½ cups sliced fresh mushrooms
- ⅓ cup sliced green onions
- 2 garlic cloves, minced
- 1½ cups brewed coffee
- 1 tsp. liquid smoke, optional
- ½ tsp. salt
- ½ tsp. chili powder
- ¼ tsp. pepper
- ¼ cup cornstarch
- ⅓ cup cold water

1. In a large nonstick skillet, brown roast on all sides in oil over medium-high heat. Place in a 5-qt. slow cooker. In the same skillet, saute mushrooms, onions and garlic until tender; stir in the coffee, liquid smoke if desired, salt, chili powder and pepper. Pour over roast.
2. Cover and cook on low for 8-10 hours or until meat is tender. Remove roast and keep warm. Pour cooking juices into a 2-cup measuring cup; skim fat.
3. In a small saucepan, combine cornstarch and water until smooth. Gradually stir in 2 cups cooking juices. Bring to a boil; cook and stir for 2 minutes or until thickened. Serve with beef.
5 oz. cooked beef: 281 cal., 10g fat (3g sat. fat), 120mg chol., 261mg sod., 6g carb. (1g sugars, 0 fiber), 39g pro. **Diabetic exchanges:** 5 lean meat, ½ starch.

CREOLE CHICKEN THIGHS

BAYOU GULF SHRIMP GUMBO

SLOW-COOKER FLANK STEAK FAJITAS

As a busy teacher, I think it's so nice to come home to a warm meal after a day in the classroom. I'm not the only one who loves this dish: The beefy fajitas always disappear fast at potlucks.

—Mary Holmgren, Mackinaw, IL

Prep: 10 min. • **Cook:** 8 hours
Makes: 8 servings

- 1 beef flank steak (2 lbs.), halved crosswise
- 1 medium green pepper, cut into strips
- 1 medium sweet red pepper, cut into strips
- 1 medium onion, halved and sliced
- 1 envelope fajita seasoning mix
- ½ cup beer or reduced-sodium beef broth
- 8 flour tortillas (8 in.), warmed
- 1 cup pico de gallo
  Chopped fresh cilantro

1. Place the first 5 ingredients in a 5-qt. slow cooker. Pour beer over top. Cook, covered, on low until meat is tender, 6-8 hours.
2. Remove beef from slow cooker. Strain vegetable mixture; return vegetables to slow cooker. (Discard cooking juices or save for another use.) Shred beef with 2 forks; add to the vegetables and heat through. Serve in tortillas with pico de gallo and cilantro.

1 serving: 361 cal., 12g fat (4g sat. fat), 54mg chol., 668mg sod., 34g carb. (2g sugars, 3g fiber), 27g pro. **Diabetic exchanges:** 2 starch, 3 lean meat.

> **TEST KITCHEN TIP**
>
> We love adding fresh toppings to slow-cooked dishes. They add color, texture and bright flavor. That's why we chose pico de gallo instead of salsa.

BAYOU GULF SHRIMP GUMBO

This recipe skips the traditional hard-to-find spices and still delivers the true seafood flavor beloved in the Louisiana bayou and beyond.

—Wolfgang Hanau, West Palm Beach, FL

Prep: 35 min. • **Cook:** 5 hours
Makes: 6 servings

- ½ lb. bacon strips, chopped
- 3 celery ribs, chopped
- 1 medium onion, chopped
- 1 medium green pepper, chopped
- 2 garlic cloves, minced
- 2 bottles (8 oz. each) clam juice
- 1 can (14½ oz.) diced tomatoes, undrained
- 2 Tbsp. Worcestershire sauce
- 1 tsp. dried marjoram
- 2 lbs. uncooked large shrimp, peeled and deveined
- 2½ cups frozen sliced okra, thawed
  Hot cooked brown rice, optional

1. In a large skillet, cook bacon over medium heat until crisp. Remove to paper towels with a slotted spoon; drain, reserving 2 Tbsp. drippings. Saute the celery, onion, green pepper and garlic in drippings until tender.
2. Transfer to a 4-qt. slow cooker. Stir in the bacon, clam juice, tomatoes, Worcestershire sauce and marjoram. Cover and cook on low for 4 hours.
3. Stir in shrimp and okra. Cover and cook 1 hour longer or until shrimp turn pink and okra is heated through. Serve with rice if desired.

1½ cups: 287 cal., 12g fat (4g sat. fat), 204mg chol., 792mg sod., 13g carb. (5g sugars, 3g fiber), 31g pro. **Diabetic exchanges:** 4 lean meat, 2 vegetable, 2 fat.

SLOW-COOKER
FLANK STEAK FAJITAS

SLOW-COOKED BEEF BURRITOS WITH GREEN CHILES

(PICTURED ON P. 200)

I created this recipe years ago, and it has become such a favorite that the wonderful aroma of it cooking makes my family instantly happy. It is hearty, flavorful and easy to prepare, and it uses the long, slow cook time that defines true comfort food.

—Sally Pahler, Palisade, CO

Prep: 20 min. • **Cook:** 7 hours
Makes: 14 servings

- 2 garlic cloves, minced
- 1 tsp. salt
- 2 tsp. ground cumin
- 1 tsp. cayenne pepper
- 1 boneless beef chuck roast (4 lbs.)
- 1 can (28 oz.) diced tomatoes
- 4 cans (7 oz. each) whole green chiles, drained and coarsely chopped
- 1 large onion, diced
- 14 whole wheat tortillas (8 in.), warmed
  Optional toppings: Shredded cheddar cheese, salsa, sour cream, sliced ripe olives

1. Combine the garlic, salt, cumin and cayenne; rub over roast. Place in a 5- or 6-qt. slow cooker. Add the tomatoes, chiles and onion. Cook, covered, on low 7-8 hours or until meat is tender.
2. Remove roast from slow cooker; shred with 2 forks. Remove vegetables with a slotted spoon; discard the cooking juices. Return beef and vegetables to slow cooker and heat through. Serve in tortillas, with toppings as desired.
1 burrito: 355 cal., 13g fat (5g sat. fat), 84mg chol., 499mg sod., 28g carb. (4g sugars, 4g fiber), 30g pro. **Diabetic exchanges:** 4 lean meat, 2 starch.

> **TEST KITCHEN TIP**
>
> We liked the coarse texture of hand-chopped chiles, but if you're trying to save time, use diced green chiles instead.

TERIYAKI PORK ROAST

TERIYAKI PORK ROAST

Since my husband works full time and attends school, I do a lot around the house, including wrangling our three kids. I'm always looking for no-fuss recipes, so I was thrilled to find this one. The juicy teriyaki-seasoned pork roast has become a family favorite.

—Roxanne Hulsey, Gainesville, GA

Prep: 10 min. • **Cook:** 7 hours
Makes: 8 servings

- ¾ cup unsweetened apple juice
- 2 Tbsp. sugar
- 2 Tbsp. reduced-sodium soy sauce
- 1 Tbsp. white vinegar
- 1 tsp. ground ginger
- ¼ tsp. garlic powder
- ⅛ tsp. pepper
- 1 boneless pork loin roast (about 3 lbs.), halved
- 7½ tsp. cornstarch
- 3 Tbsp. cold water

1. In a greased 3-qt. slow cooker, combine the first 7 ingredients. Add roast and turn to coat. Cover and cook on low for 7-8 hours or until meat is tender.
2. Remove pork to a serving platter; keep warm. Skim fat from cooking juices. Transfer juices to a small saucepan; bring to a boil. Combine cornstarch and water until smooth. Gradually stir into the pan. Bring to a boil; cook and stir for 2 minutes or until thickened. Serve with meat.
4 oz. cooked pork: 247 cal., 8g fat (3g sat. fat), 85mg chol., 194mg sod., 9g carb. (5g sugars, 0 fiber), 33g pro. **Diabetic exchanges:** 4 lean meat, ½ starch.

SLOW-COOKED CHICKEN A LA KING

When I know I'll be having a busy day with little time to prepare a meal, I use my slow cooker to make chicken a la king. It smells so good while it's cooking.
—Eleanor Mielke, Snohomish, WA

Prep: 10 min. • **Cook:** 7½ hours
Makes: 6 servings

- 1 can (10¾ oz.) reduced-fat reduced-sodium condensed cream of chicken soup, undiluted
- 3 Tbsp. all-purpose flour
- ¼ tsp. pepper
  Dash cayenne pepper
- 1 lb. boneless skinless chicken breasts, cubed
- 1 celery rib, chopped
- ½ cup chopped green pepper
- ¼ cup chopped onion
- 1 pkg. (10 oz.) frozen peas, thawed
- 2 Tbsp. diced pimientos, drained
  Hot cooked rice

1. In a 3-qt. slow cooker, combine soup, flour, pepper and cayenne until smooth. Stir in the chicken, celery, green pepper and onion.

2. Cover and cook on low 7-8 hours or until meat is no longer pink. Stir in peas and pimientos. Cook 30 minutes longer or until heated through. Serve with rice.

1 cup chicken mixture: 174 cal., 3g fat (1g sat. fat), 44mg chol., 268mg sod., 16g carb. (6g sugars, 3g fiber), 19g pro. **Diabetic exchanges:** 2 lean meat, 1 starch.

AFRICAN PEANUT SWEET POTATO STEW

When I was in college, my mom made an addictive sweet potato stew. I shared it with friends, and now all of us serve it to our own kids. They all love it, of course.
—Alexis Scatchell, Niles, IL

Prep: 20 min. • **Cook:** 6 hours
Makes: 8 servings (2½ qt.)

- 1 can (28 oz.) diced tomatoes, undrained
- 1 cup fresh cilantro leaves
- ½ cup chunky peanut butter
- 3 garlic cloves, halved
- 2 tsp. ground cumin
- 1 tsp. salt
- ½ tsp. ground cinnamon
- ¼ tsp. smoked paprika
- 3 lbs. sweet potatoes (about 6 medium), peeled and cut into 1-in. pieces
- 1 can (15 oz.) garbanzo beans or chickpeas, rinsed and drained
- 1 cup water
- 8 cups chopped fresh kale
  Chopped peanuts and additional cilantro leaves, optional

1. Place the first 8 ingredients in a food processor; process until pureed. Transfer to a 5-qt. slow cooker; stir in sweet potatoes, beans and water.

2. Cook, covered, on low 6-8 hours or until potatoes are tender, adding kale during the last 30 minutes. If desired, top each serving with chopped peanuts and additional cilantro.

1¼ cups: 349 cal., 9g fat (1g sat. fat), 0 chol., 624mg sod., 60g carb. (23g sugars, 11g fiber), 10g pro.

EASY POACHED SALMON

EASY POACHED SALMON

After 46 years of marriage, we had never tasted salmon until a friend told me about poaching it in a slow cooker. I was amazed by the delicious, moist results with so little work. I add some soy sauce to the poaching liquid for more flavor.
—Johnna Johnson, Scottsdale, AZ

Prep: 45 min. • **Cook:** 1 hour
Makes: 8 servings

- 6 cups water
- 1 medium onion, chopped
- 2 celery ribs, chopped
- 4 sprigs fresh parsley
- ½ cup dry white wine
- 1 Tbsp. soy sauce
- 8 whole peppercorns
- 1 bay leaf
- 1 salmon fillet (3 lbs.)
  Lemon slices and fresh dill

1. In a large saucepan, combine the first 8 ingredients. Bring to a boil; reduce the heat. Simmer, covered, 30 minutes. Strain, discarding vegetables and spices.
2. Cut three 20x3-in. strips of heavy-duty foil; crisscross so they resemble spokes of a wheel. Place strips on bottom and up sides of a 7-qt. oval slow cooker. Pour poaching liquid into slow cooker. Carefully add salmon.
3. Cook, covered, on high 60-70 minutes or just until fish flakes easily with a fork (a thermometer inserted in fish should read at least 145°). Using foil strips as handles, remove salmon from cooking liquid. Serve warm or cold, with lemon and dill.

4 oz. cooked salmon: 266 cal., 16g fat (3g sat. fat), 85mg chol., 97mg sod., 0 carb. (0 sugars, 0 fiber), 29g pro. **Diabetic exchanges:** 4 lean meat.

SPICY PORK & BUTTERNUT SQUASH RAGU

SPICY PORK & BUTTERNUT SQUASH RAGU

This recipe is a marvelously spicy combo, perfect for cooler fall weather and so satisfying after a day spent outdoors.
—Monica Osterhaus, Paducah, KY

Prep: 20 min. • **Cook:** 5 hours
Makes: 10 servings

- 2 cans (14½ oz. each) stewed tomatoes, undrained
- 1 pkg. (12 oz.) frozen cooked winter squash, thawed
- 1 large sweet onion, cut into ½-in. pieces
- 1 medium sweet red pepper, cut into ½-in. pieces
- 1½ tsp. crushed red pepper flakes
- 2 lbs. boneless country-style pork ribs
- 1 tsp. salt
- ¼ tsp. garlic powder
- ¼ tsp. pepper
  Hot cooked pasta
  Shaved Parmesan cheese, optional

1. Combine first 5 ingredients in bottom of a 6- or 7-qt. slow cooker. Sprinkle ribs with salt, pepper and garlic powder; place in slow cooker. Cook, covered, on low until pork is tender, 5-6 hours.
2. Remove cover; stir to break pork into smaller pieces. Serve with pasta. If desired, top with Parmesan cheese.

Freeze option: Freeze cooled sauce in freezer containers. To use, partially thaw in refrigerator overnight. Heat through in a saucepan, stirring occasionally.

1 cup ragu: 195 cal., 8g fat (3g sat. fat), 52mg chol., 426mg sod., 13g carb. (6g sugars, 2g fiber), 17g pro. **Diabetic exchanges:** 2 lean meat, 1 starch.

> **TEST KITCHEN TIP**
>
> You can substitute chicken thighs for the pork ribs in this recipe.

SLOW-COOKED FLANK STEAK

My slow cooker gets lots of use, especially during the hectic summer months. I can fix this flank steak in the morning and forget about it until dinnertime. I serve it with noodles and a tossed salad.
—Michelle Armistead, Keyport, NJ

Prep: 15 min. • **Cook:** 4 hours
Makes: 6 servings

- 1 flank steak (about 1½ lbs.), cut in half
- 1 Tbsp. canola oil
- 1 large onion, sliced
- ⅓ cup water
- 1 can (4 oz.) chopped green chiles
- 2 Tbsp. vinegar
- 1¼ tsp. chili powder
- 1 tsp. garlic powder
- ½ tsp. sugar
- ½ tsp. salt
- ⅛ tsp. pepper

1. In a skillet, brown steak in oil; transfer to a 5-qt. slow cooker. In the same skillet, saute onion for 1 minute. Gradually add water, stirring to loosen browned bits from pan. Add remaining ingredients; bring to a boil. Pour over the flank steak.
2. Cover and cook on low until the meat is tender, 4-5 hours. Slice the meat; serve with onion and pan juices.

3 oz. cooked beef: 199 cal., 11g fat (4g sat. fat), 48mg chol., 327mg sod., 4g carb. (2g sugars, 1g fiber), 20g pro. **Diabetic exchanges:** 3 lean meat, ½ fat.

MEATBALL CABBAGE ROLLS

My mother often had these cabbage rolls simmering in her slow cooker when my family and I arrived at her house for weekend visits. The mouthwatering meatballs tucked inside made these stand out from any other cabbage rolls I've tried.
—Betty Buckmaster, Muskogee, OK

Prep: 25 min. • **Cook:** 8 hours
Makes: 4 servings

- 1 large head cabbage
- 1 can (8 oz.) no-salt-added tomato sauce
- 1 small onion, chopped
- ⅓ cup uncooked long grain rice
- 2 Tbsp. chili powder
- ¼ tsp. garlic powder
- ⅛ tsp. salt
- 1 lb. lean ground beef (90% lean)
- 1 can (15 oz.) tomato sauce

1. In a Dutch oven, cook the cabbage in boiling water just until leaves fall off head. Set aside 12 large leaves for rolls. (Refrigerate remaining cabbage for another use.) Cut out the thick vein from the bottom of each reserved leaf, making a V-shaped cut.
2. In a large bowl, combine no-salt-added tomato sauce, onion, rice, chili powder, garlic powder and salt. Crumble beef over mixture; mix well. Shape into 12 balls. Place 1 meatball on each cabbage leaf; overlap cut ends of leaf. Fold in sides, beginning from the cut end. Roll up completely to enclose meatball. Secure with toothpicks.
3. Place in a 5-qt. slow cooker. Pour remaining tomato sauce over cabbage rolls. Cover and cook on low for 8 hours or until meat is no longer pink and cabbage is tender. Discard toothpicks.

3 rolls: 323 cal., 11g fat (4g sat. fat), 71mg chol., 762mg sod., 31g carb. (8g sugars, 7g fiber), 28g pro. **Diabetic exchanges:** 3 lean meat, 1½ starch, 1 vegetable.

SLOW-COOKER CLAM SAUCE

Serve this delectable clam sauce as a hot dip for holiday get-togethers. The sauce is bright and fresh with pasta, too.
—Frances Pietsch, Flower Mound, TX

Prep: 10 min. • **Cook:** 3 hours
Makes: 4 cups

- 4 Tbsp. butter
- 2 Tbsp. olive oil
- ½ cup finely chopped onion
- 8 oz. fresh mushrooms, chopped
- 2 garlic cloves, minced
- 2 cans (10 oz. each) whole baby clams
- ¾ tsp. dried oregano
- ½ tsp. garlic salt
- ¼ tsp. white pepper
- ¼ tsp. black pepper
- ¼ tsp. Italian seasoning
- 1 bay leaf
- ¼ cup sherry
- 2 tsp. lemon juice
- ½ cup water
- 2 Tbsp. chopped fresh parsley
  Hot cooked pasta

Optional: Grated Parmesan cheese, lemon juice and minced fresh parsley

1. Heat butter and oil in a skillet over medium-high heat. Add onion; cook and stir 5 minutes. Add the mushrooms and garlic; cook until vegetables are tender, 5 minutes more.
2. Drain clams, reserving liquid; coarsely chop. Place clams, reserved clam juice, mushroom mixture and the next 9 ingredients in a 5-qt. slow cooker. Cook, covered, on low for 3 hours. Remove and discard bay leaf; stir in parsley. Serve with pasta. If desired, serve with optional ingredients.

½ cup: 138 cal., 10g fat (4g sat. fat), 40mg chol., 580mg sod., 5g carb. (1g sugars, 0 fiber), 7g pro.

> **TEST KITCHEN TIP**
>
> For a creamy sauce, stir in a little cream cheese or heavy cream.

SLOW-COOKER CLAM SAUCE

SLOW-COOKED PORK WITH ROOT VEGETABLES

(PICTURED ON P. 200)

This is truly a one-pot recipe—there's no need to brown the pork, as the rub gives it rich color. The house fills with the amazing aroma of apples and pork as it slow-cooks. This makes a perfect dinner for a chilly autumn day. Use the cooking liquid as a sauce when ready to serve.
—Jackie Sharp, Suffolk, VA

Prep: 25 min. • **Cook:** 3½ hours
Makes: 10 servings

- 3 large sweet potatoes (about 2¼ lbs.)
- 2 medium turnips
- 1 tart medium apple
- ¼ cup water
- 1 medium onion, quartered
- 2 Tbsp. packed brown sugar
- 2 tsp. salt
- 1½ tsp. paprika
- ½ tsp. pepper
- 1 boneless pork loin roast (3 to 4 lbs.)
- ½ cup unsweetened apple juice
- 2 Tbsp. cider vinegar
- 1 Tbsp. Worcestershire sauce
- 1 tsp. salt
- 1 tsp. yellow mustard
- ¼ tsp. crushed red pepper flakes

1. Peel and cut sweet potatoes, turnips and apple into ¾-in. pieces. Microwave sweet potatoes, turnips and water, covered, on high until just slightly tender, 8-10 minutes. Drain; transfer to a 6-qt. slow cooker. Add apple and onion. In a small bowl, mix brown sugar, salt, paprika and pepper; rub over meat and place in slow cooker.
2. Whisk remaining ingredients; pour around pork. Cook, covered, on low until a thermometer reads 145° and the meat is tender, 3½-4½ hours.
3. Remove roast from slow cooker; tent with foil. Let stand 15 minutes before slicing. Strain cooking juices; serve pork and vegetables with juices.

4 oz. cooked pork with ¾ cup vegetable mixture: 313 cal., 7g fat (2g sat. fat), 68mg chol., 799mg sod., 34g carb. (17g sugars, 4g fiber), 29g pro. **Diabetic exchanges:** 4 lean meat, 2 starch.

AUTUMN SLOW-COOKED BEEF STEW

CARIBBEAN CURRIED CHICKEN

Having grown up in the Virgin Islands, I've eaten my share of curried chicken. This recipe hits the mark with big, bold flavors.
—Sharon Gibson, Hendersonville, NC

Prep: 20 min. • **Cook:** 4 hours
Makes: 8 servings

- 1 Tbsp. Madras curry powder
- 1 tsp. garlic powder
- 1 tsp. pepper
- 8 boneless skinless chicken thighs
- 1 medium onion, thinly sliced
- 1½ cups Goya mojo criollo marinade, well-shaken
- 2 Tbsp. canola oil
- 2 Tbsp. all-purpose flour
  Hot cooked rice, green onions and fresh cilantro leaves, optional

1. Combine curry powder, garlic powder and pepper; sprinkle over the chicken, pressing to help it adhere. Place chicken in a 3-qt. slow cooker. Sprinkle with onion. Carefully pour mojo criollo marinade along the sides of slow cooker, avoiding chicken to keep coating intact. Cook, covered, on low until a thermometer reads 170°, 4-6 hours. Remove chicken; keep warm.
2. Pour cooking juices from slow cooker into a measuring cup; skim fat. In a large saucepan, heat oil over medium heat; whisk in flour until smooth. Gradually whisk in cooking juices. Bring to a boil, stirring constantly; cook and stir until thickened, 1-2 minutes. Reduce heat; add chicken and simmer 5 minutes. If desired, serve with rice, green onions and cilantro.

1 chicken thigh with 6 Tbsp. sauce:
249 cal., 13g fat (3g sat. fat), 76mg chol., 514mg sod., 11g carb. (5g sugars, 1g fiber), 22g pro.
Diabetic exchanges: 3 lean meat, 1 fat.
* **HEALTH TIP** * Turmeric gives curry powder its intense yellow color. It's thought to have several health benefits including anti-inflammatory properties and improved digestive health.

> **TEST KITCHEN TIP**
>
> Mojo criollo (pronounced mo-ho cree-OH-yo) is a citrus-based marinade commonly used in Latin American and Caribbean cooking. We tested with Goya brand.

AUTUMN SLOW-COOKED BEEF STEW

If any dish could taste like a special occasion, it's this one with beef, pears, walnuts and sweet dried apricots. We recommend a leafy salad and rolls to complete the masterpiece.
—Amy Dodson, Durango, CO

Prep: 35 min. • **Cook:** 6 hours
Makes: 8 servings

- 2 lbs. boneless beef chuck roast, cubed
- ½ tsp. garlic salt
- ½ tsp. pepper
- 2 Tbsp. olive oil
- 2 cups dry red wine or reduced-sodium beef broth
- 1 cup reduced-sodium beef broth
- 4 garlic cloves, minced
- 1 tsp. rubbed sage
- 1 tsp. dried thyme
- ½ tsp. salt
- 2½ lbs. small red potatoes (about 20)
- 4 medium carrots, cut into 1-in. pieces
- 1 large onion, halved and sliced
- 2 medium pears, quartered
- 1 cup walnut halves
- 1 cup dried apricots
- 2 Tbsp. cornstarch
- 3 Tbsp. cold water

1. Sprinkle beef with garlic salt and pepper. In a large skillet, heat oil over medium-high heat. Brown beef in batches. Remove with a slotted spoon; transfer to a 6-qt. slow cooker.
2. In a large bowl, combine wine, broth, garlic, sage, thyme and salt; pour over beef. Top with potatoes, carrots, onion, pears, walnuts and apricots. Cook, covered, on low 6-8 hours or until meat is tender; skim fat.
3. In a small bowl, mix cornstarch and water until smooth; gradually stir into stew. Cook, covered, on high until sauce thickened, 20-30 minutes.
1¾ cups: 522 cal., 23g fat (5g sat. fat), 74mg chol., 394mg sod., 51g carb. (17g sugars, 8g fiber), 29g pro.

CARIBBEAN CURRIED CHICKEN

TENDER BAVARIAN POT ROAST

I grew up eating pot roast but disliked it until I got this recipe at a church social. My 7-year-old especially enjoys the seasoned apple gravy.
—Patricia Gasmund, Rockford, IL

Prep: 10 min. • **Cook:** 6 hours
Makes: 12 servings

- 1 beef top round roast (4 lbs.)
- 1½ cups apple juice
- 1 can (8 oz.) tomato sauce
- 1 small onion, chopped
- 2 Tbsp. white vinegar
- 1 Tbsp. salt
- 2 to 3 tsp. ground cinnamon
- 1 Tbsp. minced fresh gingerroot
- ¼ cup cornstarch
- ½ cup water

1. In a Dutch oven coated with cooking spray, brown roast on all sides over medium-high heat. Transfer to a 5-qt. slow cooker. In a bowl, combine juice, tomato sauce, onion, vinegar, salt, cinnamon and ginger; pour over roast. Cover and cook on high for 5-7 hours.
2. Combine cornstarch and water until smooth; stir into cooking juices until well combined. Cover and cook 1 hour longer or until the meat is tender and gravy begins to thicken.

4 oz. cooked beef: 230 cal., 7g fat (2g sat. fat), 96mg chol., 753mg sod., 8g carb. (0 sugars, 1g fiber), 32g pro. **Diabetic exchanges:** 4 lean meat, ½ fruit.

READER REVIEW

"This is by far the best roast I have ever made. It disappeared quick. It was moist and tender—it melted in your mouth. And the sauce had a really great flavor. We even used the sauce on the potatoes and veggies that I roasted!"
—LUCKYHILL, TASTEOFHOME.COM

SLOW-SIMMERED CHICKEN WITH RAISINS, CAPERS & BASIL

SLOW-SIMMERED CHICKEN WITH RAISINS, CAPERS & BASIL

This dish's sweetly savory flavor comes from capers, golden raisins and basil. And what's even better than that? Kids LOVE it.
—Nadine Mesch, Mount Healthy, OH

Prep: 25 min. • **Cook:** 4 hours
Makes: 8 servings

- 2 Tbsp. olive oil, divided
- 8 boneless skinless chicken thighs (4 oz. each)
- 1 tsp. salt
- 1 tsp. pepper
- ½ cup Marsala wine
- 8 oz. sliced fresh mushrooms
- 1 medium sweet red pepper, thinly sliced
- 1 medium onion, thinly sliced
- 1 can (14½ oz.) diced tomatoes, undrained
- ½ cup golden raisins
- 2 Tbsp. capers, drained
- ¼ cup chopped fresh basil
  Hot cooked couscous

1. In a large skillet, heat 1 Tbsp. oil over medium-high heat. Sprinkle chicken with salt and pepper; brown chicken on both sides in batches, adding oil as needed. Transfer chicken to a 5- or 6-qt. slow cooker.
2. Add wine to the skillet, stirring to loosen browned bits; pour into slow cooker. Stir mushrooms, red pepper, onion, and tomatoes, raisins and capers into slow cooker.
3. Cook, covered, on low until chicken and vegetables are tender, 4-5 hours. Sprinkle with basil before serving. Serve with couscous.

1 serving: 250 cal., 12g fat (3g sat. fat), 76mg chol., 494mg sod., 13g carb. (9g sugars, 2g fiber), 23g pro. **Diabetic exchanges:** 3 lean meat, 1 vegetable, 1 fat, ½ starch.

FRUITED PORK CHOPS

Here's one of my favorite slow-cooker recipes. I often prepare these tender pineapple pork chops for guests and serve them with brown rice.
—Cindy Ragan, North Huntingdon, PA

Prep: 10 min. • **Cook:** 4¼ hours
Makes: 6 servings

3 Tbsp. all-purpose flour
1½ tsp. dried oregano
¾ tsp. salt
¼ tsp. garlic powder
¼ tsp. pepper

6 boneless pork loin chops (5 oz. each)
1 Tbsp. olive oil
1 can (20 oz.) unsweetened pineapple chunks
¾ cup unsweetened pineapple juice
¼ cup water
2 Tbsp. brown sugar
2 Tbsp. dried minced onion
2 Tbsp. tomato paste
¼ cup raisins

1. Combine flour, oregano, salt, garlic powder and pepper in a shallow dish; coat chops, 1 at a time. In a nonstick skillet, brown the chops in olive oil on both sides. Transfer to a 5-qt. slow cooker.

2. Drain pineapple, reserving juice; set pineapple aside. In a bowl, combine the ¾ cup pineapple juice with the reserved pineapple juice. Stir in the water, brown sugar, onion and tomato paste; pour over chops. Sprinkle with raisins.

3. Cover and cook on low until meat is tender, 4-5 hours. Stir in pineapple chunks. Cover and cook 15 minutes longer or until heated through.

1 pork chop: 342 cal., 10g fat (3g sat. fat), 68mg chol., 341mg sod., 31g carb. (24g sugars, 2g fiber), 29g pro. **Diabetic exchanges:** 4 lean meat, 1 starch, 1 fruit, ½ fat.

FRUITED PORK CHOPS

PORK CHOP DINNER

PORK CHOP DINNER

Family and friends like to call me the slow-cooker queen. Of my many slow-cooked specialties, this dish is definitely my husband's favorite.
—Janet Phillips, Meadville, PA

Prep: 15 min. • **Cook:** 4 hours
Makes: 6 servings

- 6 bone-in pork loin chops (7 oz. each)
- 1 Tbsp. canola oil
- 1 large onion, sliced
- 1 medium green pepper, chopped
- 1 can (4 oz.) mushroom stems and pieces, drained
- 1 can (8 oz.) tomato sauce
- 1 Tbsp. brown sugar
- 2 tsp. Worcestershire sauce
- 1½ tsp. cider vinegar
- ½ tsp. salt
  Baked potatoes or hot cooked rice, optional

In a skillet, brown pork chops on both sides in oil; drain. Place chops in a 3-qt. slow cooker. Add the onion, green pepper and mushrooms. Combine the tomato sauce, brown sugar, Worcestershire sauce, vinegar and salt. Pour over meat and vegetables. Cover and cook on low for 4-5 hours or until meat is tender. If desired, serve with baked potatoes or rice.

1 serving: 338 cal., 19g fat (6g sat. fat), 97mg chol., 527mg sod., 8g carb. (5g sugars, 2g fiber), 33g pro. **Diabetic exchanges:** 4 lean meat, ½ fat.

TEX-MEX CHICKEN & RICE

Poultry and freezer basics inspired this deliciously healthy combo. I have a hard time getting my family to eat healthy, but they have no problem cleaning their plates when I serve this dish!
—Tracy Long, Bellwood, NE

Prep: 10 min. • **Cook:** 4 hours
Makes: 6 servings

- 4 boneless skinless chicken breast halves (about 6 oz. each)
- 1 can (10½ oz.) reduced-fat condensed cream of chicken soup, undiluted
- 1 can (10 oz.) diced tomatoes and green chiles

TEX-MEX CHICKEN & RICE

- 1 cup salsa verde
- ½ tsp. ground cumin
- 1½ cups (about 7½ oz.) frozen corn
- 1 cup uncooked instant brown rice
  Shredded cheddar cheese, reduced-fat sour cream, cubed avocado, chopped cilantro, and sliced ripe olives, optional

1. In a 3- or 4-qt. slow cooker, combine the first 5 ingredients. Cook, covered, on low until chicken is tender, 3-4 hours. Remove chicken from slow cooker. Cool slightly; shred chicken with 2 forks. Return meat to slow cooker. Add corn and rice; cook, covered, on low 1 hour longer.

2. If desired, serve with cheese, sour cream, avocado and olives.

1 serving: 254 cal., 4g fat (1g sat. fat), 65mg chol., 757mg sod., 28g carb. (2g sugars, 2g fiber), 27g pro. **Diabetic exchanges:** 3 lean meat, 2 starch.

TEST KITCHEN TIP

Place leftover filling in flour tortillas or lettuce cups. Or, create a Tex-Mex salad by serving the recipe with toppings over a bed of lettuce.

ALL-DAY RED BEANS & RICE

(PICTURED ON P. 201)

My family loves New Orleans-style cooking, so I make this authentic dish often. I appreciate how uncomplicated it is to make—and its smoky ham flavor is scrumptious.
—Celinda Dahlgren, Napa, CA

Prep: 20 min. + soaking • **Cook:** 8½ hours
Makes: 6 servings

- 1 cup dried red beans
- 7 cups water, divided
- 2 smoked ham hocks
- 1 medium onion, chopped
- 1½ tsp. minced garlic
- 1 tsp. ground cumin
- 1 medium tomato, chopped
- 1 medium green pepper, chopped
- 1 tsp. salt
- 4 cups hot cooked rice

1. Sort beans and rinse in cold water; place in a 3-qt. slow cooker. Add 4 cups water; cover and let stand overnight.
2. Drain and rinse beans, discarding liquid. Return beans to the slow cooker; add ham hocks, onion, garlic, cumin and the remaining water. Cover and cook on low for 8-10 hours or until beans are tender.
3. Remove ham hocks; cool slightly. Remove meat from bones. Finely chop meat and return to slow cooker; discard bones. Stir in the tomato, pepper and salt; cover and cook on high for 30 minutes or until pepper is tender. Serve with rice.
Freeze option: Freeze cooled bean mixture in freezer containers. To use, partially thaw in refrigerator overnight. Microwave, covered, on high in a microwave-safe dish until heated through, gently stirring and adding a little water if necessary.
⅔ bean mixture with ⅔ cup rice: 297 cal., 7g fat (3g sat. fat), 33mg chol., 441mg sod., 50g carb. (3g sugars, 12g fiber), 17g pro.

SHREDDED
GREEN CHILE BEEF

SHREDDED GREEN CHILE BEEF

This Tex-Mex pulled beef is tender, slightly spicy, juicy, and so delicious with mashed potatoes or rice. The beef also makes the best soft tacos you've ever had. Save any leftover pulled beef in the liquid to prevent it from drying out.
—Colleen Delawder, Herndon, VA

Prep: 25 min. • **Cook:** 7 hours
Makes: 12 servings

- 2 large sweet onions, halved and thinly sliced
- 4 Tbsp. packed brown sugar, divided
- 1 Tbsp. paprika
- 1½ tsp. salt
- 1 tsp. cayenne pepper
- 1 tsp. chili powder
- 1 tsp. garlic powder
- ½ tsp. pepper
- 1 boneless beef chuck roast (about 3 lbs.)
- 2 Tbsp. canola oil
- 1 can (28 oz.) green enchilada sauce Mashed potatoes, optional

1. Place onions and 3 Tbsp. brown sugar in a 5- or 6-qt. slow cooker. Combine the remaining brown sugar and the next 6 ingredients; coat beef with mixture.
2. In a large skillet, heat oil over medium-high heat; brown beef, 1-2 minutes on each side. Transfer to slow cooker; pour enchilada sauce over beef. Cook, covered, on low until beef is tender, 7-9 hours. Remove beef; shred meat with 2 forks. Return to slow cooker; heat through. If desired, serve over potatoes.

1 cup beef mixture: 278 cal., 15g fat (4g sat. fat), 74mg chol., 658mg sod., 14g carb. (8g sugars, 1g fiber), 23g pro. **Diabetic exchanges:** 3 lean meat, 1 starch, ½ fat.

TEST KITCHEN TIP

Try this shredded beef over pepper jack or cheddar mashed potatoes.

CAJUN-STYLE SAUSAGE & BEANS

Beans and rice make the perfect meal because they're well-balanced, an excellent source of protein, and easy to prepare. The sausage adds meaty flavor to the recipe, and traditional pork sausage lovers won't even notice that chicken sausage was used instead.
—Robin Haas, Cranston, RI

Prep: 25 min. • **Cook:** 6 hours
Makes: 8 servings

- 1 pkg. (12 oz.) fully cooked spicy chicken sausage links, halved lengthwise and cut into ½-in. slices
- 2 cans (16 oz. each) red beans, rinsed and drained
- 2 cans (14½ oz. each) diced tomatoes, undrained
- 3 medium carrots, chopped
- 1 large onion, chopped
- 1 large green pepper, chopped
- ½ cup chopped roasted sweet red peppers
- 3 garlic cloves, minced
- 1 tsp. Cajun seasoning
- 1 tsp. dried oregano
- ½ tsp. dried thyme
- ½ tsp. pepper
- 5⅓ cups cooked brown rice

1. In a large skillet coated with cooking spray, brown sausage. Transfer to a 5-qt. slow cooker. Stir in beans, tomatoes, vegetables, garlic and seasonings.
2. Cook, covered, on low until vegetables are tender, 6-8 hours. Serve with rice.

1 cup sausage and bean mixture with ⅔ cup rice: 355 cal., 5g fat (1g sat. fat), 33mg chol., 759mg sod., 58g carb. (7g sugars, 11g fiber), 18g pro.

CAJUN-STYLE SAUSAGE & BEANS

SWEET ONION & CHERRY PORK CHOPS

When I want to jump-start supper, I opt for these tender pork chops. The sweet and savory cherry sauce makes the recipe a keeper. Try serving it with wild rice pilaf.
—Stephanie Ray, Naples, FL

Prep: 15 min. • **Cook:** 3 hours
Makes: 2 servings

- ½ cup fresh or frozen pitted tart cherries, thawed
- 2 Tbsp. chopped sweet onion
- 1 Tbsp. honey
- ½ tsp. seasoned salt
- ¼ tsp. pepper
- 2 boneless pork loin chops (5 oz. each)
- 1 tsp. cornstarch
- 1 tsp. cold water

1. In a 1½-qt. slow cooker, combine the first 5 ingredients; top with pork chops. Cover and cook on low until meat is tender, 3-4 hours.
2. Remove meat to a serving platter; keep warm. Skim fat from cooking juices; transfer to a small saucepan. Bring liquid to a boil. Combine cornstarch and water until smooth; gradually stir into pan. Bring to a boil; cook and stir until thickened, about 2 minutes. Serve with meat.

1 pork chop with ¼ cup cherry mixture: 278 cal., 8g fat (3g sat. fat), 68mg chol., 425mg sod., 23g carb. (9g sugars, 1g fiber), 28g pro.
Diabetic exchanges: 4 lean meat, 1 starch, ½ fat.

TANGY TROPICAL CHICKEN

SLOW-COOKED RUMP ROAST

I enjoy a good pot roast, but I was tired of the same old thing—so I started experimenting. Cooking the beef in horseradish sauce gives it a tangy flavor. Even my 6- and 3-year-olds love this roast with its tender veggies and gravy.
—Mimi Walker, Palmyra, PA

Prep: 20 min. • **Cook:** 8½ hours
Makes: 8 servings

- 1 beef rump roast or bottom round roast (3 to 3½ lbs.)
- 2 Tbsp. canola oil
- 4 medium carrots, halved lengthwise and cut into 2-in. pieces
- 3 medium potatoes, peeled and cut into chunks
- 2 small onions, sliced
- ½ cup water
- 6 to 8 Tbsp. horseradish sauce
- ¼ cup red wine vinegar
- ¼ cup Worcestershire sauce
- 2 garlic cloves, minced
- 1½ to 2 tsp. celery salt
- 3 Tbsp. cornstarch
- ⅓ cup cold water

1. In a large skillet, brown roast on all sides in oil over medium-high heat; drain. Place carrots and potatoes in a 5-qt. slow cooker. Top with meat and onions. Combine the water, horseradish sauce, vinegar, Worcestershire sauce, garlic and celery salt. Pour over meat. Cover and cook on low until meat and vegetables are tender, about 8 hours.
2. Combine cornstarch and cold water until smooth; stir into slow cooker. Cover and cook on high until gravy is thickened, about 30 minutes.
1 serving: 378 cal., 15g fat (3g sat. fat), 113mg chol., 507mg sod., 23g carb. (6g sugars, 2g fiber), 35g pro. **Diabetic exchanges:** 4 lean meat, 1½ starch, 1 fat.

TANGY TROPICAL CHICKEN

In this colorful dish, exotic mango and pineapple beautifully complement the savory chicken. They lend a pleasant hint of sweetness that's balanced by the salty zip of soy sauce.
—Christina Aho, Naples, FL

Prep: 20 min. • **Cook:** 4 hours
Makes: 4 servings

- 1 lb. boneless skinless chicken breasts, cut into 1-in. strips
- 2 cups chopped peeled mangoes
- 1 medium onion, chopped
- 1 medium sweet red pepper, sliced
- 1 garlic clove, minced
- 1 cup unsweetened pineapple juice
- 1 cup orange juice
- ¼ cup reduced-sodium soy sauce
- 2 Tbsp. Thai chili sauce
- ¼ tsp. pepper
- 2 Tbsp. cornstarch
- 2 Tbsp. cold water
  Hot cooked rice and thinly sliced green onions

1. Place chicken in a 3-qt. slow cooker. Top with mangoes, onion, red pepper and garlic. In a small bowl, combine the pineapple juice, orange juice, soy sauce, chili sauce and pepper; pour over chicken. Cover and cook on low until chicken is tender, 4-5 hours.
2. Remove chicken mixture to a serving platter; keep warm. Transfer cooking juices to a small saucepan. Bring juices to a boil. Combine cornstarch and water until smooth; gradually stir into the pan. Bring to a boil; cook and stir until thickened, about 2 minutes. Serve with chicken mixture, rice and green onions.
1 cup: 299 cal., 3g fat (1g sat. fat), 63mg chol., 760mg sod., 42g carb. (29g sugars, 3g fiber), 26g pro.

SLOW-COOKED RUMP ROAST

SLOW-COOKER TURKEY BREAST WITH GRAVY

This quick-prep recipe lets you feast on turkey at any time of year. We save the rich broth for homemade gravy.
—Joyce Hough, Annapolis, MD

Prep: 25 min. • **Cook:** 5 hours + standing
Makes: 12 servings

- 2 tsp. dried parsley flakes
- 1 tsp. salt
- 1 tsp. poultry seasoning
- ½ tsp. paprika
- ½ tsp. pepper
- 2 medium onions, chopped
- 3 medium carrots, cut into ½-in. slices
- 3 celery ribs, coarsely chopped
- 1 bone-in turkey breast (6 to 7 lbs.), skin removed
- ¼ cup all-purpose flour
- ½ cup water

1. Mix the first 5 ingredients in a small bowl. Place vegetables in a 6- or 7-qt. slow cooker; top with turkey. Rub turkey with seasoning mixture.
2. Cook, covered, on low until a thermometer inserted in turkey reads at least 170°, 5-6 hours. Remove from slow cooker; let stand, covered, 15 minutes before slicing.
3. Meanwhile, strain cooking juices into a small saucepan. Mix flour and water until smooth; stir into cooking juices. Bring to a boil; cook and stir until thickened, 1-2 minutes. Serve with turkey.

6 oz. cooked turkey with 3 Tbsp. gravy : 200 cal., 1g fat (0 sat. fat), 117mg chol., 270mg sod., 2g carb. (0 sugars, 0 fiber), 43g pro. **Diabetic exchanges:** 6 lean meat.

CAJUN PORK & RICE

CAJUN PORK & RICE

I created this recipe after returning home from traveling. I had little food in the house, so I used ingredients already available in the refrigerator and pantry. My husband loves this pork dish because it's tasty, and I love it because it's easy.
—Allison Gapinski, Cary, NC

Prep: 20 min. • **Cook:** 4¼ hours
Makes: 4 servings

- 1½ tsp. ground cumin
- 1½ tsp. chili powder
- 1½ lbs. boneless pork loin chops
- 1 can (14½ oz.) petite diced tomatoes, undrained
- 1 small onion, finely chopped
- 1 celery rib, finely chopped
- 1 small carrot, julienned
- 1 garlic clove, minced
- ½ tsp. Louisiana-style hot sauce
- ¼ tsp. salt
- 1½ cups uncooked instant rice
- 1 cup reduced-sodium chicken broth
- 1 tsp. olive oil
- 1 medium green pepper, julienned

1. Mix cumin and chili powder; sprinkle pork chops with 2 tsp. spice mixture. Transfer to a 4-qt. slow cooker.
2. In a small bowl, mix tomatoes, onion, celery, carrot, garlic, hot sauce, salt and remaining spice mixture; pour over chops. Cook, covered, on low until meat is tender, 4-5 hours.
3. Stir in rice and chicken broth, breaking up pork into pieces. Cook, covered, on low until rice is tender, 12-15 minutes longer.
4. In a small skillet, heat oil over medium-high heat. Add green pepper; cook and stir 5-7 minutes or until crisp-tender. Serve on top of pork mixture.

1½ cups pork mixture with ¼ cup pepper strips: 423 cal., 12g fat (4g sat. fat), 82mg chol., 573mg sod., 40g carb. (6g sugars, 4g fiber), 38g pro. **Diabetic exchanges:** 5 lean meat, 2½ starch, 1 vegetable.

PEAR & POMEGRANATE LAMB TAGINE

Pomegranate, pear, and orange go together so elegantly, I decided to use the ingredients to prepare a Middle Eastern-themed tagine with lamb. The dish tastes delicious over couscous, polenta, or cauliflower mashed with feta cheese.
—Arlene Erlbach, Morton Grove, IL

Prep: 20 min. • **Cook:** 6 hours
Makes: 4 servings

2½ lbs. lamb shanks
2 large pears, finely chopped
3 cups thinly sliced shallots
½ cup orange juice, divided
½ cup pomegranate juice, divided
1 Tbsp. honey
1½ tsp. ground cinnamon
1 tsp. salt
1 tsp. ground allspice
1 tsp. ground cardamom
¼ cup pomegranate seeds
¼ cup minced fresh parsley
  Cooked couscous, optional

1. Place lamb in a 5- or 6-qt. oval slow cooker. Add pears and shallots. Combine ¼ cup orange juice, ¼ cup pomegranate juice, honey and seasonings; pour over the shallots.

2. Cook, covered, on low for 6-8 hours or until meat is tender. Remove lamb to a rimmed serving platter; keep warm. Stir remaining orange and pomegranate juices into cooking liquid; pour over lamb. Sprinkle with pomegranate seeds and parsley. If desired, serve over couscous.

½ lamb shank with 1 cup vegetables:
438 cal., 13g fat (5g sat. fat), 99mg chol., 680mg sod., 52g carb. (28g sugars, 5g fiber), 31g pro.

TEST KITCHEN TIP

Fresh-squeezed orange juice (with its pulp) can add an extra-special touch to this recipe.

PEAR & POMEGRANATE
LAMB TAGINE

**GREEK-STYLE
STUFFED PEPPERS**

GREEK-STYLE STUFFED PEPPERS

The bounty of peppers found at the local farmers market in the early fall, combined with some standard Greek ingredients, creates a dish that bursts with color and fresh flavor.
—Renee Murby, Johnston, RI

Prep: 30 min. • **Cook:** 4½ hours
Makes: 8 servings

- 2 Tbsp. olive oil
- 1 small fennel bulb, chopped
- 1 small red onion, chopped
- 1 pkg. (10 oz.) frozen chopped spinach, thawed and squeezed dry
- 3 garlic cloves, minced
- 2 each medium sweet yellow, orange, red and green peppers
- 1 can (28 oz.) crushed tomatoes, divided
- 1 lb. ground lamb
- 1 cup cooked barley
- 1 cup crumbled feta cheese, plus more for serving
- ½ cup Greek olives, chopped
- 1½ tsp. dried oregano
- ½ tsp. salt
- ½ tsp. crushed red pepper flakes
- ½ tsp. pepper
  Chopped fresh parsley, optional

1. In a large skillet, heat oil over medium-high heat. Add fennel and onion; cook and stir until tender, 6-8 minutes. Add the spinach and garlic; cook 1 minute longer. Cool slightly.
2. Cut and reserve tops from peppers; remove and discard seeds. Pour 1 cup crushed tomatoes into the bottom of a 6- or 7-qt. slow cooker. In a large bowl, combine lamb, barley, 1 cup feta cheese, olives and seasonings; add the fennel mixture. Spoon mixture into peppers; place in slow cooker. Pour the remaining crushed tomatoes over peppers; replace the pepper tops. Cook, covered, on low until peppers are tender, 4½-5½ hours. Serve with additional feta and, if desired, chopped parsley.

1 stuffed pepper: 313 cal., 16g fat (6g sat. fat), 45mg chol., 684mg sod., 26g carb. (11g sugars, 8g fiber), 17g pro. **Diabetic exchanges:** 2 starch, 2 medium-fat meat, 1 fat.

THAI-STYLE PORK

THAI-STYLE PORK

A creamy Thai peanut sauce coats tender pork in this delectable dish. The recipe is from a friend in my cooking club, and it's always a favorite.
—Amy Van Orman, Rockford, MI

Prep: 15 min. • **Cook:** 6¼ hours
Makes: 6 servings

- ¼ cup teriyaki sauce
- 2 Tbsp. rice vinegar
- 1 tsp. crushed red pepper flakes
- 1 tsp. minced garlic
- 2 lbs. boneless pork loin chops
- 1 Tbsp. cornstarch
- ¼ cup cold water
- ¼ cup creamy peanut butter
  Hot cooked rice
- ½ cup chopped green onions
- ½ cup dry roasted peanuts
  Lime juice and Sriracha chili sauce, optional

1. Mix the first 4 ingredients. Place pork chops in a 3-qt. slow cooker; top with sauce. Cook, covered, on low until meat is tender, 6-8 hours.
2. Remove pork and cut into bite-size pieces; keep warm. Transfer cooking juices to a saucepan; bring to a boil. Mix cornstarch and water until smooth; gradually stir into juices. Bring to a boil; cook and stir until thickened, 1-2 minutes. Stir in peanut butter. Add pork.
3. Serve with rice. Sprinkle with green onions and peanuts. If desired, drizzle with lime juice and chili sauce.

⅔ cup pork mixture: 357 cal., 20g fat (5g sat. fat), 73mg chol., 598mg sod., 9g carb. (3g sugars, 2g fiber), 35g pro. **Diabetic exchanges:** 5 lean meat, 2 fat, ½ starch.

SHRIMP MARINARA

SHRIMP MARINARA

Flavorful marinara sauce simmers for just a few hours. Right before mealtime, toss in the shrimp to cook quickly. Serve over hot spaghetti for a delicious dish.
—Sue Mackey, Jackson, WI

Prep: 30 min. • **Cook:** 3¼ hours
Makes: 6 servings

- 1 can (14½ oz.) Italian diced tomatoes, undrained
- 1 can (6 oz.) tomato paste
- ½ to 1 cup water
- 2 garlic cloves, minced
- 2 Tbsp. minced fresh parsley
- ½ tsp. salt
- 1 tsp. dried oregano
- ½ tsp. dried basil
- ¼ tsp. pepper
- 1 lb. uncooked shrimp (26-30 per lb.), peeled and deveined
- ¾ lb. spaghetti, cooked and drained
  Shredded Parmesan cheese, optional

1. In a 3-qt. slow cooker, combine the first 9 ingredients. Cover and cook on low for 3-4 hours.
2. Stir in shrimp. Cover and cook on high 15-25 minutes, just until shrimp turn pink. Serve with spaghetti. Sprinkle with cheese if desired.

1 serving: 328 cal., 2g fat (0 sat. fat), 92mg chol., 527mg sod., 55g carb. (9g sugars, 3g fiber), 22g pro.

TANGY PORK CHOPS

When my husband and I had our first child, we found this recipe so convenient. I could start it during nap time and we'd enjoy an easy, satisfying dinner that night.
—Karol Hines, Kitty Hawk, NC

Prep: 15 min. • **Cook:** 5½ hours
Makes: 4 servings

- 4 bone-in pork loin chops
- ⅛ tsp. pepper
- 2 medium onions, chopped
- 2 celery ribs, chopped
- 1 large green pepper, sliced
- 1 can (14½ oz.) no-salt-added stewed tomatoes
- ½ cup ketchup
- 2 Tbsp. cider vinegar
- 2 Tbsp. brown sugar
- 2 Tbsp. Worcestershire sauce
- 1 Tbsp. lemon juice
- 1 tsp. beef bouillon granules
- 3 Tbsp. cornstarch
- 2 Tbsp. cold water
  Hot cooked rice or mashed potatoes, optional

1. Place chops in a 3-qt. slow cooker; sprinkle with pepper. Add the onions, celery, green pepper and tomatoes. Combine the ketchup, vinegar, brown sugar, Worcestershire sauce, lemon juice and bouillon; pour over vegetables. Cover and cook on low for 5-6 hours or until meat is tender.
2. Mix cornstarch and water until smooth; stir into liquid in slow cooker. Cover and cook on high for 30 minutes or until thickened. If desired, serve with rice or mashed potatoes.

1 pork chop: 349 cal., 9g fat (3g sat. fat), 86mg chol., 757mg sod., 34g carb. (24g sugars, 4g fiber), 32g pro.

SLOW-COOKER BEEF TIPS BURGUNDY

Here's a heartwarming classic that's so simple thanks to the slow cooker. Mushrooms, onions and tender beef in a red wine sauce make for an easy, elegant meal.
—Deanna Zewen, Union Grove, WI

Prep: 15 min. • **Cook:** 6¾ hours
Makes: 10 servings

- 1 boneless beef chuck roast (3 lbs.), trimmed and cut into 1-in. pieces
- 2 medium onions, halved and sliced
- ½ lb. sliced fresh mushrooms
- 4 garlic cloves, minced
- 3 cups beef stock
- ½ cup dry red wine or additional beef stock
- 2 Tbsp. Worcestershire sauce
- 2 Tbsp. red wine vinegar
- 1¼ tsp. salt
- 1 tsp. crushed red pepper flakes
- ½ tsp. pepper
- ⅓ cup cornstarch
- ⅓ cup cold water
  Hot cooked egg noodles
  Minced fresh parsley

1. In a 5-qt. slow cooker, combine beef, onions, mushrooms and garlic. In a small bowl, mix the next 7 ingredients; pour over beef mixture. Cook, covered, on low until meat is tender, 6-8 hours.
2. Skim fat from juices. In a small bowl, mix cornstarch and water until smooth; gradually stir into slow cooker. Cook, covered, on high until thickened, about 45 minutes. Serve with noodles; sprinkle with parsley.

Freeze option: Omitting parsley, freeze cooled meat mixture, sauce and egg noodles in freezer containers. To use, partially thaw in the refrigerator overnight. Microwave, covered, on high in microwave-safe dishes until heated through, stirring gently and adding water if necessary. Sprinkle with parsley.

1 cup: 275 cal., 13g fat (5g sat. fat), 88mg chol., 536mg sod., 9g carb. (2g sugars, 1g fiber), 29g pro. **Diabetic exchanges:** 4 lean meat, ½ starch.

SAUCY INDIAN-STYLE CHICKEN & VEGETABLES
(PICTURED ON P. 201)

This dish always seems to develop a devoted following. Prepared sauce makes it easy to bring the rich flavors of Indian cuisine to your family. Feel free to use more or less tikka masala sauce according to your personal taste.
—Erica Polly, Sun Prairie, WI

Prep: 15 min. • **Cook:** 4 hours
Makes: 8 servings

- 2 medium sweet potatoes, peeled and cut into 1½-in. pieces
- 2 Tbsp. water
- 2 medium sweet red peppers, cut into 1-in. pieces
- 3 cups fresh cauliflowerets
- 2 lbs. boneless skinless chicken thighs, cubed
- 2 jars (15 oz. each) tikka masala curry sauce
- ¾ tsp. salt
  Minced fresh cilantro, optional
  Naan flatbreads, warmed

1. Microwave sweet potatoes and water, covered, on high just until potatoes begin to soften, 3-4 minutes.
2. In a 5- or 6-qt. slow cooker, combine vegetables and chicken; add sauce and salt. Cook, covered, on low until meat is tender, 4-5 hours. If desired, top with cilantro; serve with warmed naan.

Freeze option: Omitting cilantro and naan, freeze the cooled chicken and vegetable mixture in freezer containers. To use, partially thaw in refrigerator overnight. Microwave, covered, on high in a microwave-safe dish until heated through, stirring gently and adding a little water if necessary. If desired, sprinkle with cilantro. Serve with warmed naan.

1¼ cups: 334 cal., 15g fat (4g sat. fat), 80mg chol., 686mg sod., 25g carb. (12g sugars, 5g fiber), 25g pro. **Diabetic exchanges:** 3 lean meat, 2 fat, 1½ starch.

SLOW-COOKER BEEF TIPS BURGUNDY

TREAT
YOURSELF

> "Nothing says summer like a piece of fresh blueberry pie!
> I've been making this dessert for decades. It represents
> my home state well because Michigan is the leader
> in blueberry production in the U.S."
> —Linda Kernan, Mason, MI

STRAWBERRY-CITRUS FREEZER POPS

I knew that clementines and strawberries would be a luscious combination in a fruit pop, and I have to say these are delicious!
—Colleen Ludovice, Wauwatosa, WI

Prep: 20 min. + freezing • **Makes:** 10 pops

- 2 **cups fresh strawberries, sliced**
- 6 **Tbsp. water**
- 1 **Tbsp. sugar**
- 10 **freezer pop molds or 10 paper cups (3-oz. size) and 10 wooden pop sticks**
- 2 **cups clementine segments (about 10), seeded if necessary**
- 6 **Tbsp. orange juice**

1. Place strawberries, water and sugar in a food processor; pulse until combined. Divide among molds or cups. Top molds with holders; if using cups, top with foil and insert sticks through foil. Freeze until firm, about 2 hours.
2. Wipe food processor clean. Add clementines and orange juice; pulse until combined. Spoon over strawberry layer. Freeze, covered, until firm.
1 pop: 82 cal., 0 fat (0 sat. fat), 0 chol., 3mg sod., 20g carb. (16g sugars, 3g fiber), 1g pro.
Diabetic exchanges: 1 fruit.

STREUSELED ZUCCHINI BUNDT CAKE

STREUSELED ZUCCHINI BUNDT CAKE

Inspired by an abundance of zucchini, I created this spiced and lightly sweet cake. It even won a blue ribbon at our county fair!
—Regina Stock, Topeka, KS

Prep: 25 min. • **Bake:** 55 min. + cooling
Makes: 14 servings

- 2 **cups shredded zucchini, patted dry**
- 1⅓ **cups fat-free plain yogurt**
- ¾ **cup sugar**
- 2 **large egg whites, room temperature**
- ⅓ **cup canola oil**
- 1 **large egg, room temperature**
- 4 **tsp. vanilla extract, divided**
- 3 **cups all-purpose flour**
- 1½ **tsp. baking powder**
- 1 **tsp. baking soda**
- ½ **tsp. salt**
- 1 **Tbsp. dry bread crumbs**
- ⅓ **cup packed brown sugar**
- ⅓ **cup chopped walnuts**
- ⅓ **cup raisins**
- 1 **Tbsp. ground cinnamon**
- ½ **tsp. ground allspice**
- ¾ **cup confectioners' sugar**
- 2 **to 3 tsp. fat-free milk**

1. In a large bowl, beat the zucchini, yogurt, sugar, egg whites, oil, egg and 3 tsp. vanilla until well blended. In a small bowl, combine the flour, baking powder, baking soda and salt; gradually beat into zucchini mixture until blended.
2. Coat a 10-in. fluted tube pan with cooking spray; sprinkle with bread crumbs. Pour a third of the batter into the pan. Combine brown sugar, walnuts, raisins, cinnamon and allspice; sprinkle half over batter. Top with another third of the batter. Sprinkle with remaining brown sugar mixture; top with remaining batter.
3. Bake at 350° for 55-65 minutes or until a toothpick inserted in the center comes out clean. Cool for 10 minutes before removing from the pan to a wire rack to cool completely.
4. In a small bowl, combine confectioners' sugar, remaining vanilla and enough milk to achieve desired consistency; drizzle over cake.
1 slice: 287 cal., 8g fat (1g sat. fat), 14mg chol., 259mg sod., 49g carb. (26g sugars, 2g fiber), 6g pro.
* HEALTH TIP * Fat-free plain yogurt replaces some of the oil and helps make this cake tender and moist.

SWIRLED MINT COOKIES

No one will believe that these rich and buttery cookies are light, but they are! With their colorful swirls, each one of the minty, sugary bites has its own look.
—Lois Hill, Thomasville, NC

Prep: 40 min. + chilling
Bake: 10 min./batch • **Makes:** 4 dozen

- ½ cup butter, softened
- ½ cup reduced-fat butter, softened
- ¾ cup plus 1 Tbsp. sugar, divided
- 1 large egg, room temperature
- 1 tsp. vanilla extract
- ½ tsp. peppermint extract
- 2 cups all-purpose flour
- ½ tsp. baking powder
- ¼ tsp. salt
- 10 to 20 drops red food coloring
- 10 to 20 drops green food coloring

1. In a large bowl, cream butters and ¾ cup sugar until light and fluffy. Beat in egg and extracts. Combine the flour, baking powder and salt; gradually add to creamed mixture and mix well.

2. Divide the dough into thirds. Stir red food coloring into 1 portion of dough; stir green food coloring into another portion. Leave remaining dough plain. Cover and refrigerate for at least 1 hour.

3. Divide each portion of dough into 4 equal pieces. Roll each piece into a 12-in. rope. Place a red, a green and a plain rope next to each other. Cut through all 3 ropes at 1-in. intervals, forming sets of 3 differently colored doughs. Repeat.

4. Roll each set of doughs into a ball; place the balls 3 in. apart on ungreased baking sheets. Flatten to ⅛-in. thickness with a glass dipped in the remaining sugar. Bake at 375° for 8-10 minutes or until bottoms are lightly browned. Remove to wire racks to cool.

Note: This recipe was tested with Land O'Lakes light stick butter.

1 cookie: 59 cal., 3g fat (2g sat. fat), 13mg chol., 49mg sod., 7g carb. (3g sugars, 0 fiber), 1g pro. **Diabetic exchanges:** ½ starch, ½ fat.

SWIRLED MINT COOKIES

GLUTEN-FREE RHUBARB BARS

Rhubarb and strawberry bring spring to your table any month of the year. The crust and crumb topping are so tasty, no one will guess the bars are gluten-free.
—Lisa Wilson, Virginia, MN

Prep: 20 min. • **Bake:** 35 min. + cooling
Makes: 3 dozen

- 2 cups gluten-free all-purpose baking flour
- 1 tsp. baking powder
- ½ cup cold butter
- 2 large eggs, room temperature, beaten
- 3 Tbsp. 2% milk
- 5 cups sliced fresh or frozen rhubarb, thawed
- 1 pkg. (3 oz.) strawberry gelatin

TOPPING
- 1 cup sugar
- 1 cup gluten-free all-purpose baking flour
- ½ cup cold butter

1. In a large bowl, combine flour and baking powder. Cut in butter until mixture resembles coarse crumbs. Stir in eggs and milk just until moistened. Press onto the bottom of a 15x10x1-in. baking pan coated with cooking spray. Top with rhubarb; sprinkle with gelatin.

2. For topping, in a small bowl, combine sugar and flour. Cut in butter until mixture resembles coarse crumbs. Sprinkle over top. Bake at 375° for 35-40 minutes or until lightly browned. Cool on a wire rack. Cut into bars.

Notes: Read all ingredient labels for possible gluten content prior to use. Ingredient formulas can change, and production facilities vary among brands. If you're concerned that your brand may contain gluten, contact the company. If using frozen rhubarb, measure rhubarb while still frozen, then thaw completely. Drain in a colander, but do not press liquid out.

1 bar: 116 cal., 6g fat (3g sat. fat), 25mg chol., 58mg sod., 16g carb. (8g sugars, 1g fiber), 2g pro.

CHOCOLATE &
RASPBERRY CHEESECAKE

CHOCOLATE & RASPBERRY CHEESECAKE

You'll fall in love with this sweet treat. Each silky slice is topped with juicy raspberries. Yes, you can have cheesecake without breaking the calorie budget.
—*Taste of Home* Test Kitchen

Prep: 25 min. + chilling
Makes: 12 servings

- ¾ cup graham cracker crumbs
- 2 Tbsp. butter, melted
- 1 envelope unflavored gelatin
- 1 cup cold water
- 4 oz. semisweet chocolate, coarsely chopped
- 4 pkg. (8 oz. each) fat-free cream cheese
  Sugar substitute equivalent to 1 cup sugar
- ½ cup sugar
- ¼ cup baking cocoa
- 2 tsp. vanilla extract
- 2 cups fresh raspberries

1. Combine cracker crumbs and butter; press onto the bottom of a greased 9-in. springform pan. Bake at 375° for 8-10 minutes or until lightly browned. Cool on a wire rack.
2. For filling, in a small saucepan, sprinkle gelatin over the cold water; let stand for 1 minute. Heat over low heat, stirring until gelatin is completely dissolved. Add the semisweet chocolate; stir until melted.
3. In a large bowl, beat the cream cheese, sugar substitute and sugar until smooth. Gradually add the chocolate mixture and cocoa. Beat in vanilla. Pour onto crust; refrigerate for 2-3 hours or until firm.
4. Arrange raspberries on top of the cheesecake. Carefully run a knife around edge of pan to loosen.
Note: This recipe was tested with Splenda no-calorie sweetener.
1 slice: 237 cal., 7g fat (4g sat. fat), 14mg chol., 576mg sod., 27g carb. (17g sugars, 2g fiber), 14g pro. **Diabetic exchanges:** 2 starch, 1 lean meat, 1 fat.

EASY PECAN PIE BARS

EASY PECAN PIE BARS

I am always searching for fast and easy recipes to take to the teachers lounge. The staff goes nuts for these shortcut pecan pie bars.
—Kathro Yoder, Defiance, OH

Prep: 10 min. • **Bake:** 40 min. + cooling
Makes: 2 dozen

- 1 pkg. yellow cake mix (regular size)
- ⅓ cup butter, softened
- 1 large egg, room temperature
  FILLING
- 1½ cups corn syrup
- ½ cup packed brown sugar
- 1 tsp. vanilla extract
- 3 large eggs, room temperature
- 1 cup chopped pecans

1. Preheat oven to 350°. Line a 13x9-in. baking pan with foil; grease foil.
2. Reserve ⅔ cup cake mix; set aside. Combine remaining cake mix, butter and 1 egg; beat on low speed until blended. Press onto bottom of prepared pan. Bake 15 minutes. Cool on a wire rack.
3. For filling, beat corn syrup, brown sugar, vanilla and reserved cake mix until blended. Add eggs; beat on low speed just until combined. Pour over warm crust; sprinkle with pecans.
4. Bake until center is set, 25-30 minutes longer. Cool completely in pan on a wire rack. To serve, refrigerate at least 15 minutes. Lift out of pan; discard foil, then cut into bars.
1 bar: 223 cal., 8g fat (3g sat. fat), 38mg chol., 174mg sod., 38g carb. (30g sugars, 0 fiber), 2g pro.

TEST KITCHEN TIP

We know nuts are expensive, so when they go on sale it's time to stock up. Just pop them into the freezer, and they'll be good for about a year. Other nuts work as well as pecans; almonds are a favorite.

CHEWY COCONUT MACAROONS

These chewy cookies are my husband's favorite, so he requests them often. I like to make the macaroons on cold winter days and keep them in an airtight bowl on the kitchen counter. They never last long!
—Peggy Key, Grant, AL

Prep: 10 min. • **Bake:** 20 min./batch
Makes: 32 cookies

- 2½ cups sweetened shredded coconut
- ¾ cup all-purpose flour
- ⅛ tsp. salt
- 1 can (14 oz.) fat-free sweetened condensed milk
- 1½ tsp. almond extract

1. In a bowl, toss the coconut, flour and salt. Stir in milk and extract until blended (mixture will be thick and sticky).
2. Drop by level tablespoonfuls 3 in. apart onto lightly greased baking sheets. Bake at 300° just until golden brown, 18-22 minutes. Cool 2 minutes before removing from pans to wire racks.

1 cookie: 83 cal., 3g fat (2g sat. fat), 2mg chol., 41mg sod., 13g carb. (11g sugars, 0 fiber), 1g pro. **Diabetic exchanges:** 1 starch, ½ fat.

HAZELNUT ALMOND BISCOTTI

HAZELNUT ALMOND BISCOTTI

Pour a cup of coffee and indulge! Crisp, crunchy biscotti cookies are perfect for dunking. Hazelnuts and almonds make my favorite version even better.
—Johnna Johnson, Scottsdale, AZ

Prep: 30 min. • **Bake:** 30 min. + cooling
Makes: about 2 dozen

- 2 large eggs, room temperature
- ¾ cup sugar
- 2 tsp. vanilla extract
- ¾ tsp. almond extract
- 1⅔ cups all-purpose flour
- ½ tsp. baking soda
- ¼ tsp. salt
- ⅔ cup chopped hazelnuts, toasted
- ¼ cup sliced almonds, toasted

1. Preheat oven to 350°. In a large bowl, beat the eggs, sugar and extracts until well-blended. In another bowl, whisk together flour, baking soda and salt; gradually stir into egg mixture. Stir in nuts (mixture will be stiff).
2. Divide dough in half. Using lightly floured hands, shape each portion into a 9x2-in. rectangle on a parchment-lined baking sheet. Bake until golden brown, about 20 minutes.
3. Cool on pans on wire racks until firm. Reduce oven setting to 325°. Transfer baked rectangles to a cutting board. Using a serrated knife, cut diagonally into ¾-in. slices. Place slices on baking sheets, cut side down.
4. Bake until lightly browned, 5-7 minutes per side. Remove from pans to wire racks; cool completely. Store in an airtight container.

Note: To toast nuts, bake in a shallow pan in a 350° oven for 5-10 minutes or cook in a skillet over low heat until lightly browned, stirring occasionally.

1 cookie: 89 cal., 3g fat (0 sat. fat), 16mg chol., 57mg sod., 14g carb. (7g sugars, 1g fiber), 2g pro. **Diabetic exchanges:** 1 starch, ½ fat.

MARBLED MERINGUE HEARTS

Pretty pastel cookies are a fun way to brighten any special occasion. Replace the vanilla with a different extract for a change of flavor.
—Laurie Herr, Westford, VT

Prep: 25 min. • **Bake:** 20 min. + cooling
Makes: about 2 dozen

- 3 large egg whites
- ½ tsp. vanilla extract
- ¼ tsp. cream of tartar
- ¾ cup sugar
  Red food coloring

1. Place egg whites in a large bowl; let stand at room temperature for 30 minutes. Line baking sheets with parchment.
2. Preheat oven to 200°. Add vanilla and cream of tartar to egg whites; beat on medium speed until soft peaks form. Gradually beat in sugar, 1 Tbsp. at a time, on high until stiff peaks form. Remove ¼ cup and tint pink. Lightly swirl pink mixture into remaining meringue. Fill pastry bag with meringue. Pipe 2-in. heart shapes 2 in. apart onto prepared baking sheets.
3. Bake meringues until set and dry, about 20 minutes. Turn oven off; leave meringues in oven until oven is completely cool. Store in an airtight container.

1 meringue: 27 cal., 0 fat (0 sat. fat), 0 chol., 7mg sod., 6g carb. (6g sugars, 0 fiber), 0 pro.

COCONUT MILK STRAWBERRY-BANANA POPS
(PICTURED ON P. 228)

These four-ingredient freezer pops are a delicious way to use up a pint of fresh strawberries. You'll love the hint of tropical flavor, thanks to the coconut milk.
—*Taste of Home* Test Kitchen

Prep: 10 min. + freezing
Makes: 12 servings

- 1 can (13.66 oz.) coconut milk
- 1 pint fresh strawberries, chopped, divided
- 1 medium banana, sliced
- 2 Tbsp. pure maple syrup
- 12 freezer pop molds or 12 paper cups (3-oz. size) and 12 wooden pop sticks

Place coconut milk, 1½ cups strawberries, banana and syrup in a blender; cover and process until smooth. Divide remaining strawberries among 12 molds or paper cups. Pour pureed mixture into molds, filling ¾ full. Top molds with holders, or, if using cups, top with foil and insert sticks through foil. Freeze until firm, at least 4 hours.

1 pop: 51 cal., 3g fat (3g sat. fat), 0 chol., 5mg sod., 7g carb. (5g sugars, 1g fiber), 1g pro.

> **TEST KITCHEN TIP**
> Frozen pops may be stored up to 6 weeks.

MARBLED MERINGUE HEARTS

PEPPERMINT CAKE ROLLS

(PICTURED ON P. 229)

With angel food cake, fudge sauce and peppermints, this dessert is easy and pretty for the holidays—plus it's calorie-conscious. Even the kids like it! This makes two cake rolls, and it's a simple matter to freeze one for later use.
—Suellen Calhoun, Des Moines, IA

Prep: 25 min. • **Bake:** 15 min. + cooling
Makes: 2 cakes (10 slices each)

- 1 pkg. (16 oz.) angel food cake mix
  Confectioners' sugar
- 1 carton (16 oz.) frozen whipped topping, thawed
- 1½ tsp. peppermint extract
- 1 cup hot fudge ice cream topping
- ½ cup crushed peppermint candies, divided

1. Line 2 greased 15x10x1-in. baking pans with waxed paper. Prepare the cake mix according to package directions. Divide batter evenly into prepared pans.
2. Bake at 350° for 12-15 minutes or until tops spring back when lightly touched. Cool for 5 minutes.
3. Invert each cake onto a kitchen towel dusted with confectioners' sugar. Gently peel off paper. Roll up cake in the towel jelly-roll style, starting with a short side. Cool completely on a wire rack.
4. In a small bowl, mix whipped topping and extract until blended. Unroll cakes; spread each with 1½ cups peppermint mixture to within ½ in. of edges.
5. Cut a small hole in the corner of a food-safe plastic bag; fill with fudge topping. Drizzle each cake with half of the fudge topping; sprinkle with 2 Tbsp. crushed candies. Roll up again, without the towel.
6. Transfer cakes to platters. Frost with the remaining peppermint mixture. Just before serving, top with remaining crushed candies.

Freeze option: Omit candy topping. Place frosted cakes in airtight freezer containers; cover and freeze. Remove from freezer 10 minutes before serving. Top with remaining candies.

1 slice: 204 cal., 5g fat (4g sat. fat), 0 chol., 207mg sod., 36g carb. (27g sugars, 1g fiber), 2g pro. **Diabetic exchanges:** 2 starch, 1 fat.

CHAI-SPICED
BREAD PUDDING

CHAI-SPICED BREAD PUDDING

Nothing says the holidays to me more than a warming chai spice blend. This bread pudding incorporates the flavors I love in a dessert that everyone enjoys.
—Jessie Apfe, Berkeley, CA

Prep: 25 min. + standing • **Bake:** 35 min.
Makes: 9 servings

- 4 large eggs, room temperature, lightly beaten
- 2 cups 2% milk
- ½ cup packed brown sugar
- 1 tsp. ground cinnamon
- 1 tsp. vanilla extract
- ¾ tsp. ground ginger
- ½ tsp. ground cardamom
- ¼ tsp. salt
- ⅛ tsp. ground cloves
- 2 Tbsp. rum, optional
- 6 slices day-old French bread (1 in. thick), cubed
- ⅓ cup slivered almonds
  Vanilla ice cream or sweetened whipped cream

1. Preheat oven to 350°. In a large bowl, whisk together first 9 ingredients and, if desired, rum. Gently stir in bread; let stand 15 minutes or until bread is softened.
2. Transfer to a greased 8-in. square baking dish. Sprinkle with almonds.
3. Bake, uncovered, until puffed, golden and a knife inserted in the center comes out clean, 35-40 minutes. Serve warm, with ice cream.

1 piece: 180 cal., 6g fat (2g sat. fat), 87mg chol., 218mg sod., 24g carb. (15g sugars, 1g fiber), 7g pro. **Diabetic exchanges:** 1½ starch, 1 fat.

WHITE CHOCOLATE CEREAL BARS

A friend gave me this fresh take on traditional crispy treats. My husband loves them. They're so quick to make that you can prepare them during a TV commercial break and you won't miss much of your program.
—Anne Powers, Munford, AL

Takes: 15 min. • **Makes:** about 3 dozen

- 4 cups miniature marshmallows
- 8 oz. white baking chips (about 1⅓ cups)
- ¼ cup butter, cubed
- 6 cups crisp rice cereal

1. In a Dutch oven, combine the marshmallows, baking chips and butter. Cook and stir over medium-low heat until melted. Remove from heat. Add cereal; stir to coat.

2. Transfer to a greased 13x9-in. pan; gently press mixture evenly into pan. Cut into bars.

1 bar: 79 cal., 3g fat (2g sat. fat), 3mg chol., 58mg sod., 13g carb. (8g sugars, 0 fiber), 0 pro.

HOW-TO

To make White Chocolate Cereal Eggs, pack the cereal mixture into egg molds or clean 2-piece plastic Easter eggs. If desired, decorate the eggs with sprinkles.

OLD-FASHIONED TAPIOCA

My family loves old-fashioned tapioca, but I don't always have time to make it. So I came up with this uncomplicated recipe. It lets us enjoy one of our favorites without all the hands-on time.
—Ruth Peters, Bel Air, MD

Prep: 10 min. • **Cook:** 4½ hours
Makes: 18 servings

- 8 cups 2% milk
- 1 cup pearl tapioca
- 1 cup plus 2 Tbsp. sugar
- ⅛ tsp. salt
- 4 large eggs
- 1½ tsp. vanilla extract
  Sliced fresh strawberries and whipped cream, optional

1. In a 4- to 5-qt. slow cooker, combine the milk, tapioca, sugar and salt. Cover and cook on low for 4-5 hours.

2. In a large bowl, beat the eggs; stir in a small amount of hot tapioca mixture. Return all to the slow cooker, stirring to combine. Cover and cook 30 minutes longer or until a thermometer reads 160°. Stir in vanilla.

3. Serve with strawberries and whipped cream if desired.

½ cup: 149 cal., 3g fat (2g sat. fat), 55mg chol., 86mg sod., 25g carb. (18g sugars, 0 fiber), 5g pro.

WHITE CHOCOLATE CEREAL BARS

CLASSIC PUMPKIN PIE

CLASSIC PUMPKIN PIE

Nothing says Thanksgiving like a slice of pumpkin pie. And you can relish every luscious bite of this version since the tender crust is made with a mere hint of canola oil and butter.
—*Taste of Home* Test Kitchen

Prep: 20 min. • **Bake:** 45 min. + cooling
Makes: 8 servings

- 1 cup all-purpose flour
- 1 tsp. sugar
- ¼ tsp. salt
- 3 Tbsp. canola oil
- 1 Tbsp. butter, melted
- 2 to 3 Tbsp. cold water

FILLING
- 1 large egg
- 1 large egg white
- ½ cup packed brown sugar
- ¼ cup sugar
- ½ tsp. salt
- ½ tsp. ground cinnamon
- ⅛ tsp. each ground allspice, nutmeg and cloves
- 1 can (15 oz.) pumpkin
- 1 cup fat-free evaporated milk
  Whipped cream, optional

1. In a small bowl, combine the flour, sugar and salt. Using a fork, stir in oil and butter until dough is crumbly. Gradually add enough water until dough holds together. Roll out between sheets of plastic wrap into an 11-in. circle. Freeze for 10 minutes.
2. Remove top sheet of plastic; invert crust into a 9-in. pie plate. Remove remaining plastic. Trim and flute edges, reserving dough scraps. Chill.
3. Roll dough scraps to ⅛-in. thickness. Cut with a 1-in. leaf-shaped cookie cutter. Place on an ungreased baking sheet; bake at 375° for 6-8 minutes or until edges are very lightly browned. Cool on a wire rack.
4. In a large bowl, beat the egg, egg white, sugars, salt and spices until smooth. Beat in pumpkin. Gradually beat in milk. Pour into crust. Bake at 375° for 45-50 minutes or until a knife inserted in the center comes out clean. Cool on a wire rack. Garnish with leaf cutouts. If desired, top with whipped cream. Refrigerate the leftovers.

1 slice: 249 cal., 8g fat (2g sat. fat), 32mg chol., 295mg sod., 40g carb. (26g sugars, 3g fiber), 6g pro.

CARROT COOKIE BITES

CARROT COOKIE BITES

These soft and delicious cookies are an all-time family favorite. Their aroma while baking is absolutely irresistible! I'm always asked for the recipe.
—Jeanie Petrik, Greensburg, KY

Prep: 15 min. • **Bake:** 10 min./batch
Makes: 7 dozen

- ⅔ cup shortening
- 1 cup packed brown sugar
- 2 large eggs, room temperature
- ½ cup buttermilk
- 1 tsp. vanilla extract
- 2 cups all-purpose flour
- 1 tsp. ground cinnamon
- ½ tsp. salt
- ¼ tsp. baking powder
- ¼ tsp. baking soda
- ¼ tsp. ground nutmeg
- ¼ tsp. ground cloves
- 2 cups quick-cooking oats
- 1 cup shredded carrots
- ½ cup chopped pecans

1. In a large bowl, cream shortening and brown sugar until light and fluffy. Beat in the eggs, buttermilk and vanilla. Combine the flour, cinnamon, salt, baking powder, baking soda, nutmeg and cloves; gradually add to creamed mixture. Stir in the oats, carrots and pecans.
2. Drop dough by rounded teaspoonfuls 2 in. apart onto ungreased baking sheets. Bake at 375° until cookies are lightly browned, 6-8 minutes. Remove to wire racks to cool.

Freeze option: Drop dough by rounded teaspoonfuls onto parchment-lined baking sheets. Freeze until firm. Transfer cookie dough balls to a freezer container; seal tightly and freeze for up to 3 months. To bake, place frozen dough 2 in. apart on ungreased baking sheets. Bake at 375° until lightly browned, 10-15 minutes. Remove to wire racks to cool.

1 cookie: 50 cal., 2g fat (0 sat. fat), 5mg chol., 24mg sod., 6g carb. (3g sugars, 0 fiber), 1g pro.
Diabetic exchanges: ½ starch, ½ fat.

BUTTERSCOTCH PEARS

BUTTERSCOTCH PEARS

This grand finale simmers during dinner and impresses as soon as you bring it to the table. Serve as is, or with vanilla ice cream and a slice of pound cake. Leftover pear nectar is heavenly when added to sparkling wine or enjoyed over ice with breakfast.

—Theresa Kreyche, Tustin, CA

Prep: 20 min. • **Cook:** 2 hours
Makes: 8 servings

- 4 large firm pears
- 1 Tbsp. lemon juice
- ¼ cup packed brown sugar
- 3 Tbsp. butter, softened
- 2 Tbsp. all-purpose flour
- ½ tsp. ground cinnamon
- ¼ tsp. salt
- ½ cup chopped pecans
- ½ cup pear nectar
- 2 Tbsp. honey

1. Cut pears in half lengthwise; remove cores. Brush pears with lemon juice. In a small bowl, combine the brown sugar, butter, flour, cinnamon and salt; stir in pecans. Spoon into pears; place in a 4-qt. slow cooker.
2. Combine the pear nectar and honey; drizzle over pears. Cover and cook on low for 2-3 hours or until pears are tender. Serve warm.

1 stuffed pear half: 209 cal., 10g fat (3g sat. fat), 11mg chol., 109mg sod., 33g carb. (24g sugars, 4g fiber), 1g pro.

POWERED-UP MOLASSES COOKIES
(PICTURED ON P. 228)

These tender cookies are so soft and flavorful. You'd never guess they're also low in fat!

—Jean Ecos, Hartland, WI

Prep: 20 min. • **Bake:** 10 min./batch
Makes: 2 dozen

- ⅔ cup plus 2 Tbsp. sugar, divided
- ¼ cup sunflower oil
- 1 large egg, room temperature
- ¼ cup molasses
- 2 cups white whole wheat flour or whole wheat pastry flour
- 2 tsp. baking soda
- 1 tsp. ground cinnamon
- ½ tsp. salt
- ¼ tsp. ground ginger
- ¼ tsp. ground cloves
- 3 Tbsp. confectioners' sugar

1. Preheat oven to 375°. In a large bowl, beat ⅔ cup sugar and sunflower oil until blended. Beat in egg, then the molasses. In another bowl, whisk the flour, baking soda, cinnamon, salt, ginger and cloves; gradually beat into sugar mixture.
2. Combine confectioners' sugar and remaining sugar. Shape dough into 1-in. balls; roll in sugar mixture. Place 1 in. apart on greased baking sheets. Bake until edges are firm, 10-12 minutes. Cool on pans 5 minutes. Remove to wire racks to cool. Store in an airtight container.

1 cookie: 110 cal., 3g fat (0 sat. fat), 8mg chol., 158mg sod., 19g carb. (10g sugars, 2g fiber), 3g pro.

NO-GUILT BROWNIES

Even those watching their diet can indulge in these light but luscious brownies. They're the perfect cure to a serious chocolate craving!
—Rita Ross, Delta, OH

Takes: 30 min. • **Makes:** 16 brownies

- 3 large egg whites, room temperature
- ¾ cup 1% cottage cheese
- 1 tsp. vanilla extract
- 3 oz. unsweetened chocolate, melted and cooled
- 1 cup sugar
- ¾ cup all-purpose flour
- ½ tsp. baking powder
- ¼ tsp. salt
- 2 tsp. confectioners' sugar

1. Place the egg whites, cottage cheese and vanilla in a blender; cover and process until smooth. Add the chocolate; cover and process just until blended, about 15 seconds. Combine the sugar, flour, baking powder and salt; add to cottage cheese mixture. Cover and pulse until just moistened.

2. Spread into an 8-in. square baking pan coated with cooking spray. Bake at 350° until a toothpick inserted in the center comes out clean, 20-25 minutes (do not overbake). Cool on a wire rack. Dust with confectioners' sugar. Cut into bars.

1 brownie: 117 cal., 3g fat (2g sat. fat), 1mg chol., 107mg sod., 19g carb. (13g sugars, 1g fiber), 3g pro. **Diabetic exchanges:** 1 starch, ½ fat.

NO-GUILT BROWNIES

CHEESECAKE BERRY PARFAITS

Berry season is a real treat for me. This layered delight is an easy way to enjoy a hint of cheesecake, and it's a refreshing change from traditional pudding and fruit parfaits.
—Patricia Schroedl, Jefferson, WI

Takes: 15 min. • **Makes:** 2 servings

- 2 oz. cream cheese, softened
- 4 tsp. sugar
- ⅔ cup whipped topping
- 1½ cups mixed fresh berries
  Additional whipped topping, optional

1. In a small bowl, beat cream cheese and sugar until smooth. Fold in the whipped topping.

2. In each of 2 parfait glasses, layer a fourth of the cream cheese mixture and a fourth of the berries. Repeat layers. Top with additional whipped topping if desired. Chill until serving.

1 parfait: 146 cal., 4g fat (4g sat. fat), 0 chol., 1mg sod., 25g carb. (21g sugars, 3g fiber), 1g pro.

PEACH & BERRY COBBLER

CINNAMON ROLL MACARONS

These macarons are a winter/fall staple for me—inspired by the classic cinnamon roll, they are a delicious treat for a cold or snowy day. These pair well with a mug of tea, and can be eaten as a dessert or just a snack. Try custard, mousse, ganache, or any other buttercream as fillings, too.
—Elizabeth Ding, El Cerrito, CA

Prep: 45 min. • **Bake:** 10 min./batch
Makes: 5 dozen

- 4 large egg whites
- 1½ cups almond flour
- 1¼ cups confectioners' sugar
- ½ tsp. ground cinnamon
- ¾ cup sugar

FILLING
- 4 oz. cream cheese, softened
- 3 Tbsp. butter, softened
- 1 tsp. vanilla extract
- 1½ cups confectioners' sugar
  Additional ground cinnamon

1. Place egg whites in a small bowl; let stand at room temperature 30 minutes. Sift almond flour, 1¼ cups confectioners' sugar and cinnamon together twice.
2. Preheat oven to 325°. Beat egg whites on medium speed until soft peaks form. Gradually add sugar, 1 Tbsp. at a time, beating on high until stiff peaks form. Fold in almond flour mixture.
3. Cut a small hole in a corner of a food-safe plastic bag. Pipe 1-in.-diameter cookies 2 in. apart onto parchment-lined baking sheets. Bake until lightly browned and firm to the touch, 9-12 minutes. Keeping cookies on the parchment, transfer to wire racks; cool completely.
4. For filling, in a small bowl, beat cream cheese and butter until creamy. Beat in vanilla. Gradually beat in confectioners' sugar until fluffy. Refrigerate until mixture firms to a spreading consistency, about 10 minutes.
5. Spread about ¼ tsp. filling onto the bottom of each of half of the cookies; top with the remaining cookies. Sprinkle with additional cinnamon. Store in airtight containers in the refrigerator.

1 sandwich cookie: 60 cal., 3g fat (1g sat. fat), 3mg chol., 15mg sod., 9g carb. (8g sugars, 0 fiber), 1g pro.

PEACH & BERRY COBBLER

This is one of my favorite summer recipes because it features peaches and berries that are in season, but it's just as delicious any time of year with frozen fruit. The quick biscuit topping brings it all together.
—Lauren Knoelke, Des Moines, IA

Prep: 20 min. • **Bake:** 40 min.
Makes: 8 servings

- ½ cup sugar
- 3 Tbsp. cornstarch
- ½ tsp. ground cinnamon
- ¼ tsp. ground cardamom
- 10 medium peaches, peeled and sliced (about 6 cups)
- 2 cups mixed blackberries, raspberries and blueberries
- 1 Tbsp. lemon juice

TOPPING
- 1 cup all-purpose flour
- ¼ cup sugar
- 2 tsp. grated orange zest
- ¾ tsp. baking powder
- ¼ tsp. salt
- ¼ tsp. baking soda
- 3 Tbsp. cold butter
- ¾ cup buttermilk
  Vanilla ice cream, optional

1. Preheat oven to 375°. In a large bowl, mix the sugar, cornstarch, cinnamon and cardamom. Add peaches, berries and lemon juice; toss to combine. Transfer to a 10-in. cast-iron or other ovenproof skillet.
2. In a small bowl, whisk the first 6 topping ingredients; cut in butter until mixture resembles coarse crumbs. Add buttermilk; stir just until moistened. Drop mixture by tablespoonfuls over the peach mixture.
3. Bake, uncovered, until topping is golden brown, 40-45 minutes. Serve warm. If desired, top with ice cream.

1 serving: 279 cal., 5g fat (3g sat. fat), 12mg chol., 238mg sod., 57g carb. (38g sugars, 5g fiber), 4g pro.

CINNAMON ROLL MACARONS

FROZEN BANANA CEREAL POPS

When we want a healthy snack, we dip bananas in yogurt, roll 'em in cereal, then freeze. Ta-da!

—Scarlett Elrod, Newnan, GA

Prep: 15 min. + freezing • **Makes:** 8 pops

- ¾ cup (6 oz.) strawberry yogurt
- 2 cups Fruity Pebbles cereal
- 4 medium bananas, peeled and cut crosswise in half
- 8 wooden pop sticks

1. Place yogurt and cereal in separate shallow bowls. Insert pop sticks through cut side of bananas. Dip bananas in yogurt, then roll in cereal to coat. Transfer to waxed paper-lined baking sheets.

2. Freeze until firm, about 1 hour. Transfer to freezer containers; close tightly and return pops to freezer.

1 pop: 106 cal., 1g fat (1g sat. fat), 1mg chol., 57mg sod., 24g carb. (14g sugars, 2g fiber), 2g pro. **Diabetic exchanges:** 1 starch, ½ fruit.

TEST KITCHEN TIP

In a recipe this simple, it pays to use bananas that are ripe and sweet but still firm. Look for bananas that have little or no green on them and no brown or black spots.

SPARKLY MERINGUE SNOWMEN

SPARKLY MERINGUE SNOWMEN

For my son's first Christmas home from Iraq, I wanted everything to feel magical. He loves meringue cookies, so I made a big batch of minty snowflakes and snowmen.

—Patricia Lindsay, Independence, KS

Prep: 30 min. **Bake:** 80 min.
Makes: about 1 dozen

- 2 large egg whites
- ⅛ tsp. cream of tartar
- ½ cup sugar
- ½ tsp. mint or vanilla extract
  Black nonpareils
  Orange sprinkles

1. Place egg whites in a large bowl; let stand at room temperature 30 minutes.

2. Preheat oven to 200°. Add cream of tartar to egg whites; beat on medium speed until foamy. Gradually add sugar, 1 Tbsp. at a time, beating on high after each addition until sugar is dissolved. Continue beating until stiff glossy peaks form. Fold in extract.

3. Cut a small hole in the tip of a pastry bag or in a corner of a food-safe plastic bag; insert a #12 round tip. Transfer meringue to bag. Pipe snowmen about 4 in. tall, 2 in. apart, onto parchment-lined baking sheets. Decorate as desired with nonpareils and sprinkles. Bake until firm to the touch, 80-90 minutes.

4. Remove snowmen to wire racks to cool completely. Store in an airtight container.

1 cookie: 31 cal., 0 fat (0 sat. fat), 0 chol., 8mg sod., 7g carb. (7g sugars, 0 fiber), 1g pro. **Diabetic exchanges:** ½ starch.

ALMOND-PECAN DATE TRUFFLES

My daughter and I came across a date candy recipe when she was learning about ancient Egypt. We changed some of the spices and nuts to suit our tastes. These sweet, simple truffles are ideal for when you want something quick yet festive.
—Lori Daniels, Beverly, WV

Prep: 20 min. + chilling
Makes: about 1½ dozen

- ⅓ cup apple juice
- 1 pkg. (8 oz.) chopped dates
- 1 cup finely chopped pecans, toasted
- 1¼ tsp. ground cinnamon
- ¼ tsp. ground nutmeg
- 1 cup ground almonds, toasted

1. In a microwave, warm apple juice. Stir in dates; let stand 5 minutes to soften, stirring occasionally. Remove dates from apple juice; discard liquid. Transfer dates to the bowl of a food processor fitted with the blade attachment; process until smooth. Add pecans and spices; pulse just until combined (mixture will be thick).
2. Shape mixture into 1-in. balls; place on a waxed paper-lined baking sheet. Refrigerate, covered, 30-60 minutes.
3. Roll date balls in almonds.

1 date ball: 109 cal., 7g fat (1g sat. fat), 0 chol., 0 sod., 12g carb. (9g sugars, 2g fiber), 2g pro.

TROPICAL PARADISE MILKSHAKES

Slip away to paradise without leaving home with these fruity, coconutty shakes. A little pineapple rum or coconut rum would make them extra indulgent.
—*Taste of Home* Test Kitchen

Takes: 15 min. • **Makes:** 6 servings

- 2 medium limes, divided
- ¼ cup unsweetened shredded coconut, toasted
- 1½ cups frozen pineapple chunks
- 1½ cups frozen mango chunks
- 1 medium banana, sliced and frozen
- 1½ cups vanilla ice cream
- 1 cup light coconut milk
- ½ cup fat-free milk
- 1 cup frozen unsweetened strawberries
  Fresh pineapple, kiwifruit, strawberries, mango, starfruit and edible blossoms, optional

1. Cut 1 lime into wedges. Moisten rims of 6 margarita or cocktail glasses with a lime wedge. Sprinkle coconut on a plate; dip rims in coconut.
2. Zest and juice the remaining lime. Place zest and juice in a blender. Add pineapple, mango, banana, ice cream and milks; cover and process until smooth. Pour ⅔ cup mixture into each prepared glass. Add strawberries to remaining mixture in blender; cover and process until smooth. Pour into glasses; garnish as desired with lime wedges and optional ingredients.

1 cup: 198 cal., 6g fat (4g sat. fat), 15mg chol., 44mg sod., 33g carb. (23g sugars, 3g fiber), 3g pro. **Diabetic exchanges:** 1 starch, 1 fruit, 1 fat.

ALMOND-PECAN DATE TRUFFLES

PINEAPPLE UPSIDE-DOWN
CAMPFIRE CAKE

PINEAPPLE UPSIDE-DOWN CAMPFIRE CAKE

We make this fun recipe while camping or in the backyard around a fire. It's very yummy, but the sandwich iron should be opened only by adults to avoid burns.
—Cheryl Grimes, Whiteland, IN

Prep: 10 min. • **Cook:** 5 min./cake
Makes: 6 servings

- 6 tsp. butter
- 6 Tbsp. brown sugar
- 6 canned pineapple slices
- 6 maraschino cherries
- 6 individual round sponge cakes

1. Place 1 tsp. butter in 1 side of sandwich iron. Hold over fire to melt; remove from fire. Carefully sprinkle 1 Tbsp. brown sugar over melted butter. Top with pineapple ring; add cherry to center of pineapple. Top with cake (flat side up); close iron.
2. Cook pineapple side down over a hot campfire until brown sugar is melted and cake is heated through, 5-8 minutes. Invert iron to open, and serve cake on an individual plate.

1 cake: 211 cal., 6g fat (3g sat. fat), 38mg chol., 214mg sod., 39g carb. (32g sugars, 1g fiber), 2g pro.

TEST KITCHEN TIP

We tested these little cakes with fresh pineapple, too, but liked canned better. Fresh pineapple took too long to get tender, while canned was the perfect fit.

DOUBLE CHOCOLATE, ORANGE & HAZELNUT BISCOTTI

Biscotti are easier to make than you might think, and they're delicious with breakfast or as a snack. They store well for over a week in a sealed jar or bag. I came up with this recipe when trying to use odds and ends I had in the house. Although we love to munch on all kinds of biscotti, this variety is especially amazing—just try one with coffee or espresso!
—Sarah Knoblock, Hyde Park, IN

Prep: 20 min. • **Bake:** 25 min.
Makes: about 1½ dozen

DOUBLE CHOCOLATE, ORANGE
& HAZELNUT BISCOTTI

- ¼ cup whole hazelnuts, toasted and skins removed
- 1 large egg, room temperature
- ⅓ cup sugar
- ¼ cup 2% milk
- 1 tsp. vanilla extract
- 2 cups all-purpose flour
- ¼ cup baking cocoa
- ¼ tsp. baking soda
  Dash salt
- 2 tsp. grated orange zest
- ½ cup semisweet chocolate chips

1. Preheat oven to 350°. Place hazelnuts in a resealable plastic bag; crush nuts using a mallet or rolling pin.
2. Beat egg, sugar and milk until light and thick; add the vanilla. Whisk flour, cocoa, baking soda and salt; stir in orange zest. Gradually beat into egg mixture (dough will be thick). Fold in chocolate chips and crushed hazelnuts by hand.
3. On an ungreased baking sheet, shape dough into a 9x5-in. rectangle. Bake until a toothpick inserted in center comes out clean, about 20 minutes. Cool on pans on wire racks until firm, 5-10 minutes.
4. Reduce oven setting to 325°. Transfer baked rectangle to a cutting board. Using a serrated knife, cut crosswise into ½-in. slices. Place on baking sheet, cut sides down. Return to oven and bake until crisp, 6-8 minutes on each side. Remove from pans to wire racks to cool completely. Store in an airtight container.

Note: To toast hazelnuts, bake, stirring occasionally, in a shallow pan in a 350° oven until fragrant and lightly browned, 7-10 minutes. Wrap cooled hazelnuts in a tea towel; rub with towel to loosen skins.

1 cookie: 112 cal., 3g fat (1g sat. fat), 11mg chol., 105mg sod., 19g carb. (7g sugars, 1g fiber), 3g pro. **Diabetic exchanges:** 1 starch, ½ fat.

BANANAS FOSTER SUNDAES FOR 2

I have wonderful memories of eating bananas Foster in New Orleans, and as a dietitian, I wanted to find a healthier version. I combined the best of two recipes and added my own tweaks to create this southern treat. And with this version, it's the perfect dessert for two!
—Lisa Varner, El Paso, TX

Takes: 15 min. • **Makes:** 2 servings

- 1 tsp. butter
- 1 Tbsp. brown sugar
- 1 tsp. orange juice
- ⅛ tsp. ground cinnamon
- ⅛ tsp. ground nutmeg
- 1 large banana, sliced
- 2 tsp. chopped pecans, toasted
- ⅛ tsp. rum extract
- 1 cup reduced-fat vanilla ice cream

In a large nonstick skillet, melt butter over medium-low heat. Stir in the brown sugar, orange juice, cinnamon and nutmeg until blended. Add banana and pecans; cook until banana slices are glazed and slightly softened, stirring lightly, 2-3 minutes. Remove from the heat; stir in extract. Serve with ice cream.

1 sundae: 259 cal., 8g fat (4g sat. fat), 26mg chol., 74mg sod., 45g carb. (32g sugars, 2g fiber), 5g pro.

CONTEST-WINNING FRESH BLUEBERRY PIE

(PICTURED ON P. 229)

Nothing says summer like a piece of fresh blueberry pie! I've been making this dessert for decades. It represents my home state well because Michigan is the leader in blueberry production in the U.S.
—Linda Kernan, Mason, MI

Prep: 15 min. + cooling
Makes: 8 servings

- ¾ cup sugar
- 3 Tbsp. cornstarch
- ⅛ tsp. salt
- ¼ cup cold water
- 5 cups fresh blueberries, divided
- 1 Tbsp. butter
- 1 Tbsp. lemon juice
- 1 sheet refrigerated pie crust, baked in a 9-in. pie plate

1. In a saucepan over medium heat, combine sugar, cornstarch, salt and water until smooth. Add 3 cups blueberries. Bring to a boil; cook and stir for 2 minutes or until thickened and bubbly.
2. Remove from the heat. Add butter, lemon juice and remaining berries; stir until butter is melted. Cool. Pour into crust. Refrigerate until serving.

1 piece: 269 cal., 9g fat (4g sat. fat), 9mg chol., 150mg sod., 48g carb. (29g sugars, 2g fiber), 2g pro.

YOGURT-RICOTTA CHEESECAKE

I have always liked Italian ricotta cheesecakes, but they have too much sugar for me. I made a diabetic version and my family couldn't even tell! I serve mine with sugar-free strawberry ice cream topping and fresh strawberries.
—Diane Shipley, Mentor, OH

Prep: 35 min.
Bake: 80 min. + chilling
Makes: 16 servings

- 2 pkg. (8 oz. each) reduced-fat cream cheese
- 2 cups reduced-fat ricotta cheese
  Sugar substitute blend (made with sucralose) equivalent to 1½ cups sugar
- 2 cups (16 oz.) vanilla yogurt
- ½ cup butter, melted
- ¼ cup cornstarch
- 3 Tbsp. all-purpose flour
- 2 Tbsp. lemon juice
- 1 tsp. vanilla extract
- 4 large eggs, room temperature, lightly beaten
  Halved fresh strawberries, optional

1. Preheat oven to 325°. In a large bowl, beat cream cheese, ricotta and sugar blend until smooth. Beat in yogurt, butter, cornstarch, flour, lemon juice and vanilla. Add eggs; beat on low speed just until blended. Pour into a greased 9-in. springform pan. Place the pan on a baking sheet.
2. Bake until center is almost set, 80-85 minutes. Cool on a wire rack 10 minutes. Loosen sides from pan with a knife. Cool 1 hour longer. Refrigerate overnight, covering when completely cooled.
3. Remove rim from pan. If desired, serve cheesecake with strawberries.
Note: This recipe was tested with Splenda sugar blend.
1 slice: 246 cal., 15g fat (9g sat. fat), 91mg chol., 231mg sod., 19g carb. (16g sugars, 0 fiber), 9g pro.

CHERRY ANGEL FOOD CAKE

Not only is this cake very light, but it rises nice and high, and it's not too sweet. Pretty dots of maraschino cherry inside make the cake so festive.
—Estelle Hardin, Washington, UT

Prep: 25 min. • **Bake:** 30 min.
Makes: 12 servings

- 1¾ cups egg whites (about 13 large)
- 1 cup all-purpose flour
- 1½ tsp. cream of tartar
- 1½ tsp. vanilla extract
- ½ tsp. almond extract
- ¼ tsp. salt
- 1½ cups plus 2 Tbsp. sugar, divided
- ½ cup coarsely chopped maraschino cherries (about 30), well drained
- ¾ cup reduced-fat whipped topping

1. Place egg whites in a large bowl; let stand at room temperature for 30 minutes. Sift flour twice; set aside. Add cream of tartar, extracts and salt to egg whites; beat on medium speed until soft peaks form. Gradually beat in ¾ cup sugar, about 2 Tbsp. at a time, on high until stiff glossy peaks form and sugar is dissolved. Combine flour and remaining sugar; gradually fold into batter, ¼ cup at a time. Fold in cherries.
2. Gently spoon into an ungreased 10-in. tube pan. Cut through batter with a knife to remove air pockets. Bake on the lowest oven rack at 350° for 30-35 minutes or until cake springs back when lightly touched. Immediately invert pan; cool completely, about 1 hour. Run a knife around the sides and center tube of pan. Remove cake to a serving plate. Serve with whipped topping.
1 piece: 186 cal., 1g fat (1g sat. fat), 0 chol., 108mg sod., 40g carb. (31g sugars, 0 fiber), 5g pro.

YOGURT-RICOTTA CHEESECAKE

PUMPKIN CARAMEL CUPCAKES

Not only do kids love to eat these cupcakes, they can help bake them, too. To make things even easier, we got the idea to dunk them in premade caramel apple dip instead of using frosting.
—Donna Schaab, Belleville, IL

Prep: 25 min. • **Bake:** 20 min. + cooling
Makes: 2 dozen

- 1 pkg. yellow cake mix (regular size)
- 1 can (15 oz.) pumpkin
- ⅔ cup water
- ¼ cup maple syrup
- 3 large eggs, room temperature
- 4 tsp. sugar
- 4 tsp. ground cinnamon
  Dash salt
- 1 carton (16 oz.) caramel apple dip
  Chocolate frosting and decorating icing, optional

1. Preheat oven to 350°. Line 24 muffin cups with paper liners. Combine the first 8 ingredients. Beat on low speed for 30 seconds; beat on medium 2 minutes.
2. Fill prepared cups three-fourths full. Bake until a toothpick inserted in center comes out clean, 18-22 minutes. Cool in pans 10 minutes before removing to wire racks to cool completely.
3. Frost cupcakes with caramel apple dip. Decorate, if desired, with frosting and decorating icing. Refrigerate leftovers.

1 cupcake: 178 cal., 5g fat (2g sat. fat), 26mg chol., 242mg sod., 31g carb. (22g sugars, 1g fiber), 2g pro.

TEST KITCHEN TIP

Mashed cooked sweet potatoes can be used in place of the pumpkin.

GINGER APPLE-PEAR CRISP

GINGER APPLE-PEAR CRISP

Savor the luscious flavors of autumn —apples, cinnamon and spices—in this delicious recipe. It's even better with a scoop of vanilla or pumpkin ice cream! Whipped cream is always an option.
—Holly Battiste, Barrington, NJ

Prep: 20 min. • **Bake:** 40 min.
Makes: 8 servings

- 4 medium tart apples, peeled and sliced
- 4 medium pears, peeled and sliced
- ¼ cup sugar
- 1 Tbsp. lemon juice
- 1 Tbsp. grated fresh gingerroot
- ½ tsp. salt
- ½ tsp. vanilla extract

TOPPING
- 1 cup old-fashioned oats
- ½ cup all-purpose flour
- ½ cup packed brown sugar
- 1 tsp. ground cinnamon
- ¼ tsp. ground nutmeg
- ⅛ tsp. salt
- ⅓ cup cold butter, cubed

1. Preheat oven to 375°. In a large bowl, toss the first 7 ingredients. Transfer to a greased 2½-qt. baking dish.
2. In another bowl, mix the first 6 topping ingredients; cut in butter until crumbly. Sprinkle over fruit.
3. Bake until golden brown and fruit is tender, 40-45 minutes. Serve warm.

1 serving: 295 cal., 9g fat (5g sat. fat), 20mg chol., 250mg sod., 55g carb. (35g sugars, 5g fiber), 3g pro.

PUMPKIN CARAMEL CUPCAKES

INDEX

•Table-ready in 30 minutes or less.

HERBED PORK CHOPS,
P. 190